DRESSING UP

DRESSING UP

A History of Fancy Dress in Britain

VERITY WILSON

REAKTION BOOKS

Published by Reaktion Books Ltd
Unit 32, Waterside
44–48 Wharf Road
London N1 7UX, UK
www.reaktionbooks.co.uk

First published 2022

Supported by the Paul Mellon Centre for Studies in British Art

Printed and bound in India by Replika Press Pvt. Ltd

A catalogue record for this book is available from the British Library

ISBN 978 1 78914 529 8

CONTENTS

Introduction

FANCY DRESS DEFINED

This is a book about fancy dress. It has taken a long time to write because in the process I have done more laughing than writing. The joy it has engendered is itself one of the precepts of the fancy-dress experience, and any definition of the practice has to include its innate propensity to delight. Though most countries across the globe take great pleasure in dressing up, it is the fancy-dress endeavours of British people that are the focus of this book: the characters they represented, the manner and prevailing contexts in which they were chosen and worn, their acquisition and making. The book takes as its approximate time frame the years between 1850 and 1950, but it occasionally spills out over both the beginning and end points because events either side of these hundred years are often important to our understanding of the phenomenon. This is a sweeping period but hopefully the information presented does justice to the complexities of the subject and is not overly simplistic or reductive.

While this book does not follow a strict chronological pattern, two queens stand at the far reaches of our period. Queen Victoria came to

1 A small boy dressed as Pierrot, with his Indian *ayah*, 1920s.

the throne in 1837 and her penchant for fancy dress, of a different cast from that of the previous era, offers up a key element in defining the parameters of this book. The coronation of Queen Elizabeth II in 1953 acted as an impetus for many queenly impersonations in red, white and blue. Despite this, the first years of her monarchy presaged a waning, though not the disappearance, of fancy dress, which, until its more recent upsurge in the 1990s, was primarily associated with children in the aftermath of the Second World War. People of all ages, however, embraced fancy dress in the period covered by this book, a time when many in Britain were living more prosperous lives than previously. Fancy dress continued to reflect the vaunting appetites of the elite but also the inventive and improvisatory tactics of other social classes who were increasingly vocal in their wish to share the good life.

The profound repercussions of two world wars severely taxed the everyday habits of the British population, and the upheavals modulated fancy dress, shading its meanings and appearance. The costumes described and elucidated here were seen in big metropolitan centres and in innumerable small villages and towns across the country. But the British people who wore them were not always within the British Isles (illus. 1). A photograph of Singaporean Chinese children, still British subjects in the year Queen Elizabeth II was crowned, speaks to the dogged persistence of colonial dressing up, as patriotically inflected as any in the mother country (illus. 2).

The facts of fancy dress might seem unproblematic but, even before we enter the psychological domain of identity, expression, performance and portrayal, a lucid definition is not so very obvious. It follows, then, that one of the first questions this book asks is: 'What is fancy dress?' Competing explanations enrich our conception of it.

Trying to capture a finite definition of fancy dress is a tricky undertaking, though we think we know it when we see it. An intelligent

2 Pupils from the Bukit Panjang Government School in Singapore celebrating the coronation of Queen Elizabeth II, 1953.

3 London costermongers or 'Pearlies' in their full regalia at Epsom Racecourse on Derby Day, 1936. Costers began wearing buttoned outfits in the late 19th century, and the style was quickly copied by fancy dressers, as seen in illus. 23.

explanation appears in the prodigious dress bibliography compiled by father and son Hilaire and Meyer Hiler, published in 1939. Their long and learned introduction, 'Costume and Ideologies', defines dressing up as being costumed rather than merely clothed. Clothing is body covering, they claim, while costume is raiment of a type distinct from that worn habitually.[1] This assertion takes us some way to an understanding, though the Hilers, in avoiding the appellation 'fancy dress',

4 Children on the Hebridean island of South Uist at Halloween, photographed by Margaret Fay Shaw, 1932.

leave us with too broad a rendition and their overarching interpretation embraces many clothing styles that are not examined here. In this present book fancy dress is considered a subcategory of dressing up.

So, one way fancy dress can be comprehended is in terms of what it is not.[2] Though this might seem contrary to common sense, it brings together several sartorial pursuits that fed into, and were fed by, the practice of fancy dress. To a greater or lesser degree, these variant manifestations of clothing worn for certain distinct occasions share several characteristics with fancy dress. Theatre costume and other kinds of performance dress, notably circus and music-hall attire, are an obvious parallel. The racier side of urban nightlife that increasingly embraced showy cross-dressers, drag queens, exotic dancers and erotic performers in flesh-coloured tights, culminating in the opening of striptease clubs in 1937, is the obverse of the more respectable fancy-dress affairs described in this book, but the two have much in common as regards clothing and the limits to which it could go.[3] Garments for pageants and historical re-enactments were immensely popular at exactly the time when the fancy-dress craze reached its zenith in the nineteenth and twentieth centuries.[4] Costumed folk customs continued, were revived or newly invented (illus. 3). Some of these attempted total disguise, with the face, central to recognition, completely hidden (illus. 4). Societies and clubs extolling idealistic or utopian aims sought to capture the essence of their credos by dressing in ways that were thought to reflect their vision (illus. 5). None of these fall under our rubric of fancy dress.

In addition to all these varied kinds of garments worn for distraction and amusement, professional tailoring firms were in the business of styling more formal 'dress-up' clothes. They fashioned court, legal and academic dress, accoutred the Church and made military uniforms, all clothing classifications that involved dressing up but are not designated as fancy dress. Disguise, of a more serious kind than party attire, was another area of activity for these tailoring establishments,

5 A member of the Kindred of the Kibbo Kift dressed for a ritual in the 1930s. The organization was formed after the First World War to promote world peace.

again not strictly fancy dress. Willy Clarkson (1861–1934), the entrepreneurial wig maker and costumier, claimed to have kitted out Scotland Yard detectives with false hair and make-up, and Nathans, another famous London firm who costumed countless theatre and film productions, dressed agents to infiltrate Occupied Europe during the Second World War.[5] Falsifying appearances, in some measure, was the entire rationale behind these costumiers' trade, and many of the trappings of the assorted garment styles they fabricated reappeared as fancy dress. Costumiers were quick to realize its potential as a source of profit.

Well away from Europe and metropolitan costumiers, other British agents, or those perceived as such, were hiding their true identity

6 The plant hunter Reginald Farrer wearing a Chinese dragon robe, 1920s.

beneath divergent clothing that might, in other contexts, have been deemed fancy dress. Derring-do stories of spies appropriating 'native garb' in colonial India might be exaggerated, but they are evidence of the thrill of dressing up, something that was carried over into fancy dress.[6] In a tight situation in western China, the plant hunter William Purdom, for example, fleeing from hostile territory, wore what is described as a 'Tibetan brigand' outfit in 1911, though I do not consider this fancy dress. Reginald Farrer, another botanizing traveller who joined forces with Purdom in 1914, presents a different case. He persisted in wearing European clothing while working in the contested border region between China and Tibet in the first decades of the twentieth century but, on his return to Britain, he had himself photographed wearing the flamboyant embroidered robes of imperial China, which he must have collected en route (illus. 6). He donned other people's clothes to enhance himself, constructing his own personal image of Chinese-ness.[7] Marjory Wardrop, a pioneering translator of Georgian literature, was photographed in the dress of a lady from Tbilisi, the capital of this country in the Caucasus, on her second visit there in 1896 (illus. 7). Across the centuries, countless other Britons were pictured posing in foreign clothing, some spectacularly so, and their ostentatious indigenous outfits fall just on the borderline of fancy dress, though the posturing sitters themselves might not have categorized their clothes as such (illus. 8).[8] There were, after all, only limited opportunities for wearing such obtrusive garments from faraway places. Reginald Farrer and Marjory Wardrop's choice of clothing are emblematic of the mixed meanings of national dress. Its adoption and adaptation by Britons during the period covered by this book resonates with the rise of nationalism across the globe as well as with British imperial self-confidence or, put another way, with British attempts to compensate for Britain's smallness.[9] None of these sojourners thought that they were wearing fancy dress, though some of the garments found their way into the dressing-up box a generation later, because how else were they to be used? Many in Britain who rigged themselves out in foreign clothes certainly *did* regard them as fancy dress. 'All Nations Fancy Dress', a sweeping and durable theme that runs right through our period, stretched itself between two poles: the authentic and the

7 Marjory Wardrop in Georgian national dress, photographed by Alexander Roinashvili, 1896.
8 Thomas Hardy, *William Augustus Bowles as a Native American*, 1790, oil on canvas.

truly bogus. Native dress and fancy dress became inescapably entangled, accumulating misunderstandings and shaping uncertain identities.

Dress provided an opportunity to experiment with ethnicity and it also opened up a space to cross class. The case of Olive Malvery (1871–1914) is an engaging example of the latter. At the beginning of the twentieth century, Malvery penned a series of essays for *Pearson's Magazine* which investigated the lives of poor working women in London. A complex personality herself, she was conscious of her own mixed-race background and, on occasion, wore Indian attire, but, when she went undercover for her work, she took pains to dress like the subjects she was scrutinizing: tramp, match girl, flower girl, milliner, costermonger, waitress (illus. 9). Unusually, photographs of her wearing these plebeian garments were included in the text with several of her poses copied from the theatrical attitudinizing of contemporary actors.[10] This was not fancy dress, but photography's unresolved place on the spectrum between reality and deception worked to its benefit, and early photographs of real working men and women, despite the imputation that many were staged and idealized, encouraged people to fashion their fancy dress characters as belonging to a class other than their own.

Another form of dress, one that impinged on but was not fancy dress, involved passing: choosing to be identified as part of a group different from your own in terms of race, gender or class. The scrupulously clothes-conscious Olive Malvery swapped class and personas regularly but never permanently laid claim to a new identity. Those who did relied heavily on outward appearance. James Barry (1789–1865), a successful military surgeon for fifty years, started life as Margaret Ann Bulkley from Cork. Grey Owl, caparisoned in several different First Nations garments, embraced life in the Canadian wilderness, describing it in several well-received books. He was really Archibald Belaney (1888–1938), born in Hastings on the Sussex coast. James Barry and

Grey Owl were serious in their lifelong attempts at transformation. Fancy dress's impermanence singled out its ersatz version of passing as less dangerous than the real thing, where the accusation of being an imposter had much more serious consequences. Not necessarily linked to sexual orientation, cross-gender dressing could be discreet or rash. During the period covered by this book, with same-sex liaisons illegal for men, many homosexuals unavoidably resorted to playing multiple roles via clothes, though queer dress was not always female or loud.[11] Fancy dress drew on all this, traversing multiple limits and acknowledging extremes.

9 Olive Malvery dressed as a waitress in a London coffee house, from her book *The Soul Market* (1906). As an investigative journalist, Malvery went undercover to report on the lives of London's poor.

'Extreme clothes' certainly describes the fictional Miss Tootsie Sloper's artful designs, designated 'Fashion Fancies', which appeared in the comic paper *Ally Sloper's Half-Holiday*, published weekly between 1884 and 1923 and sporadically thereafter. In matters of dress, she outshone her comic-strip father, the massively popular Ally, with her strong sense of unconventional excess that played into readers' conceptions of what fancy dress might achieve (illus. 10). Worn with light-hearted resolve, fancy dress and frivolity were knotted together. The term 'fancy dress' itself is certainly linked to the *joie de vivre* of the eighteenth-century masquerade and in 1770 was used to refer to costume that was fancifully bedizened with accessories and only sometimes represented a particular character.

In the culture of the time covered by this book, the term 'fancy' was harnessed to many idioms besides dress, all of them pertinent to caprice and the absurd. One fitting example from many comes from the world of pet keeping, a pastime proximate with the fancy-dress craze and equal to it in terms of the commitment it demanded from its devotees. Fancy animals were bred to encourage certain prominent, sometimes frivolous and even silly, characteristics, and 'The Fancy' was the name given to a group of working-class dog-breeders bent on presentation and spectacle.[12] Charles Dickens, himself a fancy-dress devotee and a customer of Nathans, understood all this and acknowledged 'fancy' as a longing generated by enjoyment, release and wonder. The theme, never an explicit philosophy, runs through his stories.[13] Fancy dress is also implicated in Sigmund Freud's sense of the uncanny, in which the familiar becomes dreamlike and strange. The understanding of fancy dress as chimerical was not lost on contemporary commentators, and its illusory nature was at times even likened to the ideas in Freud's writings. *The Interpretation of Dreams*, translated into English in 1913, filtered through to many middlebrow publications and on 17 March 1923, for example, the woman's page of the expatriate newspaper *The North-China Herald* carried a substantial article, 'Fancy Dress and How It Reveals Our Sub-Conscious Selves', that already made reference to Freud's work.

10 Miss Tootsie Sloper's 'Polar Regions' costume from her series of 'Fashion Fancies' in *Ally Sloper's Half-Holiday*, Saturday, 20 October 1888.

Are we any closer to a definition of fancy dress? Can we identify some of its essential qualities? Fancy dress is often characterized by its apparent expendable nature. It is made for a specific occasion, sometimes from insubstantial and surprising materials. Quotidian clothes and objects appear in odd juxtaposition, transformed from the everyday into something fantastical. Colour plays a part in defining it. The norms of everyday dressmaking can be abandoned in favour of short cuts and a cursory finish. Garment shapes are eccentric or exaggerated, and hats, shoes and other accessories, essential for character recognition, are often strangely sized. However, the supposedly hastily made or frail status of fancy dress is brought into question in some instances by well-constructed, carefully designed and imaginative examples that have come down to us intact from several different kinds of maker (see illus. 11 and illus. 12). Costumes were cherished and modified to suit a new context, as surviving examples again show. Garments were enlarged to fit growing children: one instance of many is a surviving costume in the Leicester Museums, a Folly outfit. This very popular *commedia dell'arte* character was realized in several forms and colourways. The Leicester example, in green and red, was first worn in 1880. Subsequently, the bust and shoulder sections were altered and expanded and the underskirt was lengthened with lace in 1919.[14] Surprisingly, even Alexandra of Denmark (1844–1925), as Princess of Wales, had her Mary, Queen of Scots gown remodelled for a second outing.[15] Even where they are most frangible, costumes have been treasured and have outlived their wearers.[16]

Participants at fancy-dress gatherings were largely amateurs, a hallmark of the genre. Another indicator that we are dealing with fancy dress and not more formal performances is the lack of a script; the effect came from the costume itself and from simply striking an attitude dressed as someone or something else. This distinguishes it from home theatricals and pageants, which, to be sure, shared many of the same costumed characters.

The particular contexts where fancy dress was worn also help us pin it down more precisely. Indoor balls, parties and bazaars, both private and ticketed, big and small, were the setting for many fancy-dress endeavours. Commercial undertakings ran alongside charity functions. The parishioners of All Saints in Ipswich were freed from the

11 The Duchess of Devonshire's dress for Zenobia, queen of Palmyra, designed by Attilio Comelli and made by the House of Worth, Paris. The Duchess wore the dress at the Devonshire House Fancy Dress Ball held in honour of Queen Victoria's Diamond Jubilee in 1897.

last shackle of debt incurred in the building of a new church tower by the leverage of fancy dress. The *Ipswich Journal* in 1893 reported on their fund-raising 'Fair in the Forest' where young people were 'attired in costumes quaint and to use a Shakespearian phrase, "expressed in fancy"'.[17] Private high-society balls, though still attended by the glitterati, were remodelled during our period as charity functions and

12 Snakes and Ladders costume made by an unknown amateur maker, 1920–30. The bodice is decorated with commercially printed boards, and the skirt is sewn with a grid of cotton tape. The counters, snakes and ladders are cut from brown paper, card and fabric and glued to the costume.

there were affordable public balls as well. Starting in 1891 and continuing through to the First World War, the Covent Garden balls, a series of dances that ran from mid-November to April, led the way in this regard though the tickets were pricey for some. From the beginning of the twentieth century, several West End actresses both organized and appeared in costume at similar balls in other venues.[18] Not all of these functions conformed to contemporary standards of respectability, their carousing and frolicking perceived by some as violating acceptable behaviour. Some ball-goers continued the eighteenth-century custom of wearing masks, lending a frisson of excitement to the occasion. Generally fancy dress in our period renounced full disguise. Deception was not usually its intention and this marks it off from the masking convention at balls of an earlier era. Photography played a part here; the desire to be photographed in costume *and* recognized became paramount, so masking turned out to be expendable, though it did not vanish entirely. Children had a noticeable profile where balls were concerned and mayoral juvenile balls, orchestrated by city halls throughout Britain and the colonies, were civic events of great moment. Balls are discussed more fully in Chapter One.

Another context for fancy dress was the drawing room. Home entertainment, a broad category of performance prevalent before the advent of cinema, including guessing games, mime and dramatic posing, all relied on fancy dress for their effectiveness. 'The children stood so still,' marvelled Queen Victoria in 1852 when she wrote a journal account of a royal costumed *tableaux* portrayal of characters from John Milton's verse.[19] *Tableaux vivants* or 'living pictures', where participants posed in a static scene, depended on unstirring quietude and we find the queen's children and, later, her grandchildren pressed into service for this most exacting of performance styles, one to which fancy dress was absolutely central. Both children and adults well outside of the court circle engaged with *tableaux* and *pose plastique*, mimicking famous oil paintings and posing as classical statues, in addition to more knockabout dumbshows. The invention of photography, revealed by Louis Daguerre in France and by William Fox Talbot in England in 1839, turned out to be a technique that incrementally overflowed class barriers. It became thoroughly interconnected with fancy dress, so much so that feigning to be somebody else in front of the camera became an end in itself, separate from parties and parades. Along with the silent attitudes of *tableaux* and charades, we look at this aspect of posing in Chapter Two.

The camera's momentous impact on dressing up was realized early when an outfit entitled 'Photography' was seen at the Governor General's Ball in Canada in 1865, the style having been taken from a Paris fashion plate of 1864.[20] 'Kodak Girl', a figure created by the American firm synonymous with easy-to-operate, low-cost cameras, later became a fancy-dress favourite too.[21] Above all things, photography played a central part in how fancy dress evolved. Today, our understanding of earlier fancy dress is transmitted primarily through photographic images rather than figurative language. People in costume seem to escape their time and connect with us across the years. The contemplation of images showing costumed people held a fascination for contemporary spectators, and many of those same spectators would also have been the subjects of this attentiveness, dressed up for the camera.[22] The period of fancy dress's popularity considered in the following chapters is concurrent with photography's trajectory from experimental wonder to technological marvel. This simultaneity matters to such a degree that mention of the connection recurs throughout the book.

Moving outdoors, processional culture was reinvigorated during our period, giving another context for fancy dress and helping us define it: revamped carnivals, student rags, service personnel antics, Guy Fawkes and fire festivals. Several were bastions of male-only participation, quashing any notion of men's reluctance to dress up. Conspicuous skylarking attended many of these outdoor events and this was encouraged by after-dark scheduling.

Fancy dressers utilized costume to muster an extensive roll call of traditional characters as well as to comment on political or social issues of the day, a determining mark of fancy dress in the period covered by this book. Village and small-town festivals produced uniquely ingenious scenarios that revealed parochial concerns to do with swimming-pool plans, council housing and rates. The field of choice was broadened when parade floats provided relevant scenic settings for a costumed group who singly would not have made an impact. Much creative energy went into these sets, and disguising a vehicle employed several of the same skills and materials as costume making (illus. 13). Identifying the theme of a float often relied on written signboards or banners and these became a particular trait of fancy dress in our period, especially outdoors. Often there was a play on words, as seen

13 *All the King's Horses*, a float at Ryde Carnival on the Isle of Wight, September 1952.

at the Harwich Guy Carnival in Essex in 1930: 'Every Little Alps' was the slogan for a fund-raising float decorated with revellers in Tyrolean costume. Some carnivals brought international events to provincial and suburban Britain very soon after they happened. The highly contentious Johnson–Jeffries boxing match, a sporting event with disturbing racist repercussions, was quite startlingly re-enacted as a carnival float in the small west Devon market town of Hatherleigh in 1910, only a few months after the match had taken place in Reno, Nevada. This famous fight quickly caught the popular imagination for all the wrong reasons when the white Jeffries was sorely beaten by Johnson, the son of an emancipated slave.[23] While race riots erupted in the United States, in Hatherleigh, as reported by the *Exeter and Plymouth Gazette* for Friday 11 November, a couple of local lads flexed their boxing gloves on a carnival float. Outdoor fancy-dress parades of all types are discussed in chapters Three and Four.

The beauty and extravagance of the Caribbean parade that is today London's world-famous Notting Hill Carnival must not blind us to the marginalized Black British population, not to mention other immigrant communities, who were denied access to the realm of visibility and so were generally much less part of the public culture of fancy dress during our period. Minorities rarely appeared in the mainstream accounts of fancy dress and white Britons, in whatever way they were garbed, perhaps not surprisingly, provided the dominant paradigms for fancy dress. One rare instance of Indian participation is reported at the Islington Carnival in 1907. The street carnival included groups dressed as 'Robin Hood and merry men', 'the Princes at the Tower', 'the Village Blacksmith' and 'Mary Queen of Scots' along with floats representing 'Dick Whittington and his cat' (the pantomime hero famous for 'turning again' in this North London borough), 'Old English Sports and Pastimes', 'Dick Turpin's Ride to York', 'Physical Culture' and 'Hands Across the Sea', the sentiment of Sousa's military march (1899) as realized in countless picture postcards. Finally, and unusually, as reported by the *London Daily News*, 'an Indian scene' gave the opportunity 'for a number of young Indian gentlemen resident in the borough' to appear 'in the gorgeous and multi-coloured costumes of the East'. Likely these men habitually wore Western clothes in London but they declined, or else were denied, the opportunity to dress up as any number of different characters and settled instead for impersonating vague figures from 'the East'.[24]

People of colour seldom appear in any of the fancy-dress contexts already described and the Indian men living in Islington might not have participated in a carnival again. One of the built-in tenets of fancy dress for others in Britain, however, is its cyclical inevitability.[25] Carnivals and other costumed events came round every year and with them came new opportunities for trying out a costume. Mr Muxlow, who was one half of the boxing American duo in 1910, can be traced through successive Hatherleigh carnivals for fifteen years until we lose sight of him after 1925. His fancy-dress entry for that year was based on a then-popular song, 'Why Did I Kiss That Girl?'[26] The repeated costumed presence of one person throughout several years of the same carnival – Mr Muxlow is not the sole example – suggests that people became attuned and committed to fancy dress; it was assimilated into the annual round of community life. Coronations, royal jubilees and victory celebrations provided additional excuses to dress up. They add another defining context, demarcating the boundary between fancy dress and other styles of clothing. Civic and national pride coalesced, and the familiar tropes of patriotism were on display. We will cover these national rejoicings in Chapter Five, where we see children having an especially conspicuous presence.

Children and fancy dress were in fact inseparable. Many costumed events were designed for them alone and, at fancy-dress gatherings where adults were also present, a dedicated children's programme was always included in the order of events. Sometimes children dressed as scaled-down adults, sometimes they portrayed characters of their own age, and the boundaries between the two were not always clear-cut. But, whoever they depicted, children in costume lent a particular sweetness to fancy-dress parades and parties.

In all the contexts of dressing up the identification of fancy dress as a competitive pursuit is another of its designating markers. Prize-winners always got their name in the paper and, in some cases, won valuable prizes. Covent Garden balls were lavish in this respect: in 1901 the prizes included a complete set of dinner plates with cutlery in a polished oak case, a gentleman's gold watch, a silver toilet set in a Moroccan leather case, a mahogany escritoire, an afternoon tea service and a spirit and game cabinet. These and other prizes could be viewed at Mappin & Webb's store on Oxford Street, and this display of prizes in shop windows was established everywhere when a competitive costume event was imminent. In financially constrained times modest fancy-dress dances offered cash prizes. Thirty pounds was offered at a 1936 Cinema Fancy Dress Ball in Sunderland for the best impersonations of film stars or film titles, and at its Harvest Dance in 1945, the Burnley branch of the National Farmers' Union gave £3, £2 and £1 for first, second and third places respectively while offering reduced-price entry for members of HM Forces. Outfitters and paper-pattern suppliers were wise to the lure of competition and advertised certain costumes as sure winners. Celebrities frequently presented the prizes: Marie Lloyd, the famous music-hall singer, distributed them at a ball held at Kings Hall in Hackney in 1908.[27]

One framework for thinking about, if not defining, fancy dress is inevitably that of class. The extraordinarily wide reach of fancy dress as a social phenomenon and its spread well beyond its original, mostly upper-class constituency are due to the conjunction of several technological developments and capitalist enterprises. Fancy dress may be viewed as capricious, but it does not follow that its entrée into ordinary lives was by happenstance. Discounting periods of war and economic depression, the years considered in this book were years of novelty in terms of consumption. It was a period when several segments of the British working and middle class had more leisure time and more money to indulge in dressing up. Britain was transformed, albeit inconsistently, by advances in communications and by the invention of marvellous machines. Newspapers, local and national, and illustrated weeklies increased their circulation and reached a much broader section of a now more literate public. The growth of print capitalism and the popularity of fancy dress are indivisible. Queen Victoria's fancy-dress ball of 1842, right at the start of our period, was reported in the very first issue of the *Illustrated London News*, a pioneer of print journalism in its field, and this set a precedent for fancy-dress reportage and pictures that were seen by a wide swathe of the population. Provincial newspapers recorded both metropolitan and local balls and carnivals, and the format became regularized with occasionally a picture on the front page and an account on an inside page delineating the setting, detailing the charitable recipient, naming the organizers and attendees, and announcing prize-winners. Titles of many of the character costumes were usually included and while comments on the garments themselves could be perfunctory, they sometimes ran to considerable length. At every carnival there was nearly always one participant dressed as an actual newspaper or bedecked in billboard posters, the fancy-dress garments pleated and folded into shape to reveal headlines.[28] Books dedicated to the topic of fancy dress also proliferated, and costume manuals were bought or borrowed and mined for ideas and tips. Painting and sculpture, graphic illustrations, postcards, cigarette cards, cartoons and more besides depicted actual fancy dress or provided inspiration for it.

A speedy postal system and a network of railways transported both the outfits themselves and the materials for creating them but,

14 Elsie Landseer dressed as a Newhaven fishwife for the Children's Fancy Dress Ball, Adelaide, photographed by the firm of Wivell, 1887.

more importantly, they took knowledge about fancy dress to urban and remote communities alike. This new know-how often melded with older local costume lore. Conversely, in metropolitan areas there was a growing awareness of rural dress and idiosyncratic work wear, quickened by the medium of photography. Travelling away from their indigenous locales, these old forms of dress became effective fancy dress, if poor simulacra of the original, as happened, for example, with the Newhaven fisher girls whose distinctive striped skirts, originally worn kilted up, were variously copied by fancy dressers who knew nothing of life on the east coast of Scotland (illus. 14).[29]

Hidden behind the plethora of pictorial and textual representations of fancy dress are other, less recoverable histories: the sometimes frustrating world of making and making do. The potential grief inherent in any kind of practical endeavour was, in some instances at least, ameliorated by the sewing machine and the paper pattern, both of which came of age during the years explored here. Complete ready-made ensembles could certainly be purchased, increasingly cheaply, but progressively across our period, a conglomeration of materials and accessories for home creation was on offer to the aspiring dressmaker who had the potential to fabricate something outside the regular model. Many costumes, in any case, were not newly made garments but everyday clothes embellished with applied designs and cut-outs, as seen on the Snakes and Ladders outfit. The affirmed place of fancy dress in street festivities and indoor gatherings from the second half of the nineteenth century is therefore due, in part, to the availability of cheaply produced material, particularly crêpe paper, opening up fancy-dress participation to a broader section of the population. This will be examined in chapters Six and Seven.

During the course of the nineteenth and twentieth centuries, the people of Britain and its empire embraced fancy dress with considerable brio, momentarily banishing the real world for a fictitious one. We should not view dressing up as a trivial pastime but as an enriching facet of life. We will see how very thoroughly fancy dress was both encouraged and recorded. People dressed up to escape, to feel different, for amusement and fun. In some respects, it gave them a certain licence to behave differently. A whole universe of characters was laid before the carnival and party participant, though tracing the progenitors of many of the costumes can shade into guesswork. We find a bewildering assortment of fancy-dress styles along with different modes of presenting them, but in practice a range of social and cultural factors acted to set bounds beyond which certain costumes or styles were tacitly unacceptable.[30] These limits were elastic through time and varied according to context. Garments that were revealing or crossed the gender divide were always of some concern, though the intensity of the criticism ebbed and flowed. A steady trickle of angry letters to newspapers vented concerns about morals, and police constables in particular were vocal in their dislike of being impersonated.

Aside from this, fancy-dress characters underwent changes decade by decade. The scale of what was available is far too expansive to be covered in this book. Even the best-loved characters are mentioned only briefly. Some of these remained in vogue for many years, for example 'Dutch Girl', 'Dutch Boy' and 'Japanese', while others, like 'Etonian', were at first serious replicas of the real thing, then lived on as comedy characters. 'The Cure', explicated below, appeared before quickly disappearing. Some costumes were brought up to date, as happened with the Harlequinade figures, while some, such as 'New Woman' from 1896 and 'French Art Student' from the 1920s, were freshly invented. As new materials and adhesives came on to the market, differently shaped outfits could be fashioned more easily and home-made costumes took on a greater complexity, with 'Lampshade', 'Spinning Top', 'Petrol Pump', 'Billiard Table' and 'Garden Wall' exemplifying the style and providing instances of inanimate objects that upstaged human characters (illus. 15).

15 'Ye Olde Garden Wall' as worn by Mase, photographed by the firm of F. W. Clark of Forest Gate and Ilford, 1917.

Named personalities continued to appear on the fancy-dress circuit but, not unexpectedly, the names changed through time. Marie Antoinette was replaced by Carmen Miranda. With her fruit-encrusted headdress, a gift for amateur show-offs, this popular entertainer, and others like her, swept aside the once-popular powdery high-coiffed aristocrats of the *ancien régime*, though by no means exterminated them. In the face of this onslaught from Hollywood, the *poudré* characters, as the style was called, endured as ciphers.

Gender, merchandise promotion, competition and contemporary social fads were all implicated in fancy dress and the word 'modern' was applied to it in line with a general rise in the term's usage during the period 1870 to 1930.[31] Any number of Pierrots were designated 'modern' and there was even an outfit called 'Modern Art'. In the early 1920s, *The Lady Book of Fancy Dresses* devoted a paragraph to 'The Modern Touch' with a suggested costume based on Augustus John's painting *The Orange Jacket*, acquired by the Tate Gallery, now Tate Britain, in 1921. Out of the thousands of potential characters, both 'modern' and 'traditional', on offer to pleasure-seekers, Chapter Eight will examine a few in depth: 'Cowboys and Indians', Pierrot and animals.

Fancy dress's ingrained acceptance, and even ordinariness, made it an instantly understood referent in popular culture, and one with a very wide reach. Popular songs, for instance, are greatly apposite to our concerns. The theatrical phenomena of burlesque and music hall that grew out of song and supper rooms in the mid-1850s always included singing. Audience participation was encouraged and sheet music with coloured illustrated covers, in themselves inspiration for fancy dress, was on sale in the many specialist music shops that opened up in the latter part of the nineteenth century. Composers and lyricists turned out song after song to gratify the demand and in the rush to publish they naturally looked to the most topical subjects, fancy dress being one. The incomparable Dan Leno (1860–1904), most remembered for his pantomime dames but a music-hall star as well, impersonated an array of working-class characters and his song 'No More Fancy Balls For Me' dramatized the privations of the less moneyed: 'I ought to have gone as a Roman Glad / but they wanted £4 10sh for that / and I'd only got 15sh to do the evening on.' Inevitably, much knockabout ensues: as the 'King of Denmark', he has his wig pulled off, the 'King of Spain' brandishes a revolver and so on. The singer resolves to give up fancy-dress balls and leave them to the aristocracy and the parsons, a nice touch and one that would have resonated with members of Leno's audience who were aware of the fancy-dress extravaganzas of the moneyed elite.

Many of the storylines of these songs hinged on the disorganized ruckus that fancy dress balls could precipitate but the 'Song of the Perfect Cure', later sometimes called 'The Reg'lar Cure', prompted an entirely new dressing-up costume. The song was taken up by J. H. Stead (*c.* 1828–1886), who had perfected a stage dance routine during the 1850s. By the time Charles Dickens witnessed Stead in 1861 at Weston's Music Hall in London, he had settled on his oddball outfit of conical cap, red-and-white-striped trousers and close-fitting jacket with distinctive lapels giving a kinetic-like appearance (illus. 16). 'A St Vitus's Dance of incessant jumping' was how Dickens described Stead's ceaseless capers across the stage.[32] The song was an inconsequential ditty where the word 'cure' in the final line of each verse came to mean a 'curio' or a 'funny fellow'. The song, dance and offbeat costume mesmerized the public and for thirty or so years 'The Cure', or several identical 'Cures', showed up at fancy-dress parties, a front-runner preference for men of a comedic bent who were bound to elicit total recognition of their character and no doubt a request to perform the giggle-inducing jig.

Fancy dress permeated life in all manner of other ways. It appeared on a poster for the London Underground in 1913 and was used as a textile design in 1937.[33] Its ubiquity implicated it in cases of theft and bankruptcy, divorce proceedings, accidents and more. Novels of the period delineate a variety of fancy-dress entertainments, and capture some of the high tensions and emotions inherent in discarding familiar garments for more aberrant ones. Mr Rochester's artificiality is revealed to Charlotte Brontë's heroine in *Jane Eyre* (1847) by way of a costumed *tableau vivant*. The idle Lupin Pooter and Frank Mutlar's embarrassing stunt dressed as the funambulating Blondin Donkey in *The Diary of*

16 Sheet music cover for *Song of the Perfect Cure* (1861).
The red-and-white striped suit became a hit as fancy dress.

a Nobody (1892) end in humiliation for Mr Pooter Senior. Mapp and Lucia, in the E. F. Benson stories, single themselves out as fit to portray historic paragons in *tableaux* soirées, including 'The Execution of Mary Queen of Scots', 'Brunhilde' and 'King Cophetua and the Beggar Maid'. In the 1926 story 'P&O', by Somerset Maugham, a shipboard fancy-dress celebration goes ahead despite an unfortunate death. The focus of the story is not, in fact, the demise of Mr Gallagher, but rather the dilemma over inviting second-class passengers to attend the ball. In one P. G. Wodehouse novel, *Joy in the Morning* (1947), a Sinbad the Sailor suit and a policeman's uniform are the chosen disguises for a fancy-dress ball as well as an excuse for some ridiculous subterfuge on the part of Bertie Wooster and his valet, Jeeves.[34] While many fictional episodes dilute the sometimes serious content of fancy dress, many also disclose society's stunning snobbery and lay bare the precarious boundaries between one class and another.

Further scrutiny of fiction, biographical writings and diaries, including the Mass Observation survey that recorded everyday life in Britain from 1937 to the early 1950s, might possibly help to illuminate the nuances of people's felt experience of wearing fancy dress. Cartoons targeted fancy dress frequently and lampooned the ridiculous aspects and gaffes of dressing up. These sources have not been as central to this book as other kinds of historic testimony. Local and national newspapers provide limitless accounts of fancy-dress events, as do illustrated journals, and all of them comment generally on the practice and offer advice and tips. They carry advertisements and small-ad columns enriching the fancy-dress archive with information about ticketing and supply of materials. Specialist manuals, etiquette books and pattern magazines, which also contain relevant advertisements, reveal the minutiae of fancy dress, while historic photographs augment the textual and graphic evidence. Local history websites have proved fruitful here, with enthusiastic and knowledgeable volunteers posting images that otherwise would never have been seen outside the family circle. Pathé newsreels brought world affairs to British cinemas from 1910 but also documented low-profile community events, among them fancy-dress stories. Museum collections have remarkably high numbers of fancy-dress garments and although many of these are too frail to be displayed and photographed their mere survival is witness to the importance people assigned to dressing up.

At the beginning of this chapter, I enumerated several clothing customs that are not judged to be fancy dress. I then identified ways of characterizing and framing fancy dress and my hope is that a succinct definition will emerge in the pages that follow. For now, we can say that donning unusual attire of a kind incompatible with daily life and wearing it for a one-off occasion indicates fancy dress. Furthermore, attracting attention and performing, albeit wordlessly, is what fancy dress is all about. And prior to sallying forth in costumed finery, there is the anticipation of the event, a flight into a fantasy realm well before the special day itself. The whole process enfolded the party-goer in an otherworldly intensity as they metamorphosed into another being over several weeks. Dressing up was all about feeling different and, for the most part, it was enacted with thoroughgoing pleasure, a sensibility that hopefully pervades this book. The costume choices of well-to-do ball-goers made manifest the hopes and attitudes of the ruling class even though grand balls, like that organized by the Duchess of Devonshire in 1897, are arguably also a testament to incipient anxieties about the stability of that class. For all classes the photograph stands as a document in an archive imparting permanency to a sitter in transient fantasy clothes, both a record of joy and a symptom of unease in a transforming world.

17 Henry Follett dressed in mayoral regalia for the Exeter Juvenile Ball, hand-tinted photograph by Owen Angel, 1873.

One

BALLS AND PARTIES

Charles John Follett (1838–1921) was Mayor of Exeter between 1872 and 1874. In 1875, a large oil portrait of him clothed in his robes and insignia of office was commissioned by the city council of this cathedral city in the county of Devon. In 1873, Mayor Follett's son, Henry, had donned a miniature set of mayoral regalia and been immortalized not in oils but in a photograph, an increasingly popular format for portraiture (illus. 17). This aspirational image was by no means unusual and it gives us a point of entry into one facet of dressing up, namely costume balls. Henry Follett's child-size outfit was worn to a juvenile fancy-dress ball, the rituals of which were enacted all across Britain and the empire with remarkably little variation during the period covered by this book. The Exeter ball held on 14 January 1873 ostensibly celebrated the birthday of another Follett child, Marian, though other meanings can be ascribed to the event, and the essential qualities of the Follett party concur with the practices of fancy dress more broadly: the careful choice of outfits and their making, the utilization of photography to memorialize the event along with the near certainty of local or national news coverage, the implications of class, gender and social status, the involvement of children. The turn towards respectability as a corrective to the rakish costumes of eighteenth-century entertainments is also a factor.

Fifty children attended the Exeter ball, which provides us with an early example of this type of gathering. Both the written and visual records survive, and an account of this well-documented event will help to elucidate the genre and act as an introduction to the world of fancy dress in general. The young guests are attired in beautifully crafted clothes. Images of each child were pasted into an album soon after the event. The list of *dramatis personae* is long but it bears reciting here because it evokes the spectrum of characters available to party-goers. The surviving photographs are captioned: 'Mayor of Exeter', 'La Figlia de Reggimento', 'A Dresden Shepherdess', 'Queen of the Fairies', 'Queen of the Roses', 'Violet Seller', 'Bo Peep', 'Greek Girl', 'Red Riding Hood', 'Man o'Wars Man', 'Robin Hood', 'A French Flower Girl', 'Bertram and Parolles', 'Norman Peasant', 'The Princess Elizabeth (Daughter of Charles I)', 'The Princes in the Tower', 'Queen of the May', 'Italian Boy', 'Forget-Me-Not Girl', 'Cherry Girl', 'Sailor (HMS Victory)', 'Italian Brigand', 'Richard Coeur de Lion', 'Queen Mab', 'Queen of the May', 'Captain Royal Engineers', 'Prince Arthur as Betty in Shakespeare's King John from the picture by Northcote, R.A.', 'The Princess Zobeide of Bagdad', 'Haroun Alraschid Caliph of Bagdad', 'La Marquis de Clairvaulx', 'La Princesse de Lamballe', 'Dolly Varden', 'Spring Time', 'Greek Boy', 'à la Watteau', 'Aurora', 'Buy a Broom', 'A Cavalier (time of Charles I)', 'Court Page (Charles II)', 'Rob Roy'.[1] From the second half of the nineteenth century, this type of fancy dress, with some variation, as we shall see, dominated exclusive children's costume balls hosted by civic leaders and the aristocracy, as well as those organized by dancing academies for the children of the well-off.[2] The sometimes irregular nomenclature, the mingling of periods and places, and the intertwining of fact with fantasy run through all fancy-dress undertakings, and vagueness abounds. Those outfits that carry clear markers of recognition are likely to be the ones that are perpetuated across time and class, though many of these too fall out of favour and are unknowable to later generations.

So, what can we say about these 1873 garments concerning the origins of their popularity and their longevity as fancy dress? Diminutive mayors are distinctive to children's civic balls, which were widespread in provincial cities until well after the First World War. In 1912, a more demotic gathering than the Exeter one, the street carnival in Garston, Liverpool, echoed the high-class children's event with a child mayor and mayoress.[3] Many children at the Exeter ball wore historic dress and this remained a fixture on the fancy-dress scene even if specific characters were eclipsed. Named figures from France's *ancien régime*, such as the now only dimly remembered Princesse de Lamballe, faded from the costume canon in the twentieth century. Garments inspired by Watteau paintings and the closely aligned porcelain figures of shepherdesses abounded at the Exeter ball. Their bucolic prettiness meant they were never out of vogue and the *poudré* style, termed after its defining attribute of white powdered hair, lived on in many permutations (illus. 18). Certain characters from Shakespeare reappear across the years but Prince Arthur from the bard's *King John* diminished in popularity. The flaxen-haired Amyas Stafford Northcote, who dressed up as Arthur in Exeter, bore a close resemblance to the prodigiously popular child actor William Henry West Betty (1791–1874), or Master Betty, as he was known. The name 'Northcote' in the Exeter album caption must refer to James Northcote (1746–1831), an artist who painted Master Betty several times. We presume the artist's name is mentioned because he is most likely an ancestor of young Amyas Northcote, an example of the practice, particularly rife among well-connected families, of dressing up as an illustrious forebear.

Alongside Shakespeare and history, many of the outfits in Exeter derived from nursery rhymes, fairy tales, stories and legends. Several of the characters are, in fact, children. Their inclusion helped to keep the adult world at a distance though the participants themselves might have relished playing at grown-ups. With the passing of time, some characters are transformed, almost flattened out, into something less specific, more generic. Lottie and Rashleigh Porter came to the Follett ball from eighth-century Baghdad, though there was more fiction than history to their named characters. 'Haroun Alraschid, Caliph of Bagdad', as Rashleigh's character is transcribed, was a historic Abbasid ruler at the time of Baghdad's greatest magnificence in the late eighth and early ninth century. The real Harun al-Rashid crossed over into fantasy and his medieval court was the impetus behind several of the tales in the *Arabian Nights*. Lottie Porter, partnering her brother, is an apparition from the dazzling and fantastic Arabian stories too. Dressed as 'The Princess Zobeide of Bagdad', she seems to be portraying two characters in one: Sultana Zubayada, the favourite wife of the caliph, and Zobeide, the heroine in the cycle of stories 'The Porter and the Three Ladies of Baghdad'.[4] There is a play on the Porter surname here, and while this might be unintentional, it is in the nature of fancy dress to draw on such puns. The *Arabian Nights* seem predisposed to fancy dress because the costumes are singular, far different from those worn in everyday life. The siblings wear loose trousers gathered in at the ankle and Lottie's just peep below her pearl-encrusted frock. The novelty of wearing golden, pendant earrings of considerable size must have delighted the young girl, though her brother's false moustache is perhaps an example of fancy dress's pervasive potential for discomfort. As time went by, 'Arabia' was to be more or less loosened from its connection with the *Arabian Nights* and, apart from a few honourable exceptions, its realization in the twentieth century across all fancy-dress categories would be reduced to 'harem trousers', bare midriffs and flimsy face veils.

A strict division of gender was maintained at these official balls at this date. Boys dress as stout-hearted military and naval characters, legendary heroes or derring-do brigands. 'Dolly Varden' and 'La Figlia de Reggimento' ('Daughter of the Regiment'), two female characters at the Exeter ball, recur as favourites throughout the nineteenth century, and

18 Agnes Porter dressed in *poudré* style as La Princesse de Lamballe for the Exeter Juvenile Ball, hand-tinted photograph by Owen Angel, 1873.

intermittently live on in the next decades (illus. 19). Precisely who these characters were may have been lost to later generations of party-goers.

Dolly Varden, from Charles Dickens's *Barnaby Rudge*, serialized through 1840 and 1841, caught the imagination of fancy dressers to such an extent that several Dollys often appeared together. In Exeter the sisters Annie and Constance Richards both went to the ball dressed as the sweet-natured Dolly. Perhaps neither sister was prepared to countenance another costume. Whether, in truth, the children themselves played any part in choosing their characters is doubtful. This only seems to have been encouraged in the 1920s.[5] The fact that *Barnaby Rudge* is an historic novel set in the 1780s, a favourite period for fancy-dress aficionados, partly accounts for Dolly's popularity and inclusion in so many of the listings, but the magnetism of the costume also rests with Dolly's signature small straw hat and the cut of the dress itself: a flowered or quilted overskirt gathered up over a separate underskirt. This style was not confined to costume balls: the 'Dolly Varden dress' was in vogue as day dress in the early 1870s when Dickens's own oil painting of her came on to the market just at the time the Richards sisters wore it as fancy dress, an unusual, though not unknown, instance of contemporary clothing being taken up as costume.[6]

'La Figlia de Reggimento', as another Follett daughter, Harriet, is styled, is an intriguing character, vastly popular because of Donizetti's opera *La Fille du régiment*, first staged in London in 1847. The daughter of the title grows up to serve as a *vivandière* or *cantinière*, French terms for women who were official suppliers of food and drink to the army. These military followers' distinctive clothes greatly endeared them to fancy dressers who had plenty of reference material in the form of a myriad coloured prints. The great recorder of the Crimean War (1853–6), Roger Fenton, even photographed one in 1855. By dressing in the dashing *vivandière* manner, girls were able to participate imaginatively in a soldierly life. They copied real-life *vivandières* in donning an approximation of military uniform: a tight-fitting tailored jacket, a skirt just above the ankle and that most controversial of garments, a pair of trousers. The ensemble was completed with a brimmed hat and the accessory that defined the character, a brandy barrel across the shoulders.[7] Apart from the trousers, Harriet Follett conformed to this style but the pristine nature and richness of her outfit, trimmed in gold bands, swansdown and red silk ribbons, was filtered through the opera rather than the battlefield.

In the Victorian era, flowers were seen as playing an important role in the material expression of sentiment. It is therefore no surprise that many of the girls' costumes feature floral decoration. Mabel Baker as 'Queen of the Roses' wears a dress fashioned in tiers with scalloped edges in imitation of the enfolding petals of a flower. There is thus a suggestion that Mabel is the embodiment of the rose itself, personifications being a compelling component of fancy dress. In the Follett album, 'Aurora' and 'Spring-Time' provide other examples of the cultural preference for depicting young women as personifications of the natural world. In the same vein, Feodore Mary Ellis and Alice Maud Milford, both dressed as 'Queen of the May', embody spring and the May Day celebrations. Their white dresses and flower crowns mark them out as these familiar allegorical female figures associated with the European-wide custom, well established by the sixteenth century, of celebrating springtime fertility. The May Day rite in the towns and villages of England was still flourishing at the time of the Follett ball in 1873. Later in the century, it was to be further reinvigorated by Victorian folklorists and the art critic John Ruskin (1819–1900), and in certain locales it became part of carnival and included other forms of fancy dress. May Day remained overwhelmingly a working people's celebration, as evocatively portrayed in Flora Thompson's *Lark Rise to Candleford*, published in 1945 though recording events at the end of the nineteenth century. The Devon children at the Follett ball were from

19 Harriet Follett dressed as 'La Figlia de Reggimento' (The Daughter of the Regiment) for the Exeter Juvenile Ball, hand-tinted photograph by Owen Angel, 1873.

a social milieu that may have excluded them from taking a major role in this working-class holiday. In dressing as May Queens for a private party they are not only crossing over into a fantasy realm, but crossing class. The fluidity of fancy dress allows ball-goers to move up the social scale as well as down but, perhaps because of their already high status, there are more depictions of common people than the reverse among the Exeter children. With only imprecise and sanitized notions of the life of a real flower girl, Violet Barnes, who would go on to be a successful actress under the name of Violet Vanbrugh, came to the ball as 'Violet Seller' (another play on words). Mary Buckingham was 'A French Flower Girl', Sophia Harding and her sister, Isabel, 'Forget-Me-Not Girl' and 'Cherry Girl' respectively. Any suggestion of their working lives, as with the *vivandière*, has been erased. The flower seller is as clean as the princess; there are no scuffed shoes or dirty hands here. These young girls, and certainly their mothers, would have been familiar with another aspect of the culture of flowers, one they would have acknowledged more openly than that connected to the earthy life of a street flower seller. The interest in the symbolic meanings of flowers was nearing its height at the time of the Follett children's ball. Partly based on mythology and traditional floriculture, the 'language of flowers' was reworked and reinvented in many different formats, so much so that floral messages and their interpretation became a defining aspect of Victorian culture. It is small wonder that flowers and fancy dress were inseparably linked at this time. And both were bound to the feminine because the language of flowers was suffused with communicating the sentiments of love.

By way of dressing up, ordinary mortals could be elevated to sempiternal beings as well as having regal status bestowed on them. Marian Follett, the mayor's young daughter, and Bertha Lloyd assumed the form of immortal queens for the duration of the party, Marian as 'Queen of the Fairies' and Bertha as 'Queen Mab', really the same being.

As with Lottie Porter's earrings, great attention was paid to jewellery, trimmings and accessories for all the outfits at the Follett ball, but the fairy accessory that was to find its most persistent expression in the later Victorian period through to the present day is remarkable for either its absence or smallness here. Wings are unseen on Marian and Bertha's costumes though tiny ones like those depicted on the slender back of the ballerina Marie Taglioni, performing *La Sylphide* in the early 1830s, may be present. While we think of these iridescent flying mechanisms as completing and even defining a fairy costume, according to Thomas Keightley's authoritative two-volume work *The Fairy Mythology*, first published in 1828, wings are rare in folklore, for fairies flew by magic and sometimes hitched a ride on the back of birds. The fairy extravaganza, awash with wings, of Gilbert and Sullivan's opera *Iolanthe* (1882) was still a little way in the future for the Devon children, but pantomime and the images reproduced of it could have played a part in the imagining of fairyland.[8] Like a stage set, the *mise en scène* of the ball itself was designed to be a wonderland and to frame the costumed children.

Under the auspices of the Lady Mayoress, a prominent figure in all these civic gatherings, the Exeter boys and girls were taken to the theatre a few days after the ball itself decked out in their party outfits. Costumed children looking at costumed actors served up a double helping of illusion. The youthful companions were on display in a way they had not been at the party, their distinctive clothes singling them out as privileged young people. They were on show yet again when they posed for the camera, giving them a third opportunity to wear their special apparel. On this occasion, they were required to be immobile. Though speeding up, exposure times were still long throughout the nineteenth century, with management of the sitter viewed as a necessary part of the photographer's craft.[9] If we could see beyond the frame of the final photograph, we would learn much more about fancy dress and posing.

Sometimes photographers rigged up makeshift studios at party venues, but the controlled misrule of these fancy-dress balls, and their surprisingly late finish, meant that over-excited children and crumpled costumes were not ideal subjects for photography. For some children visiting the studio was a way to perpetuate the pleasure. For others there might be an ambivalence about stretching the conceit too far and spoiling a singular experience.

We interrupt the narrative of the Exeter images here to note that all costumed ball-goers throughout our period, children and adults alike, persisted in presenting themselves to the camera. When electric light was installed in photographic studios in the late 1880s fancy dressers of modest means could have their portraits taken before a ball to ensure the costume looked its best prior to an evening of dancing. The Electric Light Studio of Mayall in Brighton, for instance, opened by appointment after 6 p.m. especially for ladies en route to balls and dinner parties and this arrangement was convenient for those who had to return hired outfits to a costumier.[10] For photography studios up and down the country, this type of work became commonplace. The inexpensive box Brownie camera, needing no tripod, became available in the early 1900s and ineluctably linked the British enthusiasm for family snapshots with their love of dressing up. Nonetheless, studio photography continued to prosper, partly owing to the challenge faced by amateurs of lighting indoor spaces.

A great deal of bulky equipment would have been needed by Owen Angel (*c.* 1821–1909), the photographer charged with recording the Follett children in 1873. He is the emissary between us and the children. Photographs and presentation albums became key features of fancy-dress parties, commemorating their celebratory elements and enhancing the status of organizers and participants alike. When photography turned out to be a viable financial practice – early pioneers moved the craft forwards surprisingly swiftly, though there was much innovation to come in the years that followed this album's creation – Owen Angel saw an opportunity for his already thriving printing business and, by the time he was commissioned by Mayor Follett, Angel already had nearly twenty years of photographic experience behind him. Charles Follett would rightly have regarded him as one of Exeter's most successful photographers, though it was a crowded profession. The gilded album containing the cabinet portraits of the named children binds fancy dress to photography, a persistent coupling throughout our period.[11]

Children's fancy-dress balls were not an invention of Queen Victoria's reign, though they gathered pace at this time and the royal court certainly fostered the idea of dressing up. Queen Victoria's children were often portrayed in fancy dress. In 1859, the queen and Prince Albert gave a *bal costume* for one of their children, Prince Leopold, on his sixth birthday. He and his brother, Arthur, were arrayed in cream and pale blue satin as the sons of the English king Henry IV, while two of their sisters were in Swiss costume.[12]

Mayoral children's parties, like the one in Exeter, were doubtless swayed by royal exemplar. These juvenile balls, defined by fancy dress, came to great prominence in the second half of the nineteenth century and increasingly became annual civic affairs opulently staged in municipal guildhalls. In Liverpool in 1877, council workers laid down a crimson carpet, festooned the hall with evergreen boughs and hothouse plants, affixed long mirrors to the walls and rigged up lighted globes supported on statuary. We know that this Liverpool ball was viewed by the mayor, Alderman Walker (1824–1893), a wealthy brewer and benefactor of the Walker Art Gallery, as an attempt to include a wider section of the Liverpool citizenry in civic festivities rather than confining these festivities to the male cliques in political power at the time.[13]

We are not told on what basis the Liverpool children were chosen so we cannot determine their social status, but a letter in one local paper, just prior to the event, hints at, but does not spell out, the possible financial burden of attending such a gathering. The correspondent recommends 'Highland Scotch' dress because it can be made in many variations, and leather ankle bands with buckles can serve for shoes. Moreover, the outfit had a cost advantage because it could be used time and again as ordinary outdoor wear.[14] We do learn from a report later in that same year that Mayor Walker 'brought all classes to share in the festivities furnished by his liberal purse and open heart' but we cannot gauge exactly what this meant.[15] As the Scottish outfit demonstrates, home-made costumes were acceptable alongside those supplied by costumiers. MacTaggart of Bold Street advertised apparel specifically for the forthcoming Liverpool children's ball, and made colour plates and costume books available to make a selection.[16]

Between five hundred and six hundred children attended the Liverpool ball, a much larger number than the more private ball in Exeter and a sign of what was to come throughout Britain and the empire. In Adelaide around the same number of young guests were photographed caparisoned in their costumes for the 'complimentary return' mayoral ball there in November 1887.[17] These 'return balls', seemingly very popular in Australia, for several are recorded, provided an excuse to dress up twice in the space of less than a month, such was the ardour for fancy-dress functions. The Adelaide ball was in celebration of Queen Victoria's Golden Jubilee and, as we shall see in Chapter Five, national rejoicings provided many opportunities to dress up. We can discern several parallels between these three mayoral balls – Exeter, Liverpool and Adelaide – and between many similar ones of the period.[18] Where there are surviving photographs, single and sibling portraits are favoured, and poses are limited to a fairly narrow range. Importantly, while we expect the choice of costume to vary over nearly twenty years, we find many characters reprising their roles. Fairies, flower girls, variant forms of shepherdesses and peasants, nursery-rhyme characters,

20 Beatrice Hardy dressed as 'Cherry Ripe' for the Children's Fancy Dress Ball, Adelaide, photographed by the firm of Wivell, 1887.

fisher folk, powdered aristocrats, soldiers, sailors, Robin Hood, Dick Whittington and the Daughter of the Regiment, nearly all of which featured in Exeter, stand their ground at later balls.

But among the tried-and-tested outfits, 'Carmen', after the first London production of the opera in 1878, finds favour and spawns many permutations of 'Gypsy'. Sportsmen and women begin to appear in line with a greater understanding of the benefits of exercise: 'Cricketer', 'Footballer', 'Jockey' and 'Lawn Tennis', this last a widely adopted fancy-dress conceit of labelling a character as an abstract noun. 'Cherry Ripe' infiltrates the fancy-dress ball in Adelaide several times over and from 1880 onwards the little girl with the outsize mob cap, a cluster of cherries at her side, continued to appear at all levels of costume party (illus. 20). John Everett Millais (1829–1896) painted the original picture as a commission to be reproduced and stapled into the centrefold of *The Graphic* Christmas Annual in 1880. The inspiration for it was a young guest at a fancy-dress ball organized by the journal. Its reliance on a portrait by Sir Joshua Reynolds (1723–1792) helped it on its way to become a fancy-dress norm because the eighteenth century, and Reynolds in particular, were viewed by the Victorians with nostalgic reverie as the epitome of Englishness. 'Cherry Ripe' added another pretty costume to the fancy-dress ranks, joining those other mainstays of sweetness, 'Dresden Shepherdess', 'Dolly Varden', 'à la Watteau' and 'Cherry Girl', that had gone before. Boys were not exempt from this aura of innocence and posed in pastel blue satin and lace after Gainsborough's painting *The Blue Boy* (*c.* 1770), known to a Victorian audience through many print reproductions, and itself a homage to an even earlier artist, Van Dyck (1599–1641).[19] Release from this saccharine honey trap comes by way of 'Girl Graduate' in gown and mortar board, a gratifyingly popular costume unseen, and perhaps unimagined, at Exeter but replicated several times over at the later balls. By the time of the Adelaide ball, a few women were beginning to enter higher education and wear gowns, though the fancy-dress version was still highly aspirational.

The Adelaide gathering had the advantage of a broader choice of characters by way of what became the bible of fancy-dress guides, Ardern Holt's *Fancy Dresses Described or What to Wear at Fancy Balls*, first published in 1879. Holt helped to sanction inanimate concept costumes more broadly for party-going communities. However, several years before domestic telephones were installed in Adelaide and prior to its appearance in a later Holt listing, a young Adelaide guest,

21 Antonia Bircher dressed as a telephone for the Children's Fancy Dress Ball, Adelaide, photographed by the firm of Wivell, 1887.

ten-year-old Antonia Bircher, appeared as this newfangled contrivance in 1887, a surprisingly early date for the telephone, the culmination of much experimentation with the electric telegraph (illus. 21).[20]

Portraits of dressed-up children by several renowned studios in London survive in some numbers from the Lord Mayor's Juvenile Balls, still held annually at the Mansion House in the City. They are preserved in albums and were also published, first as engravings and later as half-tones, in the illustrated pages of weekly journals with national and empire-wide circulation (illus. 22). This is childhood as spectacle. The time span between the Exeter ball of 1873 and the very many later London Lord Mayor's balls stretching through to the Second World War and beyond tells a significant story of both certain continuities and obvious innovations in the practices surrounding children, photography and fancy dress. The collaged image of the 1925 Mansion House event published in *The Sphere* shows the children dressed as characters that appear right across most decades of our period: cowboy, pirate, Italian peasant, Stuart and Georgian costume, Harlequin and

22 The Lord Mayor's Juvenile Fancy Dress Ball at the Mansion House, London, *The Graphic*, 12 January 1895.

Columbine, Gordon Highlander, Madame de Pompadour.[21] They are conservative choices. When photographed individually, however, more contemporary characters are seen to have been present at what *The Sphere* termed a 'Lilliput Ball'. In 1925, as in many subsequent years, the Lord Mayor had commissioned the famous London-based photographer Alexander Bassano to photograph the children in a portable studio set up within the Mansion House. The firm was an obvious choice for this civic occasion, for it regularly photographed mayors in their regalia and, right from the start, photography had been an unquestioned adjunct to civic grandiloquence, as it was to dressing up. In the 1925 studio shots, the children were photographed against a plain, uncluttered background, affirming that change for this particular domain of fancy dress was in the mode of iconographic representation (illus. 23).

A more distinct break with the past, however, comes with the advent of moving pictures. In 1936, in a Pathé newsreel of the event, the London children are seen crowding into the Mansion House and shaking hands with their hosts, though a traditional album of still photographs commemorates the occasion as well.[22] The newsreel breathes life into the garments and we fleetingly see close-up details of pleats, trimmings and fastenings. At least two costumes at this 1936 ball, 'Umbrella' and 'Paint Box', correspond directly to paper dressmaking patterns from Weldons, a firm who played a part in keeping fancy dress in the mainstream. An acknowledgement of modernity was provided by 'Flight', a dress strewn with birds and aeroplanes worn with a winged headdress. A hint of decorous cross-dressing was supplied by Miss Freshman, who appeared in eighteenth-century male *poudré* attire comprising a satin coat worn over knee breeches, a lace jabot and buckled shoes. This was one of the first ensembles to be acceptable for both genders. Earlier, Victoria, the Princess Royal, was dressed this way in a Winterhalter watercolour of 1850 of her dancing with her sister.[23] Before boys became seriously interested in ballet, girls took male and

23 Robert and Cynthia Brown dressed as a 'Pearly King' and 'Powder Puff' for the Lord Mayor's Juvenile Fancy Dress Ball, London, photographed by the Bassano Studio, 1925.

24 A young guest books a dance partner at the Lord Mayor's Juvenile Fancy Dress Ball, London, 1934.

female parts at amateur shows and the fashion seems to have spread to fancy dress. Other cross-dressers in 1936 are the Shipton sisters, both dressed in the style of Fred Astaire, the Hollywood star famous for his flawless dance routines. The humour implicit in cross-dressing was slow to take off at these formal children's balls and even as late as 1936 many of the costumes were carbon copies of what had gone before. A telling shot from the Pathé newsreel shows a young boy as Harlequin holding a pad and pencil in his hand. Is he noting down his impressions of the ball? A similar still image from 1934 and surviving stationery from the 1938 and 1939 Mansion House Balls confirm that this was a programme card used to record the names of partners for successive dances (illus. 24).[24] This touching custom lived on in the face of irreversible changes in fancy-dress practices outside of this closed circle.

Those changes – manifest in their disparate venues and modes of organization – opened up the opportunity for children of different backgrounds to attend costume parties. Fancy dress was recast as something accessible to a greater number of children, though balls for the privileged are better documented than more modest gatherings. The brief notice on the front page of the *Ripley and Heanor News and Ilkeston Division Free Press* for Friday, 27 December 1929, can stand in for many similar ones in the 1920s, '30s and '40s:

> CHILDREN'S FANCY DRESS PARTY
> Outram Street Schools, RIPLEY, FRIDAY, DEC. 27th, at 6 p.m.
> Tickets: 1/- (refreshments inclusive)
> In aid of Sunday School Funds
> Come and spend a Happy Evening.
> A Treat in store for all.

Cost, both of tickets and of costumes, is more in evidence from the First World War on. In 1927, the competition classes at a children's

25 The Palmer and Godfrey children at a fancy-dress party aboard RMS *Orion*. George Palmer compiled an album of photographs on his migrant voyage from England to Australia with his wife Gertrude and their two daughters, Shirley and Lesley, in March 1947.

fancy-dress party in Farndon, a village on the banks of the River Dee in Cheshire, were divided between those costumes costing less than five shillings and those over that sum.[25] Many of the characters portrayed in Farndon duplicate those at the 1873 Exeter ball, notably fairies, flower girls and peasants, and some Farndon costumes also match up with those from contemporaneous Lord Mayor's Balls, 'Powder Puff', for example. The visual evidence for these more relaxed fancy-dress get-togethers is piecemeal but newspaper reports sometimes include a grainy, often cheerily shambolic, line-up of attendees, a formation that would never have passed muster at a Lord Mayor's Ball. Other pervasive testimony for less polished children's parties survives in the form of

British migrant family snapshots taken on board ship (illus. 25). Fancy dress was a customary way to pass days at sea and perhaps it helped fend off anxieties about the future. Apart from sea voyages, indoor children's fancy-dress events lived on in the 1940s and '50s mostly in the form of birthday parties for a small group of friends, but dressing up really prospered when it moved outdoors, as we shall presently see.

Adult costume balls encapsulated many of the same elements that defined their child counterparts. Queen Victoria played a part in establishing fancy dress as respectable for adults as well as for children. Her three themed balls – Medieval, early Georgian and Restoration – put in place an ongoing vogue for grand affairs centred on tradition and history. The costumes for the first in 1842 looked back to the reign of Edward III (1312–1377), a king remembered for re-establishing royal authority. Inspired by the Westminster Abbey effigies of Edward and his wife, Philippa of Hainault, Queen Victoria and Prince Albert took on the roles of this regal couple themselves and were immortalized wearing their costumes by Edwin Landseer (1802–1873). His resplendent painting makes plain one of the constants of fancy dress: beneath an historic veneer, it unfailingly discloses the clothing styles of the time. Vouillon & Laure, the royal dressmakers, fashioned Queen Victoria's costumes for all three balls and a surviving dress, a confection of Benares silk and carefully copied seventeenth-century Venetian lace, exposes a stark disparity with the materials more ordinarily equated with fancy dress.[26]

Inexpensive faux materials were certainly used for fancy dress, as we shall see in Chapter Seven, but costly textiles are also synonymous with dressing up. Lush fabric and haute couture coincide with ball costumes on which moneyed heiresses were prepared to spend ostentatiously, as was the case with the Devonshire House Fancy Dress Ball of 1897. Held in honour of Queen Victoria's Diamond Jubilee and orchestrated by the Duchess of Devonshire (1832–1911), the surviving documentation for this ball, like that of the Follett's, is substantial and can help us make sense of other such events even though they were not on such a lavish scale.[27]

The place of high fashion within fancy dress comes into play in this affluent stratum of society. At the end of the nineteenth century, Paris and London were establishing themselves as burgeoning centres of fashion. A new breed of dress designer took inspiration from, and contributed to, the visual and performing arts of the day. Their clients' requests for fancy dress, apparitions of fantasy brought to corporeality by the skilled manipulation of luxurious cloth, appealed to their creative sensibilities. For the 1897 Devonshire ball Evelyn James, to give just one example, a very wealthy guest, acquired her Empress Elizabeth costume at Maison Lucile, a flourishing couture business run by Lady Duff-Gordon (1863–1935), the originator of theatrical catwalk shows.[28] These shows can be equated with the sequential parade of costumed guests at the start of many balls. The very obvious link between the theatre, high fashion and fancy dress is evidenced by the couturier Charles Frederick Worth (1825–1895), who worked with some of the most famous actresses of the day. Several affluent women chose the House of Worth, which continued after Charles's death, to dress them for the Devonshire ball. The costumes for Cleopatra, Marie Antoinette, Empress Theodora of Byzantium and, for the hostess herself, Zenobia, queen of Palmyra, all emanated from the Worth studio (illus. 26).

The 1897 Devonshire ball appropriated the over-reaching indulgence and arrogant hauteur of its several predecessors, the most recent of which had been the Marlborough House Ball held 23 years before, in 1874. The Duchess of Devonshire's guest list included royalty, members of the aristocracy, notable celebrities and politicians, and she summoned invitees to appear in allegorical or historical costume prior to 1820. She gave further instructions to some of the crème de la crème to cluster into pre-arranged groups, called quadrilles, who would process in formation and dance together, having rehearsed beforehand. This format was common to many balls. Like fancy dress itself, the quadrille themes at the Devonshire Ball proved to be rather porous. Apart from royal quadrilles – the courts of Elizabeth I and of Empress Catherine II of Russia, for example – another group formed around King Arthur and his Knights of the Round Table, headed by Guinevere. The presence of a quadrille of 'Orientals', led by the Duchess herself as the Palmyran queen, lent an indeterminate Eastern flavour to the evening. The gauzy draperies, ornate jewellery and peacock-feather fans of this group were all exoticizing elements distilled from a charmed world beyond Europe. 'Oriental' fancy dress provided an opportunity for seductive dressing and sultry posing, as well as an excuse to abandon corsets.

26 The Duchess of Devonshire dressed as Zenobia, queen of Palmyra, for the Devonshire House Fancy Dress Ball, photographed by the Lafayette Studio, 1897. The Duchess's dress is shown in illus. 11.

Contrary to the rhetoric of fancy dress as fun, this self-regarding extravaganza had far less to do with enjoyment than it did with the maintenance of class and the upholding of tradition, the empire and the monarchy. Celebrating Queen Victoria's sixty years on the throne, the many queenly costumes devised for this jubilee ball paid homage to a sovereign who loved dressing up. Queen Victoria did not attend in person but her imprint was everywhere. As the embodiment of the nation, Lady Wolverton as Britannia stood in for the ageing queen and other guests invoked a deliriously haphazard chronology of queens and empresses selected from classical, biblical and literary sources. Queen Elizabeth I was the only queen at Devonshire House who had ruled England in her own right. Other queens regnant such as Mary Tudor and the Stuarts Anne and Mary appear from the published material not to have been prominent and may indeed have been absent altogether. Maybe this tells us that although the abundance of queens at the ball was deliberate, the choice of particular regal women ensured that Victoria could be favourably compared with them. To single out Elizabeth I was to align Victoria with the achievements of both royal houses.

Men and women party-goers were drawn to Shakespearean characters, to opera heroes and heroines, to historic figures and to personifications of the Moon and Night. Greek goddesses attracted several ladies, and the Countess of Gosford contrived to portray Minerva by combining mythology with the ever-popular *poudré* style. Appearing across several groupings at the duchess's ball, this powdered effect, as we have seen with children, became an amorphous category of dress that could easily accommodate any number of characters spread across a fairly wide spectrum of historic, painterly and fictional subjects. It appealed to those of all classes and it lingered on endlessly in the fancy-dress canon, but its *ancien régime* associations of rank, superiority and wealth ensured it an extremely high profile at Devonshire House.

Out of the costumed throng of seven hundred, only a handful of people whose photographs still exist were, or pretended to be, people of colour. Prince Victor Duleep Singh (1866–1918) had been brought up in England and outwardly retained few of his Sikh forebears' practices despite being the head of the Royal House of the Punjab. He attended the ball attired as the Muslim Mughal emperor Akbar (r. 1556–1605). The gentleman acting as a train bearer in Lafayette's photograph of Gladys, Countess de Grey, as Cleopatra is unquestionably of African descent. He is used as a prop and a foil to her magnificence, though his own costume – 'a real old Egyptian slave's attire' as reported by the

Lady's Pictorial – has not been overlooked and is a fanciful concoction. Major George Cornwallis-West wore black make-up to play a minor role as one of four attendants to his sister, Princess Daisy of Hess as the Queen of Sheba. In the photograph Cornwallis-West wears a long-sleeved, full-length gown and his face gleams with sweat beneath his make-up. Reports make mention of other 'Black Attendants' accompanying costumed guests but we know nothing of them. Doubtless there were servants of African and Asian descent working in the Devonshire House kitchens and gardens.[29]

The renowned firm of Lafayette secured the original commission for photographing the Devonshire guests in a specially erected tent in the garden of the Piccadilly house. Lafayette's proprietor, James Stack Lauder (1853–1923), claimed to have continued photographing until five in the morning, when fatigue overtook his camera operators. The fact that the fancy-dress outfits, and indeed their wearers, appear pristine must be due to the robust tailoring of the gowns as well as to the largely unexplored work of the Devonshires' major-domo and the many, perhaps hundreds, of stewards and servants who orchestrated this visual register of guests and ensured that the costumes remained immaculate, intact and unsullied by food and sweat stains. We know that these bone-weary menials were also dressed in costume: Egyptian, Elizabethan or the Devonshire livery of the eighteenth century. Permanent house staff wore made-to-measure garments and the casual labour made do with clothes hired from a theatrical outfitter.[30]

But despite the servants' best efforts, a number of the guests extended the photographic sessions to the ensuing days, resuming sittings at the Lafayette Studio and at other society photographers' premises to ensure the perfect picture. The presentation album produced in 1899, *Devonshire House Fancy Dress Ball, July 2nd, 1897: A Collection of Portraits in Costume of Some of the Guests*, is a startling work. The vanity of the sitters, intensified by the astonishing way they are dressed, is plain to see. For connoisseurs of fancy dress, this ball is the gold standard for late Victorian grandiloquence and there were others in a similar vein right across the empire.[31]

Beyond question, decor and setting were cardinal ingredients of any fancy-dress experience and Covent Garden theatre became a venue for wildly ambitious costumed entertainments (illus. 27). In a more louche style than the Devonshire event but no less baroque, the annual series of balls held at the opera house from 1891 were also about class and reflected the changing mores of the time. Sandwiched in between opera performances to extract the maximum profit for the theatre impresarios, this particular series of balls, started by the manager, Augustus Harris (1852–1896), were commercial undertakings. They were overblown and even notorious affairs. Despite this, or perhaps because of it, the Covent Garden phenomenon laid down a blueprint for the many hundreds of other similar, less ostentatious paying balls.

Open to the general public with tickets priced on a sliding scale, the Covent Garden balls were advertised in a broad range of newspapers read by several different sectors of society. This seems to presage a more open event, one that did not differentiate on the basis of income, with fancy dress acting as the leveller. However, when we consider the layout of a theatre like the Royal Opera House, with its tiered balconies and boxes, we can understand how, for some people, spectating rather than parading in costume became part of the pleasure. Furthermore, we know that the desirable seats with the best views were substantially more expensive than mere 'admission to the ball': eight or ten guineas as opposed to one guinea, though the latter was still a hefty price for many working people. A situation thus arose where the rich, or at least the richer, were looking down on the less well-off and exhibitionists of any class, all in fancy dress. Illustrations and reports of these balls tell us that those who were elevated, both literally and by virtue of wealth, tended not to dress up but wore conventional evening dress.[32] Fancy dress may have permeated several classes who had not previously dressed up but no class barriers had fallen.

A correspondent for *The Bystander*, a weekly read by the upper-middle class, expected to make friends on the spot at a Covent Garden ball: 'I did not like the "friends" I made,' he reported haughtily, having been addressed by his masked dance partner as 'dearie' and asked to stand her a bottle of champagne.[33] Within this narrative, we learn that

THE FANCY DRESS BALL AT COVENT GARDEN
DRAWN BY ARTHUR HOPKINS, R.W.S.

27 The Fancy Dress Ball at Covent Garden, from *The Graphic*, 12 March 1895.

masking, a feature that was dropping out of use elsewhere, positions this particular type of ball as a continuation of the earlier masquerade, an entertainment with a risqué reputation for deviance introduced from Venice at the beginning of the eighteenth century and famous for illicit assignations in darkened, outdoor settings like London's Thameside Vauxhall Gardens.[34] The adjudged brazen behaviour of the Covent Garden correspondent's companion also bears comparison with this type of earlier entertainment, and unescorted women were encouraged by free tickets to don fancy dress and come incognito. Miss Ada Foster, for example, was likely admitted to the ball this way, for she was both a dressmaker and a semi-professional singer.[35] Dancers from the Covent Garden corps de ballet were also given free entry, as were music-hall stars, the latter conferring great éclat on the proceedings.

The lyrics to many music-hall songs recounted tales of mishaps at fancy-dress balls, with Covent Garden liberally referenced. A song called 'Domino' of 1908 is named after the all-enveloping hooded cloak of that name, worn with an eye mask, and the words relate the dangers of masking at a ball 'up West', especially for Gladys, the protagonist of the piece. Her partner unmasks as they settle into a cab after the ball, whereupon he is revealed to be her uncle. These songs were full of such sly imputations. Music-hall favourite Kittee Rayburn (1875–1930) sang about Susannah, who is intent on winning first prize at a Covent Garden fancy-dress ball, wearing not much more than a wreath of roses. The inherent innuendos of 'She Wore a Wreath of Roses and One or Two Other Little Things' would not have been lost on those who dressed up for more reputable balls and family parties. Here the limits of fancy undress were more strictly policed than at paying balls like Covent Garden, though this is not to disregard the possibility of easy-going conduct everywhere there was fancy dress.

With her minimal rose costume, Susannah in the song was hopeful for a prize and Covent Garden organizers offered immensely valuable ones. With the aim of winning, competitors spent an inordinate amount of time and money on their get-ups (illus. 28). We can speculate that for some participants this was a gamble they thought worthwhile. The *Strand Magazine* in 1895 reported that £5 had been spent on 'Our Back Garden' and it won a solid-silver coffee service worth £60 at Covent Garden and no less than a carriage and pair worth 100 guineas at a skating carnival at Olympia. Back at Covent Garden, in 1897, the substantial first prize of a 75-guinea evening dress went to a butterfly costume. It must have been sparklingly opulent to outshine the runners-up: 'The Central Railway', 'A Gordon Highlander', 'A Christmas Bazaar' and 'Oysters and Champagne'. Through the years, Covent Garden costumes were more 'construction' than 'dress', with theatre stagehands and property-masters designing and wearing many of them.[36] The Augustus Harris Covent Garden balls in their original form continued until the outbreak of the First World War and an increasing number of costumed charity events, well established at other venues, ran alongside them at Covent Garden from the beginning of the twentieth century. These were organized for the most part by titled women whose undimmed love of display right through our period ensured that fancy dress was a defining component of any successful fund-raising evening.

28 Mr Stanford at the 1898 Covent Garden Ball dressed as 'The Kitchener', photographed by Langfier, *The Sketch*, 23 November 1898. The costume referred to the British army leader Earl Kitchener, and the punning words across the front of the kitchen range read 'Our Kitchener's grate'. Cumbersome costumes were not unusual at Covent Garden balls.

Society drama queens were, however, not the only ones involved in charity dress-up events. The close bond between the world of theatre, costume and celebrity set in motion a succession of fancy-dress balls not only attended but organized by famous actresses, both at Covent Garden and at other suitably showy venues. In the years just prior to the First World War, Gladys Baly, for example, a tireless organizer of events for the Three Arts Club, a residential and rest space for performers, could outshine any aristocratic woman where grandiose display of costume was concerned. The balls she helped stage matched any of those presided over by wealthy heiresses. She was, however, reluctant to reproduce the exclusivity of society events and strove to broaden participation.[37] Later, in the 1920s and '30s, the Three Arts Balls went on to have a presence outside the capital.[38]

The old protocols surrounding class and gender were to some extent cracked open by the imperatives of war after 1914. Fancy dress became the beneficiary of these changed conditions as well as the object of opprobrium. Balls burgeoned after 1918 and party-goers used fancy dress to be rakish or ethereal in a variety of settings. The Victory Ball held in 1918 in the Royal Albert Hall does not at first seem to reflect these changes. Society women paraded in national and symbolic costumes representing the Allies and, in the words of *The Tatler*, were among the 'numerous victims of the veracious camera', testament to both the endurance of an upper class bent on dressing up and their unremitting craving for publicity.[39] However, the ball was notionally open to anyone who could pay the price of a ticket. Like Covent Garden, the Royal Albert Hall lent itself to segregation and ranking by virtue of its boxes and banked tiers and, although prices started at £100 for the most expensive Grand Tier Box, a single ticket – you did not even have to have a partner – cost three guineas, and for ten shillings you could view the proceedings from the gallery.[40] Gawpers were an indispensable constituent of fancy dress, and here, in what seems to be a reversal of the rankings at Covent Garden, the dressed down are ogling the dressed up. The gorgeous domed amphitheatre of the Royal Albert Hall created an alluring ambience for costumed balls and so many were held there that practically the entire history of the capital's love affair with fancy dress is inscribed within its walls. The remarkable interior, further decorated and artistically lit for a ball, was an ideal space to promenade and pose. Yet there was much in this seemingly innocent pleasure to irritate eyebrow-raisers. Strong protestations against the Victory Ball came from the Royal British Nurses' Association, who likened it to 'dancing over the graves of the dead'. Growing condemnation of the same event in the years that followed set in its place the poppy-filled commemoration we know today, with Dick Sheppard (1880–1937), a prominent Anglican clergyman, objecting more to the fancy-dress element than to the dancing.[41]

The morality of pretending to be somebody other than yourself was also brought into question, as evidenced by Lady Malcolm's Servants' Ball held between 1923 and 1938. Organized for domestic servants from the great houses of London and beyond, it was a fun-filled night at the Albert Hall. In line with all balls of the period, there was a competitive element to the evening and in 1933 the composer and actor Ivor Novello and his glamorous co-star Dorothy Dickson presented prizes in several classes – the most original, the most humorous, the best home-made, the best pairs and the best advertisement – giving us a good overview of the categories of outfits chosen for this event, as well as for smaller gatherings. In 1930, Lady Malcolm in haute couture and a pearl tiara led off the dancing with an unnamed butler dressed as a Mexican (illus. 29). The fancy-dress code was designed by the patroness of the ball to make it accessible to those who might not own suitable evening clothes, though the elaborate costumes recorded in press photographs are evidence that money had been spent and the working-class guests were as keen as any ball-goers to shine (illus. 30).[42] Borrowing finery from your moneyed employer might have been one solution. Photographs confirm that attendees dressed with obvious pleasure and

29 A service-flat butler, dressed as a Mexican, dances with Lady Malcolm, the organizer of the Servants' Ball at the Royal Albert Hall, London, 1930.
30 Guests in costume at Lady Malcolm's Servants' Ball, London, 1930.

also with a touch of class resentment: cleaning products, alarm clocks, indigenous servants from around the British empire and members of the aristocracy all materialized as costumes at the Royal Albert Hall.

But, returning to the question of correct conduct, one of the most remembered aspects of the Lady Malcolm balls concerned gender identity and deviation. In 1929, the *Daily Mail* could report with amusement the presence of a group of twenty men dressed as a cavalcade of women through the ages, but in 1934, the London Metropolitan Police records registered overt intrusion of what they deemed to be male prostitutes wearing lipstick, rouge and tight trousers, though noticeably not dresses. As a consequence, the ball authorities the following year issued tickets bearing the words: 'No man impersonating a woman and no person unsuitably attired will be permitted to remain.'[43] The choice of costume for a fancy-dress ball had always been hedged about with societal checks and curbs, so this stricture on cross-dressing, although blatant, was nothing new. Like many such controls it apparently failed and a gay component continued to mingle undetected among the gaudily rigged-out crowd.

Many in that crowd were probably culpable of unwittingly cross-dressing: the correct clothing styles of foreigners, for example, were of little consequence to fancy dressers who used unfamiliar male and female dress indiscriminately. These costumes went unnoticed and were not the kinds of clothes that instigated the ban on men dressed as women. The most censorious remarks by those who railed against fancy dress were reserved for cross-dressers of a more flamboyant type who were assumed to be intent on same-sex liaisons. Throughout our period, the sensationalist *Illustrated Police News* reported raids on balls where those clad in women's clothing were taken into custody and charged with offences 'unnameable', referring to the then illegal practice of homosexuality, for which the penalties were heavy. In Manchester in 1880, the hapless revellers appeared in the dock still wearing their feminine ball clothes.[44]

A queer presence was certainly a fixture at the Chelsea Arts Club Ball, an event that very much caught the zeitgeist. It started in the early 1900s and continued until 1958. From 1910, it was held at the Royal Albert Hall (illus. 31). These Chelsea divertissements spawned other such balls throughout the country and over the years this annual fiesta consistently dispensed innovation and exaggeration. Although it was a ball by name, it was more akin to carnival, with statues and scenery paraded to the hall through the streets of West London, and a constant ebb and flow of people and moving floats inside (illus. 32). Pathé newsreel footage from several Chelsea balls more fully captures the event's shifting, motile patterns than still photography.[45] The distinctive participation of artists and art students in the ball's devising and execution is key to the unexpected and turbulent nature of the event. While understanding the ball's transience, they were not afraid to think on a grand

31 The Chelsea Arts Club Ball at the Royal Albert Hall, London, 1926.

scale. Their virtuosic practical skills expertly transformed the hall into a volatile lotus land with bizarrely or beautifully costumed inhabitants peopling the realm.

Each occasion pivoted around a sculptural centrepiece dominating the space, and figures in apposite costume harmonized with this focal point. Fancy dressers also accompanied specially constructed floats, or turned up as part of a group in coordinated outfits. In 1923, the overall theme was the Antarctic. A cubist South Pole, 30 feet (10 m) high, was erected and surmounted by a futurist statue of Barbara, the recently deceased bear from London Zoo. Costumed penguins, 'Eskimos', Icelanders, human snowballs and icicles reinforced the sub-zero scene, but a clutch of Roman gladiators also attended, and the recent discovery of the tomb of Tutankhamun, an irresistible find for fancy dressers, provided one group with an excuse to abandon the snow altogether and fashion an impeccable float with carefully delineated pharaonic designs and costumes.[46] Ordinary ticket-holders who came along to enjoy the hedonistic atmosphere dressed from the pantheon of stock characters that had for long been the mainstay of fancy-dress gatherings: gypsies, pirates, *poudré.* Add into this mix the uniforms of regimental bands and the Dagenham Girl Pipers hired to perform after the Second World War, as well as the stage costumes of the many professional entertainers, and we see how several genres of dress collide at the Chelsea balls. Although there was still a lingering dalliance with an A-list hierarchy, guests seem not to have been as socially stratified as those at the Victory Ball and all the different strands blended together, suggesting a turn to a more inclusive orientation, one that was simultaneously occurring at open-air carnivals where constant movement, parade and spectacle were also paramount.

32 *The Talking Bird* mounted by students from the Grosvenor School of Art for the Chelsea Arts Club Ball, 1938. The theme for that year was the *Arabian Nights*, with Edmund Dulac designing the Royal Albert Hall centrepiece and sets.

33 Poster for a St Patrick's Day fancy-dress ball organized by students of Goldsmiths' College, London, 1923.

Art students can be identified as one driving force in the artistic and innovative presentation of fancy dress (illus. 33). Institutions, associations, clubs and colleges of many different persuasions held fancy-dress functions at various levels of society throughout Britain (illus. 34). Women's Institutes, hospital committees, military regiments and hunts were especially active. For public ticketed events, many accessibly priced, the only allegiance necessary was to the art of dancing and dressing up. Especially from the 1890s, character costumes of long-standing shared space with new forms of party attire, and fancy dress was recalibrated to accord with music-hall jokes, topical songs and ingenious wordplay. The Ryde Exhibitions and Horticultural Association staged a St Valentine's Day Ball in 1895 and Nellie Stamp won first prize dressed as 'The Order of the Bath' in Turkish towels, a bathing cap and sponges 'judiciously arranged'. Mr W. Stamp appeared as a skein of wool with 'Real English worsted' written across the top and 'Made in Germany' across the bottom.[47] Thousands of organizations sponsored balls across our period and the following list of some length only begins to cover the range: Boots, the pharmacy chain, in Nottingham in 1920; the Dalziel Co-Operative Society in 1924; the Young Men's Recreation Club of St Luke's Church in Milngavie in 1929; the Riccall British Legion in East Yorkshire in 1931; the Louth Canine Society in 1935; and the Morpeth Highland Pipe Band in 1937.[48]

During and after the Second World War, adult fancy-dress balls and parties survived, though in declining numbers, in crowded *palais de danse* as well as grand hotels. The phenomenon was just one among a number of manifestations of fancy dress.

Evidence of the reach of fancy-dress balls is provided by a surprising example held in 1910 at the Claybury Asylum, a large mental health

34 A group in fancy dress at a boys' club, 1931.

institution in suburban East London. It is not an isolated example. Patient participation in formal social occasions, including fancy-dress balls, was actively encouraged in such institutions.[49] Here the concern was for the interior life, the *Chelmsford Chronicle* reporting that 'entertainments of this kind are in every way refreshers to the jaded mind.'[50] The curative value of these events, with patients designing and making their own costumes, was high and the benefits sustained over a long period. An affection for the aristocracy and royalty of the past, for admirals of the fleet and generals, and for peasants of various nationalities are indicated by their appearance in high numbers at the Claybury Ball. Also present were a jockey, an organ grinder, Pierrot, several *vivandières*, Cupid with wings of gauze, Mephistopheles with wings of fire, the Lady of Shalott and, singled out for special mention, Nurse Gale attired as the North Pole. There were no named historic grandees as at the Devonshire Ball just over a decade earlier, though masked characters, the *raison d'être* of the eighteenth-century masquerade, were in abundance at Claybury and give pause for reflection on the psyche, identity and disclosure.

Two

POSES AND TABLEAUX

Fancy dress was the default mode for many home entertainments during the Victorian and Edwardian eras. Increased literacy and a flourishing publishing trade encouraged the production of books that suggested and described many different types of leisure activity. The lengthy title of one book, published in 1854 by the London publisher David Bogue, gives a flavour of the very wide range of drawing room diversions on offer: *Round games for all parties: a collection of the greatest variety of family amusements for fireside or pic-nic: consisting of games of action, games simply taxing the attention, games of memory, catch games, depending on the assistance of an accomplice or secret knowledge for the purpose of mystification, games requiring the exercise of fancy, intelligence, and imagination, directions for the crying of forfeits, &c., &c.: for the use of old and young, and adapted to the understandings of children from the age of seven to seventy*. Several of these distractions were animated by fancy dress, as were charades, living waxworks, statuary and *tableaux vivants*.

Costumes for guessing games and charades were often of the most rudimentary kind. In what appears to be one of the foundational books on charades, *Acting Charades or Deeds Not Words: A Christmas Game to Make a Long Evening Short* (1850), the Brothers Mayhew speak of the 'unbounded mirth' these sketches are designed to provoke, and this is mirrored in the extremely improvisatory, and often ridiculous, nature of the costumes to which 'the mind must be exerted with high-pressure ingenuity'. The Mayhews continue: 'The most prominent characteristic of the costume must be seized and represented,' an opinion reiterated throughout the contemporary fancy-dress literature. The finesse we find at balls and the clever thoughtfulness behind carnival is frequently absent from the more spontaneous character-acting of charades. Where necessary the Mayhews add little asides on costume beside each charade title: for 'court' in 'courtship', the usher holds a carpet broom of office, and counsel are 'properly wigged in nightcaps'. The captain in the 'ship' section of the same charade wears 'a noble cocked hat made out of yesterday's *Times* and hair-brushes stand in for epaulettes'. As with other kinds of fancy dress, the costumes for charades relied on signifiers that were well understood by all, and most were produced at home using materials to hand. Where fictional and historic characters are incorporated into word-guessing games, they are the same ones that show up at fancy-dress balls and parties. The 'All Nations' theme, likewise much favoured across the broad sweep of fancy dress, regularly makes an appearance in charades. In the Mayhews' book, the 'courtship' charade includes eight wronged wives, all from different countries, each wearing her national dress.[1] *The Book of Drawing-Room Plays and Evening Amusements* (1868) by Henry Dalton gives an introductory list of useful costume items: old bonnets and ball dresses, court dress too shabby for appearance at court, ancient parasols, umbrellas, garden hats, college caps and gowns, servants' aprons and the housemaid's cap. A Spanish lady's mantilla, he suggests, can be contrived out of an old book cover. These items situate the readership of Dalton's volume in the better-off middle class, the costs negligible for this spontaneous type of home entertainment.[2]

While many charades ended with an *exeunt omnes*, some finished with a picturesque grouping of motionless characters. In the public staging of plays in the Victorian era, the concluding scene was often 'frozen' into a picture, and it is this lack of motion and quietude that defines this chapter. We can immediately see the implications for photography here, with its ability to capture a performance and enchant spectators in the manner of painting, and below we look at the ways people dressed up especially for the camera. First, though, other posed expressions that offered up opportunities for fancy dress are considered.

Tableaux vivants are narrative scenes formed by stationary and silent groups of actors. The trend for this form of entertainment peaked at the end of the nineteenth century but was popular from 1830 to 1920 with continuing, though diminished, coverage in newspapers through the 1930s and '40s. Some of this media attention was directed towards professional performances. The Palace Theatre in London regularly staged programmes of stand-alone *tableaux*, making constant changes and additions to the repertoire to keep the audiences coming. Customarily inspired by paintings of near-naked nymphs, the costumes must have been scant and diaphanous, the figures distinctly titillating: in 1894, 'The Bathers', after a picture by Colin Hunter, 'A Naiad' after Henrietta Rae and 'Fairy Tales' after Cuno von Bodenhausen were realized on the Palace's stage. As late as 1930, no less an august establishment than the Royal Academy of Arts mounted a series of professional *tableaux* at the Coliseum inspired by contemporary paintings, among them Laura Knight's *A Musical Clown* (1930) and William Russell Flint's *Silver and Gold* (1929–30), depicting a woman reclining provocatively on a day bed.[3]

Professional *tableaux* performances were matched by those of enthusiastic laypeople, the commercial and the home-produced existing side by side and often sharing themes and sometimes personnel. Like professional *tableaux*, many amateur ones copied famous artworks, an indication of the immense interest in painting and its subjects fostered by widely available reproductions. An early recorded example from the colonies was staged in 1870 in Hobart, Van Diemen's Land, now Tasmania, under the auspices of the British governor, Sir William Denison, whose collection of prints provided the inspiration. Amid 'perpetual bursts of laughter', Edwin Landseer's 1834 painting *Scene in the Olden Time at Bolton Abbey* was mounted in *tableau*, the dead stag realized by an opossum-skin rug with a pair of horns on the top of it, and a small boy lying under it to stuff it out.[4]

Late Victorian art critics often made moral rather than aesthetic judgements on the paintings they reviewed.[5] Consequently, many of these paintings as *tableaux* have a moralistic subject-matter. Three examples cited in an article on *tableaux vivants* in the *Strand Magazine* of 1891 were *The Gambler's Wife*, *Scandal or Private and Confidential* and *The Tiff*, all based on favourite contemporary paintings.[6] In 1907, the costumes for the *tableaux vivants* in Ipswich Lecture Hall were designed specially and the evening was entirely devoted to recreating famous paintings by Joshua Reynolds, George Romney, Thomas Lawrence and Dante Gabriel Rossetti, all British artists who painted clothing with great flair and tactility. The local paper thought the programme too artistic for the Ipswich public.[7] Nevertheless, paintings continued to inform *tableaux vivants* right through the 1920s and '30s at both small, local events and upper-class charity galas (illus. 35).

35 *Tableau vivant* of Ford Maddox Brown's *The Last of England* (1864–6), *Illustrated London News*, Saturday, 2 June 1928. It was staged as part of 'A Famous Picture Gallery' at the Empire Day Ball, May Fair Hotel, London.

Painting was not, however, the only inspiration behind *tableaux* and, as with fancy-dress balls, the practice reached across class. In 1894, at the height of the public's

36 *Auld Robin Gray*, an 18th-century Scots ballad by Lady Anne Lindsay, performed as a *tableau*, in Simla, India, 1881. The participants included the editor of the *Civil and Military Gazette*, Lahore and Mrs Lockwood Kipling, the mother of Rudyard.

infatuation with *tableaux*, and apropos class, the *Pall Mall Gazette* somewhat condescendingly reported: 'The Living Picture, like many another *fin de siècle* sensation, is but an ancient device modernised, furbished up to date, and prepared for the million.' True to its upper-class readership, the same journal had earlier published an account of the very varied *tableaux* staged at the spacious home of Lady Alexander Gordon-Lennox in 1889: 'The Death of William IV', 'A Roman Slave Market', 'Queen Elizabeth on Her Deathbed', 'Mr Gladstone' (in a bath towel reaching for a slippery bar of soap emblazoned with the words 'Home Rule'), 'Pepita' and 'Farewell to Charles I' (with Henrietta Maria in an historically perfect coiffure), along with other groups representing the empire and the British Isles paying homage to the queen.[8] The elite often hired theatres and hotels to stage their extravagant *tableaux*, though humbler ones were enacted in drawing rooms, clubs and parish halls, the majority for charitable causes.

An admixture of themes and emotions was typical of *tableaux* entertainments wherever they were performed, and standard portrayals were duplicated across geographical and class boundaries. Their subject-matter ranged widely over legend and allegorical tales, history, literature and contemporary topics (illus. 36). They also portrayed humorous, even farcical, everyday incidents, and people's understanding of the appropriate costumes for differing moods was an implicit part of the culture.

History and genre scenes with obvious melodramatic overtones were favourite subjects for *tableaux*. They could be painterly in aspect but not slavishly copied from actual works of art, with participants imaginatively disposed and dressed. Interest in this type of scene was fanned by stereograph photography, a craze which dovetailed with the vogue for *tableaux vivants*. These binocular pictures, intermediaries between two- and three-dimensional space, gave the illusion of reality when viewed through a stereoscope, manufactured commercially after its debut at the 1851 Great Exhibition. Professionally produced stereographs were collected and perused at home, and the costumes and attitudes of the artists' models who posed for them were noted and remembered for future actualization. Depth of field, artfully created on a flat plane in paintings, was more immediate in stereographs, and a *tableau vivant* was able to optimize this effect. Out of the thousands of surviving stereographic cards, many subjects approximate to recorded performances of *tableaux* and several match up very closely. *The Mistletoe Bough* is a case in point (illus. 37). The cover of the sheet music of the popular ballad of the same name was replicated in stereograph form, and this wonderfully eerie tale of the missing bride whose skeleton is found fifty years later was both regularly sung and staged as a *tableau* through the second half of the nineteenth century, giving ample opportunity to dress in ghoulish costume.[9]

Though *tableaux vivants* are closely allied with theatrical presentations, silence and stillness position them as something apart. They

37 Stereograph of *The Mistletoe Bough* from the popular ballad about a missing bride, 1880–1900.

had no speaking lines, and, in lieu of learning a script, *tableaux* actors must have practised holding a pose, though the literature says nothing about the length of time required for each attitude. Most people were familiar with standing in front of a camera and waiting for the shutter to complete its work, but a *tableau* performance required a more dramatic, even melodramatic, positioning of the body and there were props to contend with as well. Performers had to be closely marshalled and directed.

Postures and facial expressions of *tableaux* actors were enhanced by lantern footlights, candles against tin reflectors or limelight, which was produced by flaring up calcium oxide. Gauze curtaining stretched in front of the statue-like posers created an illusion of diffused wonder and, even where a famous painting was not being realized, the front of the stage was often built to resemble an outsize gilded picture frame. We can see how learning to handle an unfamiliar costume was essential both for safety reasons and for credible character portrayal. Affecting costumes, more substantial than those for charades, were an indispensable component in the construction of the picture but, as with charades, amateurs were enjoined to fit their performances to readily available clothes and props, as described in 'Tableaux Vivants: How to Achieve Artistic Results', an article in the *Sheffield Evening Telegraph* of Friday, 12 December 1913. Other articles and handbooks published as guides to the successful staging of *tableaux* vary in tone; some are more prescriptive than others, and some are illustrated. All, however, presume a familiarity with the cultural happenings of the day as well as an acquaintance with the miscellanea of fancy dress current at the time.

The text of the 1891 article in the *Strand Magazine* is mostly concerned with scenery and lighting. The illustrations are almost the only guides to costuming. Though the original paintings would have been highly coloured, the magazine calls attention to the dresses of near-white, an inevitable result of the monochrome print process. In performance, the pale costumes would have been enhanced by coloured stage illumination.[10] Henry Dalton's chapter on *tableaux* in *The Book of Drawing-Room Plays and Evening Amusements* also puts an emphasis on lighting but, along with technicians, he does suggest a ladies' dresser as one of a trio of people essential for a successful performance. In Dalton's book, the stage manager and artist take the masculine pronoun while the wardrobe assistant takes the feminine.[11]

Queen Victoria may not herself have sewn a seam but she is certainly linked to the popular craze for *tableaux vivants* and must have been partially instrumental in its spread. They were one of several pastimes that the royal family shared with tens of thousands of their British subjects. *Tableaux vivants* enmeshed the court in a middle-brow world, though queenly advantage made for a superior kind of production beyond the realization of many drawing-room amateurs. As the years passed, the queen seems to have taken a commanding part in their preparation. Her visual aptitude and prior experience of all manner

38 Queen Victoria's children in the final pose of the *Tableaux of the Seasons*, photographed by Roger Fenton at Windsor Castle, 1854. Princess Helena as 'The Spirit Empress' stands in the centre, with Prince Alfred sitting beside her as 'Autumn'. To the left are Princess Alice as 'Spring' and the Princess Royal with Prince Arthur as 'Summer'. Albert Edward, prince of Wales, and Princess Louise representing 'Winter' are to the right.

of theatrical performance from circus to high tragedy meant she was attuned to costuming requirements.[12] At first, the entire process of orchestrating a set of *tableaux* in the royal household seems to have been put in the hands of Edward Henry Corbould (1815–1905), art tutor to the queen's children and the illustrator of Henry Dalton's book. Corbould's own watercolours show the princes and princesses posing in two pictorial groupings illustrating John Milton's poems *L'Allegro* and *Il Penseroso* in 1852. In 1854, the children staged the *Tableaux of the Seasons* and for the first time these are recorded both in watercolour and in photographs, an instance of Victoria and Albert's early patronage of the camera, inseparably linked to fancy dress (illus. 38). The *Seasons tableaux* photographs were not publicly displayed until after Queen Victoria's death and the master adept behind the camera was the soon-to-be eminently famous Roger Fenton (1819–1869). Renowned today as one of the earliest war photographers, his interest in the camera's possibilities for creating visual fictions extended to donning fancy dress himself. He posed as an Ottoman official for his own photograph *Pasha and Bayadère* of 1858. While Fenton's Ottoman garments were brought back from Egypt by his artist friend Frank Dillon (1823–1909), the queen's children were garbed in winsome dressing-up clothes, and the photographs reveal, in a way that the watercolours do not, a slight air of the makeshift: Prince Alfred's animal kirtle is rather short, revealing what appears to be his winter underwear. If the children's garments seem to some extent provisional – a mark of many fancy-dress costumes – headdresses and, more especially, sandals give the impression of being specially and expertly made.

Queen Victoria recorded her pleasure at seeing her children in fancy dress, a sentiment shared by parents across her empire. As queen she was matriarch of the nation but her enjoyment of costumed *tableaux* casts her in a more homely, motherly role, one her public understood from their own experience of this popular domestic pastime.[13] As the royal children grew into adulthood, they continued to dress up and pose in character in these silent dramas and in this they were no different from many people in Britain. Fancy dress gave the royal family a reassuringly ordinary veneer, notwithstanding their ability to hire the best skilled artists and makers to carry through their ideas.

Most people relied on their own resourcefulness to put together *tableaux* performances. Charles Harrison's 1882 guide, *Theatricals and Tableaux Vivants for Amateurs*, suggested simple set-ups, designed for the private drawing room. His entry for *Charity* (illus. 39) is typical: 'Little girl presenting old man with money. Old-fashioned costume.'[14] 'Old-fashioned costume', 'old-fashioned costume of the Kate Greenaway type' and 'costume of the old style as near as possible' appear regularly in Harrison's and other texts and readers would have immediately understood his reference to the illustrations of Kate Greenaway (1846–1901). Her best-selling books, here just at the start of their unstoppable trajectory, showed children in dainty eighteenth-century clothing styles, and her sugary inventions, along with those of Walter Crane (1845–1915), another prolific illustrator in the Arts and Crafts tradition, never fell out of fancy-dress favour. Those charged with providing costumes for this prettified style were well versed in fashioning oversized mob caps or straw bonnets, fichu necklines and flounced and sprigged skirts with wide sashes.

39 *Charity*, a *tableau* for home staging from Charles Harrison, *Theatricals and Tableaux Vivants for Amateurs* (1882).

Accounts of *tableaux*, like those at Cherkley Court in Surrey in aid of the Leatherhead Church Restoration Fund in 1891, are markedly numerous. Familiar fancy-dress types were pressed into service for these community charity events and, though we often know the names of some of those involved, we hear nothing from them personally about the experience of posing. The live picture-making at Cherkley included: 'How Happy Could I Be With Either', 'Joan of Arc', 'You Dirty Boy!', 'A Love Set', 'My Lady's Bower', 'A Slave Market', 'The Reign of Terror', 'The Queen of Hearts', 'Past, Present and Future', 'Nydia', 'The Last Dance', 'The Waning of the Honeymoon', 'Cross Purposes', 'The Mistletoe Bough', 'Bluebeard' and 'Britannia', a classic, sundry assortment of sketches and topical songs, plus the dirty child in a famous Pears soap advertisement.[15] 'Joan of Arc', the cross-dressing daughter of French peasants, gripped fancy dressers with an intensity reserved only for a few other characters and at Cherkley the young visionary was personified by one Miss Utterton who, true to the spirit of amateur *tableaux* productions, also posed in the *tableaux* 'Future' and 'A Slave Market'. The dramatic posturing and silent interaction of the players must have been part of the appeal of *tableaux* both for performers and audience. The close intermingling of the participants, particularly where performers of different genders acted together, added a frisson of excitement.

Interspersed with more serious themes, there was also a chance for comedy, as seen at Cherkley. This was a fixed ingredient of many an evening's *tableaux*. Some of the costumes for droll *tableaux* seem to have been modelled on an amusement-park aesthetic or else on Madame Tussaud's waxwork displays of the famous and infamous. The comic-strip character Ally Sloper, ever in tune with the times, amused his readers with sketches of waggish *tableaux* in an 1888 edition of *Ally Sloper's Half-Holiday*.[16] G. J. Goodrick's late Victorian publication on *tableaux vivants* and living waxworks includes Archimedes wearing a college cap with a corkscrew for a tassel, and William the Conqueror in pasteboard armour, topped with a sou'wester. There is a suggestion here that only men can play the fool. Across all the domains of amateur fancy dress, it is the male who largely provides the comedy, though this does begin to erode in the twentieth century. Goodrick assigns the 'Babes in the Wood' to two grown men, one of whom crossed both generational and gender boundaries. By the mid-1890s, if not before, this had come to be an accepted practice. 'The grotesque effect . . . may be exaggerated to the hilt,' Goodrick tells us, referring generally to living waxwork entertainments.[17]

Goodrick was taking his cue from an American author, George Bradford Bartlett (1832–1896), who in turn revived a memorable, though minor, character from Charles Dickens's *Old Curiosity Shop* (1840–41): Mrs Jarley, the proprietor of a travelling show. Bartlett's *Mrs Jarley's Far-Famed Collection of Waxworks*, designed for amateur staging, sets out a bantering script for 'Mrs Jarley' to recite in front of a range of ill-assorted 'waxwork' mimes who sit forever silent and mostly immovable until they are wound up one by one. The debt to the fairground is clear from the list of characters in Bartlett's book: 'Chinese Giant', 'Two-Headed Girl', 'Captain Kidd', 'The Victim', 'The Mermaid', 'The Siamese Twins', 'The Dwarf' and 'The Cannibal' appear alongside nursery-rhyme figures and 'Lord Byron' (with Childe Harold seated on his knee). The instructions for these freakish characters are more about contriving an aberrant body shape than they are about fancy dress: 'Two girls standing back to back, one red skirt around both' describes Bartlett's 'Two-Headed Girl'.[18] The characters in a Jarley entertainment laid on at a seaside boarding house in 1910 are, however, less outlandish. A picture taken at 'Holmlea' in Bexhill, Sussex, includes 'Darby and Joan', 'Sleeping Beauty and Prince Charming', 'Belle and the Bobby', 'Florence Nightingale with dying soldier', 'Escaped Nun', 'the Woman in White' and 'Mother Sawday'.[19]

William Gurney Benham, an Essex newspaper editor and English collaborator of Bradford Bartlett, wrote about the non-professional staging of waxworks in a syndicated article in 1892. His general explanation was that they should be inexpensive and, for Jarley-type performances, well adorned with tinsel. Eyebrows and lashes were to be heavily pencilled and cheeks rouged with a bright spot of red. Mrs Jarley, according to Gurney Benham, can be portrayed by a man or a woman and, as was usual across the whole span of fancy dress, men's impersonations of women were invariably stereotypical, comedic parodies. Mrs Jarley wears a gaudy dress and a false nose. She is padded out and carries a bottle of drink.[20] 'Jarley's Waxworks' were well enough known that even the suffragist writer Cicely Hamilton (1872–1952) produced an activist performance version before the First World War.[21] 'Jarley's Waxworks' were still performed by amateur groups into the 1920s, but by that time many pleasure-seekers had transferred their allegiance to other laughter-inducing experiences of a more modern kind, such as rollercoaster rides at the newly thrilling amusement parks.[22]

Another branch of *tableaux vivants*, that of living statuary or *poses plastiques*, takes picture-making to a more serious level (illus. 40).[23] Again, stereoscopic photography can, in some measure, be yoked to these bodily enactments. Statues were popular subjects for stereographs and these pictures' rounded, haptic qualities surely appealed to draped posers. Women are explicitly aligned with living statuary, though men are not excluded. Ardern Holt's final edition of *Fancy Dresses Described or What to Wear at Fancy Balls*, an influential guide, includes 'Marble Bust' as one of the choices for a costume ball and its addition to this 1896 volume speaks of statuary's popularity and acceptance as a costume at that time. This manifestation of marble ladies is not perhaps as oddly outré as we might at first suppose. In the nineteenth

40 A *pose plastique*, the endpiece of O. J. Wendlandt, *Living Statuary* (1896).

century, stone statues of allegorical females proliferated across European and American cities, seemingly holding up public and commercial buildings, standing astride bridges and embellishing parks and civic squares.[24] Their prototype ideals were the sculptures of ancient Greece, examples of which had been on display at the British Museum since its foundation. These ancient Greek forms were thought to embody ideas about beauty, and in turn morality itself, but when plaster casts of classical statuary were exhibited at the Crystal Palace in London in 1854, the stark nakedness of many of them overstepped the boundaries of propriety for the largely working-class and lower-middle-class visitors.[25] Fig-leaf manufacturers enjoyed an employment bonanza because the controversy was primarily over naked men; the female statue of Venus was acceptable, as it had already been absorbed into the 'nude as art' category.

In a quite different context, near-nudity was equated with women acrobats and professional troupes of trick cyclists, and many Crystal Palace visitors would have seen these types of performance as well as viewing classical statuary. At the beginning of the twentieth century, a nearly nude Australian called Pansy Montague posed on the London stage as 'La Milo' and was thought by some to have crossed the lines of decency, though many paid to gaze at her statuesque representations of Venus.[26] Mindful of the disrepute a flesh-coloured body stocking as worn by Miss Montague might engender, aesthetic drapery allowed women to pleasingly pose as statues in an amateur setting without being castigated.

Artistic taste and perception were the first requirements for this type of winter amusement, according to O. J. Wendlandt. In his 1896 book *Living Statuary*, he cautioned against revealing too much flesh by advocating 'a little more clothing and drapery than is given in the original picture'.[27] Flirtatious states of undress stretched notions of respectability and several authors on living statuary included admonitory asides about immoderately scant clothing. Nudity was permissible in the Academy but not in the parlour, though these drawing-room amusements must sometimes have come perilously close to the *pose plastique* of the music hall.

Statuary clothing and make-up were very distinct from other forms of fancy dress. To be convincing, the human actors had to resemble stone, so the costumes, the props and the body itself were limited to the colour white. Drapery was easily procured and fashioned into a passable facsimile of chiselled robes, though lengths of actual textile do not in reality behave like the original stone clothes.[28] Flair wins out over expert sewing. 'Statues' were garbed in classic raiment with sheets or inexpensive, stout cotton held together with that essential accomplice to dressing up, the safety pin, in widespread production by the mid-nineteenth century. Wendlandt's book, especially designed to help amateurs successfully produce plausible statues, gives instructions for a standard costume that can be used across several different settings:

> First, stitch three widths of calico together in lengths reaching from the shoulder to the feet; hollow out the neck; stitch together over the shoulders, and then gather the neck up in a narrow band, leaving an opening large enough for the head to pass through; shape out the arm-holes and attach short sleeves . . . Cords or tapes from each shoulder to the waist, crossing each other over the breast, indicates a matron or married lady.[29]

A plain white towel twisted around the head for a turban and a white, fringed bed quilt for a mantle complete the ensemble.[30] Compared to many real statues as seen in museums and reproduced in stereographs, some drawing room live sculptures appear almost overdressed. The prevalence of folds of cloth on these living figures was not only an indication of the need to be decorous but a way to camouflage female bodies marked and disfigured by corsets, which were temporarily discarded for these poses. While much high fashion and fancy costume was the antithesis of ongoing dress reform, classical drapery can be seen as an exception. Greek sculptural clothing influenced the refashioning of women's everyday dress into softer styles. From the mid-Victorian era, the Rational Dress Society and the Healthy and Artistic Dress Union advocated garments shaped according to the natural contours of the body with minimal or no boning, and the latter organization arranged *tableaux vivants* for public performance as part of its crusading mission.[31] For statuary costume, there was no insistence on tight, tailor-made apparel and several of Wendlandt's examples are very free-flowing and audacious for their era.

While effective dress is indispensable to the statues' credibility, other persuasive components are necessary to produce an accomplished statuary *tableau*. This is why several pages of the preamble to Wendlandt's guide, prior to the expounding of the themes, are taken up with the technicalities of the staging. These specialized details include the platform draped in black to show up the figures, the curtain, the pedestal, the limelight and gaslight, the musical accompaniment, and the distinctive accessories and body make-up. Wendlandt rejects bismuth, magnesium and common chalk as skin whiteners, and recommends instead oxide of zinc mixed with glycerine and applied with a paintbrush. Helpfully, for those organizing this ticklish but key part of the proceedings, he tells us that half a pound will suffice for twenty people and that a dusting of violet powder improves the look.[32] The final touches of white make-up are added once the 'statue' is in position and before the curtain is raised. If the figure is full-length, an article in *Every Woman's Encyclopaedia* recommends whitening the feet after the correct pose has been taken up so as not to leave a trail of footprints across the platform. The eyelids, eyebrows and eyelashes are also whitened

41 An illustration from *Every Woman's Encyclopaedia* showing the last touches of white make-up being applied to a 'statue', 1910–12.

at the last moment and blanched accessories were vital to a correct reading of the statue portrayed (illus. 41).[33]

In lieu of make-up, white gloves and stockings were an easier way to achieve bodily whiteness. Cast-off slippers could be whitewashed or covered in calico. Hair was a particularly irksome challenge, hence the towel turban. Otherwise, flour or violet powder could be sprinkled through the hair after first priming it with soft soap. Home-made wigs were fiddly to make: long hanks of cotton had to be bleached with chloride of lime, then stitched to white calico caps.[34]

Both the *Encyclopaedia* and Wendlandt's *Living Statuary* are ambitious in scope and offer up several formidable *coups de théâtre.* The implicit pursuit of authenticity leads the anonymous contributor to *Every Woman's Encyclopaedia* to propose 'mutilation' as a device to enhance several of the statues described. Mention of this stark practice brings a jarring note into the world of make-believe, until we read on. By the simple expedient of pulling a homely pair of black stockings over the arms, the onlookers are deceived into perceiving a broken statue: the actor's limbs completely disappear when set against a black background. For a damaged head, the only extra costuming required is a black skullcap. 'The curiosity of those of the audience who suddenly recognise the familiar features of a near relative or friend in some armless and semi-headless marble bust standing upon a pedestal can better be imagined than described,' enthuses the writer.[35] If they are to imitate a bust, the performer kneels inside a whitened and upended box.

The head and shoulders rise above the top of the makeshift plinth. Living statues with eyelids caked shut and painful knees are an extreme illustration of fancy dress as the apogee of torment: a kind of costume martyrdom. 'All sorts of beautiful *plastiques* can be done by a graceful man and woman together,' conceded the Butterick's fancy-dress manual, so this unusual intimacy may have negated the suffering.[36]

Wendlandt's scenarios were extraordinarily demanding and grandiose. Amateurs who attempted his exacting poses would have needed considerable pluck to stage *The Fountain* (illus. 42). Threads of very fine woven glass, it is suggested, can simulate the falling water. It is an entrancing composition but we remember that this ashen scene demands heightened bodily control on the part of the models who, moreover, are clad in pinned and tacked sheeting that might pucker or even come adrift. The watery females, eyes closed throughout and daubed from head to toe in make-up, must withstand the scrutiny of both lights and audience. We might question how feasible Wendlandt's suggestions were. Other challenging subjects for living statuary outlined in this quite extraordinary book are 'Faith, Hope, and Charity', 'The Albert Memorial' and 'Niobe' from Greek mythology, who turned to stone after all her children were murdered. Children were positively encouraged to participate in living statuary and there was an expectation that they could remain in mute stillness with their lightened skin and their oddball clothes. The children masquerading as Niobe's deceased offspring must have been told to keep very still as if they were asleep. Victorian post-mortem photographs were mementos of recently deceased children who are often posed to look as if they

42 *The Fountain*, a suggested *pose plastique* from O. J. Wendlandt, *Living Statuary* (1896).

are sleeping.[37] Living statuary and funerary photography reached the height of their popularity at the same period (1860–1910), so the conceits of picture creation, with the central concern of stillness, travelled across these different genres. In the late 1930s, reminiscent of funerary pictures, one popular girls' fancy dress was 'Doll in a Box', with a child lying motionless, eyes closed, in imitation of a china doll.

Charades, *tableaux vivants*, living waxworks and *poses plastiques* were characterized by wordless attitudinizing. All entailed dressing up and they make a distinctive contribution to any account of fancy dress. In staging them the performers are quite literally in the spotlight for thirty seconds or so. We have seen how the manuals stress the importance of effective *tableaux* lighting, with new innovations such as coloured tints enthusiastically promoted to enhance the experience of the audience. In such a scrutinized setting, costumes accrue a significance vital to the sentiment of the silent scene. Particularly in a domestic setting, *tableaux* and living statuary have a palpably physical fascination because the audience is very close to the stage and, in the absence of speech, is intent on *looking*. The players are exposed to a level of visual contemplation different from that accorded to masquerading partygoers or carnival participants and, though the duration of each scene is never precisely mentioned, this determination to remain still is often acknowledged, as in the following news item from Dundee, where:

> the spectators were so delighted with every representation that they were not content with a brief sight of each enticing vision, and so long was it sometimes before the curtain was dropped that the ordeal of appearing as statues must have been most trying to mortals of flesh and blood.[38]

Local newspaper reportage of community *tableaux* ventures is positive and praiseworthy and the prescriptive 'how-to' texts are not, of course, accounts of what actually happened. Homespun outfits, unsteady platforms, jammed curtains and perilous lighting must, however, have been common. In 1891, the *Strand Magazine* noted the danger from artificial lights and recounted one *tableau* participant attempting to pinch out a large speck of burning soot that had floated down from the ceiling onto her dress.[39] As well as physical dangers, the nascent unruliness – Wendlandt called it 'larking in the dressing rooms' – inherent in the genre would doubtlessly have surfaced during the rehearsals, if not the staging, of domestic *tableaux*. This must be why the handbooks encourage firm leadership. Harrison suggests bringing in a professional with ready-made costumes, props and sets.[40]

Christian New Testament dramatizations stand apart from most other costumed diversions. Forerunners of the school Nativity Play were often *tableaux* scenes, performed in many churches across Britain. The Christian nativity favours the sequential configuration of living pictures. Their solemnity and distinct appropriation of Holy Land attire help illumine another facet of fancy dress. One early instance illustrated in *The Graphic* of 1882 shows the villagers of Rous Lench in Worcestershire dressed up as biblical characters performing a succession of eleven nativity *tableaux*.[41] These Christian *tableaux* were at the height of their popularity around 1920, with Loughborough High School unusually maintaining the tradition today and continuing to feature a scene *en grisaille* with figures painted and dressed completely in grey.

These *tableaux* endeavours came out of an established practice of amateur religious drama and there are good reasons for including them in a survey of fancy dress. Religious figures from the New Testament are rarely portrayed in fancy dress outside of a church framework, so we must include these popular and widespread parochial performances in our survey in order to gain a much truer insight into the habit of dressing up across the country. Though regular attendance at church was declining throughout our period, it still provided a focal point for social life, particularly in rural places. Folk performances and the reinvention of waning traditions were often parish-based, if not strictly religious, and fancy dress borrowed from all the different expressions, Christian and pagan alike. Furthermore, biblical scenes are especially implicated in orientalism: Christian *tableaux* were based on a certain set of received ideas about the Holy Land, different from the more melodramatic and often worldly pictures used as inspiration for dressing as characters from the *Arabian Nights*.[42]

Nativity performances – plays, pageants, *tableaux* – and the setting up of a manger have a fragmented history in the British Isles because of sectarian strife and, although their roots have been traced back to medieval mystery or miracle plays, by the nineteenth century many had been recast and absorbed into the phenomenon of the 'Victorian Christmas'. However, in the twentieth century, in the years following the First World War, church *tableaux* performances were wholly meditative, ruminative pictures that were perhaps a way to make sense of a changed post-war world.

From 1918, a mostly female company organized and enacted the Christmas story in *tableaux* format in the church of Buckland Dinham, a small village near Frome in Somerset. Especially after the loss of so many men in the war, women had a high profile in church affairs; they were no longer confined to costume-making. This particular Christmas nativity stands out from others in that it was described in detail and photographed in *Bethlehem Tableaux*, a book designed to give guidance and encouragement to others who might wish to stage something similar (illus. 43). The Buckland Dinham *tableaux* took place annually for several consecutive years. The performers – a few schoolboys, but mostly young girls who bicycled to rehearsals straight from work – arranged and rearranged themselves in a sequence of pictures, the curtain falling between each episode to allow for a hushed changeover of scene.

"The Child grew in wisdom and stature . . . . and the grace of God was upon Him."

43 Christ in the carpenter's shop from *Bethlehem Tableaux* performed at Buckland Dinham in Somerset and photographed in the Bath studio of Herbert Lambert, 1920.

A natural expression was recommended for the participants and, unlike several other forms of *tableaux*, there was to be no make-up and no disfiguring wigs and beards. Likewise omitted are the ox and ass. Animal disguises were popular by the 1920s but they introduced a humorous note and were therefore inappropriate for serious striving after holiness. For this was the *raison d'être* of the event, the concentrated attention by both players and audience designed to engender sanctity. To this end, the drafting and detailing of these *tableaux* is carefully set down by Cynthia Starey in *Bethlehem Tableaux*.[43]

As in other guides to mounting *tableaux*, she spends time on the construction of the stage and set. She takes for granted a prior knowledge of 'biblical dress' and recommends a perusal of watercolours by William Hole (1846–1917) reproduced in his very widely disseminated *The Life of Jesus of Nazareth* (*c.* 1908). Looking to art was espoused as a foundational necessity for credible fancy dress. Hole's illustrations appealed to costume-makers because he had travelled to Palestine in the first years of the twentieth century and, like several other contemporary artists, brought back examples of local clothing as models for his work. The supposed authenticity that Hole's paintings were thought to enshrine did not take account of changing dress traditions in Palestine or of differing regional styles, and his pictures, in fact depicting nineteenth-century Bethlehem, were used in all seriousness as near-accurate images of the first centuries of the Christian era. In *Bethlehem Tableaux* the correct procedures as regards costuming are set down with some deliberation and the *tableaux* were praised for not being 'amateur'. The author emphasizes the importance of dress rehearsals to correct any faults and to accustom the performers to wearing their character clothes. She stresses the care needed when dressing prior to the performance and draws attention to the maintenance of the costumes between performances. Another concern was to ensure a harmonious colour scheme: the host of angels, for example, are to be clothed in green and blue so as to blend with the Virgin's cloak and to contrast with the copper-coloured bracken on the stable roof and the tints of gold and auburn in the angels' hair. Here is true picture-making, a flawless example of the proximity of fancy dress to art.

This theatricalized notion of the Holy Land and the unfolding story of the saviour's birth was photographed by Herbert Lambert (1881–1936). Reflecting on the reciprocal affiliation between photography and fancy dress, we can see how *tableaux vivants* summoned up atmospheric, motionless images for an audience in much the same way that the camera did. Static photographs are enduring versions of costumed *tableaux vivants*. The Buckland Dinham photographs come late in the amateur trend for staging secular living pictures, and the considerable technical difficulties involved in the photography, as related in Cynthia Starey's book, help to explain the absence of more widespread photographic evidence for this popular phenomenon. Conditions inside the church were unsuitable and the same applied to domestic drawing rooms and parish halls, despite continuing advances in flash photography.[44] The eighteen youthful performers from Buckland Dinham, along with props, stage sets and costumes, had to be transported 12 miles (20 km) to Lambert's Bath studio.

Photographic technology was tangled up with the way people posed and presented themselves. It is no wonder they dressed up specifically to stand in front of the camera lens. There are many portraits throughout this book where the sitters were not necessarily going to a ball, taking part in carnival festivities or acting in a *tableau* but just recording a costumed moment, sometimes in borrowed fancy dress provided by a studio. While commercial and home photographers up and down the country produced images of people pretending to be someone other than themselves, a separate group of artistic originators, some of them luminaries from the very founding of photography, viewed camera technology as a way to investigate the magnetic relationship between character and identity, and in doing so they used dress to help express essential virtues or the drama of a narrative setting. What follows is a new way of looking at these now canonical compositions, focusing on the sitters' clothes and their meanings. Whether 'fancy dress' was a term these famous practitioners themselves used is uncertain. They may have eschewed its perfunctory and frivolous undercurrents, but it is evident that costume was critical to the aesthetic effect of their photographic compositions.

When photography was newly invented, the Scottish artist David Octavius Hill (1802–1870) and his chemist collaborator, Robert Adamson (1821–1848), produced costumed groups to illustrate Walter

44 *The Game of Life*, photographed by Thomas A. Rust, *c.* 1895.

Scott's novels. Later they would photograph Newhaven fish workers, the women's distinctive striped skirts becoming inspiration for fancy-dress outfits, as seen in illustration 14.[45] William Lake Price (1810–1896) was diligent in his attention to the detailing of the clothes as well as the set for his realizations of Don Quixote and Robinson Crusoe, two favourite characters for fancy dressers. Henry Peach Robinson (1830–1901) layered negatives together to produce stagey pictorialist scenes. His models were mostly clothed in artistic versions of contemporary dress or generalized drapery and he evidently took great pains with the setting for *The Lady of Shalott* (1861), perhaps his most famous photograph.[46] Robinson's ideas about photography and aesthetics would have been appreciated and understood, if only vaguely, by amateurs mounting *tableaux vivants*.[47] Thomas A. Rust's image *The Game of Life* (*c*. 1895) shows a contrived scene with all three protagonists – an angel, an eighteenth-century gentleman and the Devil – wearing clothing familiar to dressing-up cognoscenti (illus. 44). Rust's photograph is a mute moralizing homily. It was an acceptable topic for photography as well as the kind of narrative that would have been staged as a *tableau vivant*.

Richard Cockle Lucas (1800–1883) was more interested in the expression of emotion than in dress but as an artist he intuited its power. This unconventional man garbed himself from a ragbag wardrobe and marshalled a whole gallery of photographic self-portraits that filled sixteen albums. He transformed himself into a sort of living sculpture and his tatty, perfunctory garments were designed to help draw out something deeper than the superficial.[48] The masculine self-regard of Lucas is also present in another series of photographic portraits which position dress much more centrally as the defining component of the image. Between 1863 and 1868, David Wilkie Wynfield (1837–1887) pictured fellow artists in the style of 'Old Master' painters. The Victorian group's own work often referenced medieval and Renaissance subjects and so they were attuned to Wynfield's endeavour and must have relished the idea of aligning themselves to the past by dressing up in the style of their revered forebears. In this, of course, they were no different to hundreds of sitters and party-goers who looked back into history for their costume inspiration. In placing his models close to the camera, Wynfield emphasized the soft silk and fur of the gowns, the lace of the cuffs and ruffs and the feathers in the hats. He arranged them in an attempt to offset any suggestion that they were masquerade costumes, a judgement that nonetheless was levelled at them at the time. We know that at least two of his sitters wore the same costumes to a fancy-dress tea party in Surrey, and that all members of the set regularly enjoyed amateur theatricals. Certainly, items of dress moved between the different spheres.[49]

The intensely touching photographs of children in fancy dress produced by Lewis Carroll (Charles Lutwidge Dodgson, 1832–1898) further implicate costume with the workings of the camera (illus. 45). Carroll and his near contemporaries who worked in a similar vein were, for the most part, comparatively wealthy and from educated backgrounds. Foremost among them were Clementina, Viscountess Hawarden (1822–1865), whose beautiful daughters posed for their mother if not in fancy dress then in fanciful costume, and the pioneering photographer Julia Margaret Cameron (1815–1879), who clothed friends and family for what she herself categorized as 'Fancy Subjects for Pictorial Effect'. Their photographs are well known today and recent scholarship has interpreted, theorized and scrutinized their work and lives to great effect.[50] We do not know much about the logistics of clothing their models but, in the easy-going climate of Carroll's Oxford, it seems he borrowed some of his material from museum stores.[51] We also know that he kept a rotating stock of costumes in a dressing-room annexe to his studio and persuaded the mothers of his child models to make or purchase suitable garments.[52] The very absence of much information about costume makes clear that making and acquiring it was unexceptional and routine even though a lot of labour might be involved. The artistry was in the *wearing*, meaning that what these images have in common is a conscious preoccupation on the part of the artist/photographer to pose their subjects in persuasive configurations that reveal them as something more than portraits. As part of this illusion, they appropriated dress to accentuate an allegorical theme or infuse the picture with an ethereal quality.

Costume was conducive to artistic manipulation, giving these photographers scope to experiment with gesture and look, as well as to sculpt and light the textile material for the camera. On the sitter's side,

45 *Lorina and Alice Liddell in Chinese Dress*, photographed by Lewis Carroll (Charles Lutwidge Dodgson), 1860.

46 Leopold Myers posing as 'The Compassionate Cherub' for his mother, Eveleen Myers, in the 1880s.

we can speculate that, despite uncomfortable moments, fancy dress helped the models to feel different and thereby to respond appropriately to the lens. Costume had a formative effect on the subject's body, reshaping and recomposing it. What is apparent is that the practical considerations inherent in dressing up for the camera are the same as those for donning costume in a *tableau vivant*. The mundane paraphernalia of a costume wardrobe – needle and thread, tape and scissors, pins and glue – was essential but always out of sight. A photograph from the 1880s by Eveleen Myers (1856–1937), who herself had sat for Millais and so understood the tireless patience required of a model, encapsulates this concept of the pragmatic and the poetic (illus. 46). Her son poses as 'The Compassionate Cherub' and the picture exemplifies just how convincingly real a photographic image could be. Though we know that children are not gravity-defying and do not possess wings, these gorgeous appurtenances are persuasive. However, for the photograph, they might have been precariously positioned and fixed to young Leopold Myers's back in a less than visually appealing manner.

The idea of narrative dissimulation as exemplified in these early images was not obviously or immediately carried forwards into the twentieth century. In its place, fashion photography became a creative force and the flourishing and diverse world of the theatre provided dramatic studies of celebrated actors and actresses in character and in costume. However, the almost headlong rush into hedonism by some members of the moneyed class in the late 1920s and '30s ensured that the desire to perform and dress up for the camera was never extinguished. Glamorous fancy-dress balls continued to attract attention, with *tableaux* frequently part of the evening's entertainment. Cecil Beaton (1904–1980) captured their classy seductiveness, as we shall see in Chapter Seven.

Another photographer, a woman who suffused her mannered portraits with colour, produced a series of arresting representations of classical heroines as an artistic endeavour unconnected with a ball or theatrical performance, even though they were undeniably staged. Madame Yevonde (Yevonde Philone Cumbers, 1893–1975), a highly innovative colourist, created dramatic images of society women, styling them as goddesses (at the time of writing, these were in the care of the National Portrait Gallery, London). There is no trace of the trappings that an earlier generation had employed for their living statues. Gone are sheets and white make-up. Costume of any kind is minimal but two aspects of these very deliberately composed photographs are often equated with fancy dress: there is no attempt to disguise the identity of the models and bold props do duty as markers of mythological recognition. Tendrils of seaweed appear to float up from the head of Arethusa (Lady Bridget Poulett), a Nereid who fled from her home beneath the sea to become a fountain (illus. 47). Baroness von Gagern, another of

47 Lady Bridget Poulett as Arethusa, photographed by Madame Yevonde, 1935.

Yevonde's subjects, acknowledges the classical in a loose robe of yellow satin. Her face, in profile, rests against a bull's head defining her as Europa. An owl and books elucidate the character of Aileen Balcon, who appears startlingly up to date carrying a revolver as the armed Minerva. Allegedly classical deities, many of Yevonde's assured sitters wore red lipstick and gloss nail varnish along with ropes of heirloom pearls, confirmation that fancy dress was always of its time.

Accentuating and manipulating the colours of the photographic plates at the processing stage did not do away with the need for effective posing on the part of Madame Yevonde's models. Angus McBean (1904–1990), another ingenious twentieth-century photographer and dresser, used montage tricks and double exposure to produce dreamlike portraits of famous actors and celebrities. His self-portraits often brought to the fore his inventive costume artistry. He regularly attended the Vic-Wells Costume Balls – an event organized to raise funds for the two London theatres the Old Vic and Sadler's Wells – and was awarded first place for a fabulous Chinese outfit worn with astonishing eye make-up in 1930. He scooped the prize again the following year for his impersonation of Queen Victoria, walking on his knees beneath a long black dress and wearing a mask of his own making. For the 1933 ball, he prepared for his part as the near-naked sea king Neptune by removing his body hair and oiling his skin. A fin of plaster down the length of his spine caused his skin to peel when it was removed, reminding us of the pain as well as the pleasure of fancy dress. In homage to the spirit of masquerade, he fashioned a stunning painted and gilded mask with a lofty carapace-like forehead that completed his transformation to the ruler of the deep.[53] In 1939, he photographed himself as Neptune, dramatically rising from a shell, and this time wearing a high rope crown (illus. 48).

McBean had long been a consummate creator of highly dramatic mantles and masks, having enthusiastically participated in the costumed

48 Angus McBean, self-portrait as Neptune, 1939.

gatherings and pilgrimages of the Kindred of the Kibbo Kift, a youth movement set up in the aftermath of the First World War to redress some of society's ills. Native American iconography, borrowed from Baden-Powell's Scouts, was augmented by Egyptian, Norse and Anglo-Saxon symbolism for the organization's hieratic rituals, and we can see in McBean's later guises the influence that this early pageant-like costuming had on his work. While the tabards, cloaks and masks of the Kibbo Kift might not be classified as fancy dress, the group's penchant for dressing up fed into ideas about artistic self-expression through clothing redolent of the interwar period.[54] The picturesque apparel championed by Liberty's was also suggestive of these notions, and we know that McBean worked at the Regent Street store for a time. He went on to photograph himself over a fifty-year period in a wholly individual way, often sending out the resulting images as Christmas cards. A match for Richard Cockle Lucas in the previous century, both men were unfazed by dressing up and unabashed in front of the camera, and their confident attitude thwarts the accepted trope of male disinclination to don fancy dress. Their oeuvre draws towards what today is thought of as a queer aesthetic. Like many devisers of fancy dress, McBean utilized unusual or everyday materials to conjure up his costumes. Blue sugar-bag paper and old legal documents on vellum are mentioned by his biographer.[55] His zany imagination and outstanding practical dexterity were superior to most people's but all fancy dressers were striving after the best effects, taking inspiration and materials from whatever was near at hand.

49 'Louis XIII Mousquetaires' at Bridgwater Guy Fawkes Carnival, 1897.

Three

GUY FAWKES AND UP HELLY AA

This chapter addresses two contexts for dressing up which were both exclusively male and share the feature of having a bonfire as a central part of the ritual. One is the Up Helly Aa parade in the Shetland Isles, far from any metropolitan centre and closely tied to a strong sense of identity, while the other, a particular manifestation of Guy Fawkes Night, is patchily documented and geographically wider spread throughout the southern and western parts of England. Both Up Helly Aa and the Guy Fawkes celebrations have affinities with British street carnival. Fire festivals and carnivals took on a particular shape at the end of the nineteenth century, with the two under discussion here having clearer historic antecedents than carnival. All three are paramount in any account of fancy dress because they represent a clear about-face concerning class: they were primarily working-class occasions.

One of the best-known outdoor processional spectacles in Britain is connected with the sixteenth-century Roman Catholic plotter Guy Fawkes (1570–1606). The failure of the Gunpowder Plot, an audacious attempt by Fawkes and his band of co-conspirators to blow up parliament and the Protestant King James I of England, is commemorated annually on 5 November with fireworks, bonfires and the burning of effigies. These activities occur across Britain but an extended form of the

Guy Fawkes festival, more robust and mostly confined to certain towns in south and west England, grew from the same roots and developed an idiosyncratic fancy-dress aesthetic.

Sermons and bell-ringing were part of the original Guy Fawkes custom and fancy dress was mostly absent. The creative energies of the participants were channelled into the fashioning of dummies or 'guys', whether of the pope, the Pretender, the Devil, Guy Fawkes himself or contemporary public figures. From early on, however, concealment and clownish costumes had been part of some of the celebrations. Many of these got seriously out of hand and, when disguised roisterers could not be identified and thus brought to heel, fancy dress, more disclosing than disguise, was advocated and seemingly enthusiastically adopted. Several Bonfire Nights' espousal of fancy dress occurred in the 1880s at one of the high points of dressing up's popularity. Until recent times, participants were working men who, increasing in numbers over the years, created and paraded in decorative costumes while retaining the core tradition of making and burning larger-than-life guys. From the mid-nineteenth century, men from towns in Sussex, Kent and Somerset were organizing themselves into societies, sometimes called squads and sometimes gangs, for the production of costumes and other trappings of display.[1] Over the years, the allegiance that members felt towards their own group was strengthened by wearing thematically linked or matching costumes. Close cooperation between society members, together with the pooling of finances, resources and talent, in some cases shifted fancy dress away from the more privileged milieu of costumiers.

Today, the most famous of these Guy Fawkes celebrations is that held in Lewes, a town situated in a gap of the South Downs near the seaside resort of Brighton on the south coast. Here, as elsewhere, the transformation from disguise to costume quickened as the nineteenth century came to a close and fancy dress, while not always the main focus of Bonfire Night, added immeasurably to the powerful aura of theatricality each November. In Lewes, women may have had an early presence and certainly they participate fully today. The costume themes do not vary from year to year: the characters and the societies they come from are well-recognized. It is unclear when this format was established and it is likely to have evolved piecemeal over the years. 'Vikings', 'French Revolution', 'North American Indians', 'American Civil War Soldiers', 'Zulu Warriors' (controversially only foreswearing black make-up in 2017), 'Tudor', 'Colonial Period (1750s)' and 'English Civil War' are listed today as costume themes for some of the Lewes societies, though lack of precise archival evidence precludes a clear history for any of them. Some certainly are familiar preferences shared with other forms of fancy-dress display from the nineteenth century. At decorous balls powdered party-goers were mostly on the opposing side to 'French Revolution', affirming the supposedly more radical, working-class spirit of the Lewes event which today's participants are always keen to foster. The origin of the distinctive striped jerseys and caps worn as a uniform by the Bonfire Boys or Smuggler groups within each Lewes society is obscure but the costume was established by 1853.[2]

Along with Lewes, several other towns remodelled their tradition of Bonfire Night and, as we shall see, some celebrations coalesced into street carnivals while preserving the November date and the bonfire. In 1880, disguise was still an element, though a fading one, of the Guy Fawkes Carnival in the Somerset town of Bridgwater. In 1860, one young man mimicked the latest feminine fashion – a crinoline – and was repaid by a shower of lighted firecrackers thrown by ladies standing at an upstairs window.[3] Such hazardous horseplay brought the event into disrepute and by 1880 masqueraders were persuaded to dress differently if still festively.[4] Photographs of the reorganized event testify to the talent of the fancy-dress makers. Resplendent apparel appears in a line-up of 1897 (illus. 49). It shows a detachment of Louis XIII's musketeers in a rather good rendering of the swashbuckling style made famous by Alexandre Dumas (1802–1870) in his novel *Les trois mousquetaires* (The Three Musketeers) of 1844, translated into English by 1846. Their outfits are lavishly fashioned from lengths of rich-looking stuff. The effect is heightened by their broad-brimmed hats, shoulder-length hair and cleverly contrived moustaches. Their footwear is ingeniously devised out of textile-covered card resembling high boots and shaped to go over everyday shoes. This sartorial solution hints at an attempt to economize on what might have been a costly undertaking. Some of the musketeers carry firework squibs on poles and these were ignited along the length of the entire procession, the sudden bright line of fire bringing the garments into sharp relief.[5] The firing of the squibs in Bridgwater is one of the few times when members of different gangs, variously costumed, are seen standing motionless in close proximity to one another and this commingling of motley characters from widely different historic periods remained a compelling feature of fancy dress and one of its defining attributes whatever its context.

The high sense of adventure and derring-do inherent in many of the Bridgwater clubs' costume themes was regularly encountered in similar kinds of Guy Fawkes parades elsewhere in Britain. Over the years, the Bridgwater musketeers have been joined by other heroic bands of brothers: 'Assyrian Warriors' in 1906, 'The Sons of Erin' in 1909, 'Italian Brigands' in 1910, 'Robin Hood and his Merry Men' in 1911, 'Knights of the White Eagle' in 1911, and, later in the twentieth century, 'Antarctic Explorers' and 'Aviators'. At odds with most modern people's sensibilities, 'Dahomey Warriors' appeared in 1898 and 'Zulu Warriors' in 1908. These choices were a constant across carnival towns in Britain. Several African and Asian kingdoms that were all but wiped out by European warmongering on a colossal scale came to rest in the Western imaginary as fearless martial domains, and images of their valorous fighters entered popular culture through songs, illustrated newspapers and the popular attraction of the human exhibition. Fancy

50 'Set of Playing Cards' at Bridgwater Guy Fawkes Carnival, 1886.
51 'Fairy Princes and Princesses' at Bridgwater Guy Fawkes Carnival, 1898.

dress of this type, seen as an amusement by the Bridgwater carnival gang, was just one of the numerous expressions of imperialism and racism that pervaded the British psyche.

The Bridgwater revellers lined up to be photographed as part of the whole experience of dressing up, as many surviving images testify. Over the years, when not depicting fighting men, they have had a taste for the historic elite, for animal camouflage and for the absurd and visually appealing. They embraced cross-dressing. In 1886, for example, one of the chosen themes was a set of playing cards with the participants dressed imposingly as queens, kings and jacks in a hazily medieval style (illus. 50). The whole effect is splendidly stately and we have to look quite closely to perceive that the 'queens' are men. Likewise the

52 'Aeroplanes' squad at Up Helly Aa, Lerwick, Shetland, photographed by A. Abernethy, 1926.

'princesses' in an 1898 group entitled 'Fairy Princes and Princesses' (illus. 51).

The Bridgwater event transformed itself into a more recognizable street carnival over the years. It still maintained competing male clubs in costumed *tableaux*, though a 1935 report makes clear that sometimes women supported them as musicians and dancers: Miss Betty Spraggs, Miss Winnie Hurford and Mrs E. Kingston appeared in 'Revels of Old Seville' and we presume they were appropriately costumed. Masquerading women as single entries were also insinuating themselves into the masculine world of Guy Fawkes parades. King George V's silver jubilee gave several of them at the Bridgwater festival of 1935 a felicitous excuse to bedizen themselves in silver: Nellie Staples, for example, appeared as 'Silver Butterfly'. Winifred Clark, Gladys Baker, Gwendoline Cann and Lilian Binding even made up a ladies' group to rival the men, posing as 'League of the British Isles'. Unusually, some of the Bridgwater women dressmakers and designers are acknowledged and named.[6]

53 A.R.M. Mathewson as the Guizer Jarl at Up Helly Aa, Lerwick, 1933.

Women's infiltration of bonfire parades, however, is not reflected in a northern spectacle that continues all but unchanged to this day. The Shetland fire festival in Lerwick known as Up Helly Aa is a *rara avis* and, because it invites a series of questions and is well documented, the remainder of this chapter is devoted to this arresting marvel.[7] Although, on occasion, men have to be persuaded to dress up, the evidence suggests that many have a burning compulsion to do so. This absolutely holds true for the Shetland festival. Groups of men unblushingly dress up and record their participation in the event by lining up for the camera in their unorthodox apparel every year (illus. 52). These are the same groups, in Shetland called squads, that parade through Lerwick, the main town of the islands, an archipelago off the northeastern tip of the British mainland. They clothe themselves in outlandish attire, newly created for each January festival and different every year. The one exception to this is a squad of warriors wearing burnished Viking outfits which do not vary greatly year on year. By custom, this group's chieftain is elected annually to the high office of 'Guizer Jarl' (literally 'earl in disguise') (illus. 53). For that year only he and his personal squad dress as Norsemen, in contrast to the other participating squads, who devise fresh character costumes each year. The Jarl's squad, in their familiar regalia, are an expected part of the ceremony while the novel clothes of the others provide an anticipatory aspect to the proceedings. The configuration of the predictable with the unexpected in terms of dress is particularly effective and the balance between the two is a byword for fancy dress generally. Although in Shetland dressing up preceded the institution of the Jarl's squad, the introduction of the first Norse longship into the Lerwick celebration in the late 1880s, followed by the regular appearance of a Jarl, was pivotal in setting the scene for some unique and genuinely astonishing costumes. Any account of Up Helly Aa has to be configured around the conception, construction and subsequent burning of this galley, which took its place at the heart of the festival and accrued its own traditions as time went by. The ship is impressive but was made markedly more so by the introduction of its costumed posse of seafarers and the Viking Guizer Jarl himself at the beginning of the twentieth century. The record of past Guizer Jarls goes back to 1906 so the convention fits neatly with the rise of other outdoor presentations of fancy dress at the same period.

So, why did these Shetlanders disguise themselves as Norse warriors? A change of emphasis was needed in the 1870s because the age-old festival of Up Helly Aa, celebrated at the end of the twelve days of Christmas, the Yule season, was, like the Guy Fawkes festival, becoming increasingly rowdy and uncontrollable with blazing tar barrels rolled through the streets. Torches replaced flaming barrels and the upsurge in interest, both amateur and professional, in Shetland's past provided an opportunity to take Up Helly Aa in a new direction, one that was genuinely engaging. How did they accomplish this and where did their perceptions of Viking dress come from?

When Scandinavian lands became overpopulated, Shetland was colonized by Norsemen in the ninth century. Shetlanders are therefore quite correct to claim Norse ancestry, though 'Viking', an appellation full of preconceptions and misconceptions, has only been used in English since around 1800.[8] A potent word and a key one for fancy dress, 'Viking' is a term used for Northern European raiders and traders of the eighth to the eleventh centuries and it had become part of the accepted fancy-dress repertoire before it appeared in this specific context in the Northern Isles. Arthur Conan Doyle (1859–1930), the creator of the Sherlock Holmes detective stories, dressed as one in 1895 and other whimsical Norse pretenders turned up regularly at fancy-dress balls, cycle carnivals and even a swimming gala in 1897.[9] Through the years the fascination for heroic helmets has never wavered and the idea of these Northern strongmen took hold via a combination of scholarship and sentiment.

Several translations of *The Saga of Frithiof*, all imaginative renderings of an eighth-century Scandinavian narrative, breathed life into medieval Norway for many readers across the British Isles, and these Northern sea kings became the subject of lectures and learned papers. For the inhabitants of Shetland and prospective Guizer Jarls, nineteenth-century translations of the *Orkneyinga Saga*, an Icelandic work of legend and history, kindled a particular interest in their Viking antecedents, recounting tales of Norwegian kings and earls not only in Orkney but in Shetland as well.[10] Short stories from Norwegian history were printed in the *Shetland Times* and Shetlanders became familiar with the trappings of the Viking world when early manuscripts were used as inspiration for both the interior and exterior decorations of Lerwick Town Hall, completed in 1884. One of the stained-glass windows, for instance, depicts the figure of King Harald the Fair-Haired, first king of Norway, wearing full armour, a blue mantle fastened at his throat with a brooch, and a raven helmet. His long fair hair streams down over his shoulders, a feature given much prominence by early Guizer Jarl squads who sported blond wigs.

The discovery of a real Norse ship at the Gokstad burial site in Norway in 1880 was reported locally and certainly heightened interest in these seafarers and their boats. The Oseberg ship, dating to the ninth century, another sensational find in Norway, perhaps quickened the establishment of the line of Shetland Up Helly Aa chiefs, for the excavation was carried out between 1904 and 1905 and reported in the *Shetland Times* less than a year before J. W. Robertson took on the role of the first Guizer Jarl.[11] At that time the festival committee thought their chieftain 'should have a dress more in accordance with Norse costume' and they were prepared to meet the expense of such an outfit from a subscription fund.[12] The lustrous mail rig-out attracted some national attention, with *The Sphere* publishing a picture of Robertson under the headline 'A Strange Festival at Lerwick'.[13]

We do not know where the suit itself came from but we can reliably say where the inspiration for its look originated. Here we move right out of the domain of history and straight into the arms of romanticism, for the Guizer Jarl's habiliments are unambiguously pilfered from Wagner via Gilbert and Sullivan. We might suppose the horned helmet, that assured beacon of old north manliness, reigned supreme in Shetland and, through the years, horns *do* appear on some of the headgear in the Lerwick festival, but a glance at Carl Emil

Doepler's (1824–1905) designs for the early productions of Wagner's *Der Ring des Nibelungen* (first staged in Bayreuth in 1876) tell us that Shetland Guizer Jarls take their helmet excrescences from the exuberant expanded-wing decorations of Wagner's principal characters: horns are reserved for their retinues.[14] The *Ring* came to London in 1882, the same year Gilbert and Sullivan's *Iolanthe* premiered there. Gilbert and Sullivan, whose operas were often mined for fancy dress, costumed Alice Barnett (1846–1901) as a Viking fairy queen resembling several Brunhildes. The overlapping segmented armour worn by all Lerwick Guizer Jarls from 1906 is the version often worn by the female characters in both Wagner and Gilbert and Sullivan operas.

This is not to assume that Shetlanders saw either of these productions, though they might just have caught the D'Oyly Carte Opera Company on one of its extensive tours of the Scottish mainland, and we know a Shetland man was singing with the Company in the 1890s.[15] Many Shetlanders would certainly have been aware of the work of a local blind scholar, James John Haldane Burgess (1862–1927), whose writing was one of the catalysts for the fervent interest in Shetland's Nordic past and who is thought to have been greatly influenced by Wagner's *Ring* cycle. Haldane Burgess advised on the festivities, including its costuming, until his death.[16] Shetlanders would also have seen illustrations and descriptions in books and magazines saturated with Viking imagery of all sorts. R. M. Ballantyne's *Erling the Bold: A Tale of the Norse Sea-Kings*, for example, a very popular story for boys, included drawings by the author showing winged helmets in all eight editions before 1880 and horns in editions thereafter. While horns won out generally and became a fancy-dress staple elsewhere, Shetlanders persisted in their allegiance to wings. Before we become too sentimental about successive Guizer Jarls' awareness of their historical past, we remember that neither wings nor horns are verified as 'Viking' by archaeological evidence (though Celtic and Germanic ones exist).[17]

The first Jarl's outfit could have been purchased from a professional costumier with little input from the Lerwick guizers themselves, though we have no evidence of this. It was described as follows:

> He wore a silver helmet, with raven's wings rising high on either side, a corselet with sleeves of silver mail was worn over a jerkin, fastened round the neck and hung loosely from the shoulders. On the legs were thigh length black stockings and on the feet were rawhide sandals fastened with tan leather thongs which criss-crossed over the instep and all the way up the thighs. He carried a round silver shield on which was engraved a raven, a large silver-headed battle axe and dagger hung from his belt.[18]

Criss-crossed fastenings, extensively utilized by fancy dressers to give an ancient period feel, were often misinterpreted, as in the description above: Roman footwear had attached leather thongs to hold sandals in place, whereas Germanic cross-gartering was separate from the shoe and held down the trouser leg. Successive Jarls' apparel included this gartering feature along with all the other accessories mentioned in the original list. Subsequent photographs show only small variations. The costume is passed on to the next Jarl and only the colour and design of his tunic, originally called a 'jerkin', and cloak vary. He must stand out from the men of his squad. Over the years the chiefs pose differently for the camera. The 1907 Jarl, H. J. Anderson, looks like an invitee to the Duchess of Devonshire's Ball. He stands against an incongruous backcloth painted with foliage and rococo plasterwork. The last Jarl before the First World War, Laurence Sandison, presents himself in 1914 in front of a more appropriate studio backdrop of sea and dark clouds; he would die on the battlefields very soon after. A. P. Hawick, the Jarl in 1921, was photographed outdoors on flat rocks at the water's edge

54 'Tennis Girls' squad at Up Helly Aa, Lerwick, photographed by R. Ramsay, 1922. Peter Moar, the Guizer Jarl in 1932, is standing second from the right.

against a real seascape, his squad positioned well behind him, giving their chief prominence and authority.[19]

In 1931 considerable improvements were made to the outfit and it is notable that Shetland men were involved in this refashioning. Peter Moar (1888–1983), the Guizer Jarl for 1932, must be wearing some of these new pieces in his Jarl photographs for that year. The redesigned raven is certainly in evidence on the shield of A.R.M. Mathewson, who took on the role of Jarl in 1933, as seen in illustration 53. We can trace these particular Jarls' sartorial progress through squad photographs in other years. In 1922, for example, Peter Moar was decked out as a tennis girl (illus. 54). In 1923, both he and Mr Mathewson were Persian dancers, giving us an insight into the varied stances and characters these Shetland men enacted each year. Another image taken in 1929 shows Moar in a suit and tie lining up with fellow Up Helly Aa Committee members. Quite away from festival connections, still more photographs of Messrs Moar and Mathewson register the several complementary roles they played in civilian and army life.[20] Fancy dress might be way out on the far reaches of the clothing continuum but these images of ordinary men in different dress styles tell us that most people routinely changed their clothes to suit the occasion and the circumstance and, in that sense, they became accustomed to different ways of dressing.

When he was nominated as Guizer Jarl for the year 1932, Moar may already have been an enthusiastic searcher for Norse period settlement sites; we know that later on he certainly was.[21] So, alongside the reading of the landscape and the scholarship of the archaeological record, Shetlanders reclaimed their Scandinavian ancestry by dressing as Norsemen. Over the years, awareness of this specific heritage has not waned and the silvery costume continues to transmit a potent virility. The specificity of the January festival and the exclusive participation of indigenous male Shetlanders ensure that the ideals of Up Helly Aa are not dissipated even though certain aspects might be modernized.

Other than the Guizer Jarl's squad, topical fancy dress is the primary way that the festival is brought up to date, but even the Jarl's men made adaptations to their vestiary habits as the years went by. Through the 1920s and '30s, the Jarl and his squad are clean-shaven. By the end of our period in 1953, the men on the galley are sporting beards that look like their own.[22] The exaggerated long blond wigs gradually disappear and are replaced by shorter ones and then by the men's own hair, grown long for the occasion. This speaks of the participants' commitment to the festival proceedings and perhaps also of their desire to render themselves as dignified Norsemen rather than as caricatures of fair-haired pillagers. Contrary to the supposed ephemeral nature of fancy dress, the Jarl's costume (should we really be calling it 'fancy dress'?) is carefully preserved and passed on, with damaged sections regularly replaced. His squad's outfits are not worn again but stored away and preserved; it is a once-in-a-lifetime opportunity to be a Norseman at Up Helly Aa.

Unique as it is in many aspects, Up Helly Aa is not a totally atypical pagan festival but a rich mix of sights and sounds taken from multiple contemporary sources. However far out on the margins Shetland is judged to be by people further south, crucially in the period under discussion, certain aspects of cultural life were shared by almost everyone throughout the British Isles. The Devonshire House Fancy Dress Ball in 1897, the grand affair detailed in Chapter One, was reported in the *Shetland Times*. It was by no means the first account of a costume ball to be recorded in the Shetland newspaper. Edinburgh and London balls regularly featured in its columns. Determined not to seem parochial, it even published a notice of the fancy-dress ball given by the 'Purbhoos of Bombay' in India in May 1873.[23] The Devonshire ball, however, can be seen as one of the key moments for dressing up in Shetland. In that same year, 1897, the Thule Quadrille Club organized a copycat event, a masked fancy costume ball, an innovation for Lerwick, with many of the outfits acquired from London.[24] Up Helly Aa was a costumed spectacle of a different kind, but the Thule Quadrille Club, whose membership just might have overlapped in some measure with the festival squads, could have strengthened the disposition to dress up and to validate the time and money expended on it. The photographic archive absolutely confirms just how much attentive thought and skilful making went into the final look of each Up Helly Aa group.

Today's countdown of preparation, beginning almost as soon as each January festival is over, must resemble lead-in times of the past.

Though the carnival itself is brief, the decision-making, planning, building and tailoring that precede the parade are evident from the many surviving images of the line-ups. This Shetland costuming is not lightly undertaken. The costumes are such an inherent and important part of the proceedings that their preparation is viewed as anything but frivolous. Notionally no repeat themes are allowed year on year, so ideas have to be constantly refreshed and competition between the groups, including the Guizer Jarl's flashily conspicuous squad, acts as a strong incentive to produce original and striking outfits. There is secrecy too surrounding the theme of each squad and this sometimes results in duplicates when the costumes are revealed on the festival day. The pervasive tendency towards masking, whether as an integral part of a suit or as a separate visage covering the face, perpetuates the original sense of the old term 'guizing', as in disguise, and 'guizer' is the word used for all the costumed contributors, although the term is not unique to Shetland or even Scotland and it has a long history of use prior to Up Helly Aa.

When the Lerwick guizers take up their positions to be photographed, a rite that is annually observed within the broader rituals of the festival itself, some groups pose twice, first masked and then unmasked and revealing their identities (illus. 55 and illus. 56). Elaborate costuming seems to have been introduced in the 1870s and 'male-ladies' and caricatures of local celebrities in 1876 presaged a trend that continues to this day. By the end of the nineteenth century, Lerwick must have been influenced by the costumed street carnivals then getting under way all over Britain but no firm date can be given for the start of matching fancy dress themed for each squad, a trend, as we have seen, that runs through several of these male-oriented festivals. Photographic evidence suggests that at first uniformly dressed groups took part alongside those dressed more arbitrarily. Lookalike dressing was certainly practised in the 1890s when Arthur Abernethy photographed an Up Helly Aa squad

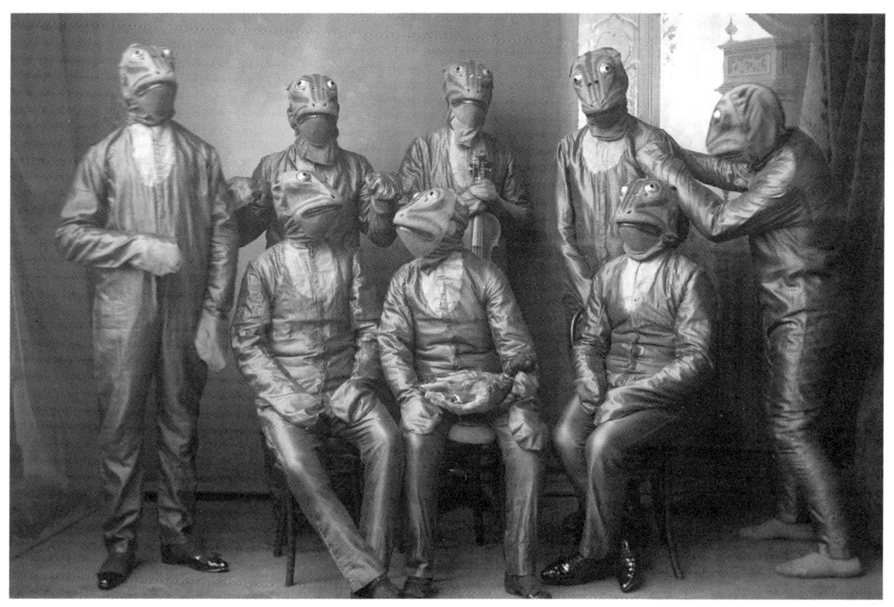

55 Masked frog squad at Up Helly Aa, Lerwick, photographed by R. Ramsay, 1911.
56 Unmasked frog squad at Up Helly Aa, Lerwick, photographed by R. Ramsay, 1911.

kitted out as lancers.[25] The only figure dressed differently from the rest of the group is a fiddler, an immediate marker of Shetland identity who makes an habitual appearance in the foreground of many squad fancy-dress line-ups. Identical dressing fostered a sense of camaraderie within the group and gave those less sure about donning wacky clothes the necessary daring to fall in with their fellow impersonators. Beyond doubt, the effect of lookalikes is visually powerful and, on a practical note, the production line is simplified and cost-effective if a whole squad's garments are similar.

The rich archive of surviving Up Helly Aa images allows us to reflect on the changing habits, mores and fads of the time as evidenced in the fancy-dress choices of these men of Shetland. Characters and costumes across the decades sometimes fall in line with fancy dress elsewhere and appear to come straight out of dress guides or pattern books. However, time and again there is a twist that belies the customary. In 1904, a squad representing 'Night' were bedecked in floor-length robes of shining, dark material appliquéd with celestial bodies. Though the concept of 'Night' could be assigned any gender or none, it is rendered as female in the popular costume books of the time, with fancy-dress photographs confirming the feminine. These Shetland masqueraders were therefore going against the accepted norms of contemporary gender assignation though not against eighteenth-century European carnival conventions, according to which switching clothes with the opposite sex was customary.[26] We do not know if this particular Shetland instance was intentional cross-dressing though we know for certain that there was plenty of deliberate gender-swapping right from Up Helly Aa's beginnings. It was a practice that never fell out of favour. Doubtless there was joking and innuendo among these Shetland men dressed up as women. Irrefutably, there are hints of the distorted parody that characterizes cross-dressing elsewhere but most Shetland squads avoided the lurid in their annual photograph.

In 1909, not one but two squads dressed as suffragettes, a fancy-dress style that became generally popular with males at this time. Did they support these campaigning women? It is very doubtful because both Shetland squads apparently distributed pamphlets couched in comedy language, and a banner in one photograph reads 'Votes for We-Men'. There is no indication of whether the purple, green and white colour scheme, devised by Emmeline Pethick-Lawrence (1867–1954) only in 1908, was taken up in Shetland. So, what did these interlopers trespassing into the world of crusading women wear? One group dressed in sensible jerseys and long skirts, and the all-important accessories, diagonal sashes and chains with padlocks, were what distinguished these men as vote-seeking strategists.[27] The second squad look to be wearing bloomers, which turns out to be just about right (illus. 57).

57 'Votes for Women' squad dressed in *jūjitsu* suits at Up Helly Aa, Lerwick, photographed by R. Ramsay, 1909.

According to the *Shetland Times,* their entire outfits are *jūjitsu* suits, a clever fancy dress in which to impersonate forceful women. The newspaper report is silent as to whether the clothes are authentic. Kanō Jigorō (1860–1938), a Japanese master of judo, a form of *jūjitsu*, introduced the sport to Europe and America from the end of the nineteenth century and there are reports of local demonstrations of this unarmed combat by Shetland service men in the same year that the Up Helly Aa squads chose to impersonate suffragettes. A year later, *Every Woman's Encyclopaedia* was extolling the benefits of this form of self-defence for women.[28] Fancy dress, sometimes viewed as a vehicle for revivifying the nostalgic past, surprises by its contemporaneity and the ability of its proponents to think creatively about signifiers. The Lerwick squad superimposed the idea of judo and conflict on to the notion of women's fight for universal suffrage. The irony is, of course, that no woman to this day has taken part in a costumed procession in Up Helly Aa though they play major roles in Shetland society, more so than in many other communities.[29]

There is another element to the suffragette squads in Lerwick and it provides us with an additional example of the way different forms of entertainment fed into each other and channelled fancy dress in certain directions. In April 1908, ten months or so prior to the festival in January 1909, Calder's Royal Cinematograph toured to Lerwick and Scalloway, providing the same sort of entertainment for Shetland Islanders as for people in the larger centres further south. The cinematograph was both a moving-picture camera and a projector and in 1908 this 'entertainment incomparable in its variety, freshness, and originality' included a new sketch, *The Suffragette*, described as 'a witty, breezy burlesque'.[30] Whether this played into the Shetland squads' plan of action for their forthcoming suffragette makeovers we cannot know, but we can say that Shetlanders, geographically positioned on the periphery of Britain, were in no way out of step with the centre.

Over the years both the number of squads and sometimes the number of men in each squad increased. In 1911, there were 27 squads and the list of entries gives a flavour of the fancy-dress choices. In procession order, and in the terminology of the times, they were: 'Indian Sikhs', 'Chinese Ladies', 'Irishmen', 'Schoolboys', 'Elizabethan Noblemen', 'Lerwick Patent Slip', 'Would-Be Toffs', 'Lord Nelson', 'Fairy Princes', 'Lerwick Cookery Class', 'Punch', 'Shoe-Shine Parade', 'Fashions for All' (a surprising inclusion, based on the successful women's fashion magazine of the same name that began publication in 1908 and included fancy-dress ideas), 'Army and Navy', 'Bon-Bons', 'King of Spades', 'The Mad Hatters', 'Saxon Peasant Women', 'German Peasants', 'Frogs', 'Scalloway Sma'-Drinks', 'Hobble Skirts', 'Pierrots' and 'Man-o'-War's Men'. Also joining the parade were visiting fishermen from Lowestoft, Yarmouth and Peterhead in their oilskins, sou'westers and boots.[31]

Music-hall entertainers featured in Lerwick fancy dress, as they did everywhere throughout Britain. In 1913, for example, one squad presented two of these performers, Happy Fanny Fields (*c.* 1881–1961) and Little Tich (1867–1928).[32] They were not a double act, as their pairing in Shetland might suggest, but both artistes caught the mood of the times and were rife for impersonation by fancy dressers. In 1913, the year the first fixed cinema in Shetland opened its doors, the film *Happy Fanny Fields and the Four Little Dutchmen* made Fanny, with her distinctive Dutch-inflected stage costume, a star. Tich's exaggeratedly long shoes and checked jacket became his signature garments, easily copied by the guizers and instantly recognized by spectators.

Other crazes of the moment were frequently chosen by Lerwick squads. In 1908, the diabolo squad presented their themed *tableau*, which was almost certainly based on pictures of the lissom Annette Kellerman (1886–1975), exhibition swimmer and popularizer of the one-piece swimming costume, juggling with the twin-cupped contrivance on a string. She was one of the first women to appear nude on film,

58 'Council Housing' squad at Up Helly Aa, Lerwick, photographed by A. Abernethy, 1920s. The fiddler, here dressed as Pierrot, appears in many group photographs and is a mark of Shetland identity.

though the Shetland men fought shy of both nakedness and swimsuits in their characterization of her. 'Pogo Fiends' depicted another current fad. The 'spring end hopping stilt', refined by German inventors in the 1920s, had made it to Shetland by 1922 when an Up Helly Aa squad used it as an excuse for depicting cross-dressed men flirting with their pogo partners. In both cases, it was the accessory that was vital to the squad's identification: real props were used to fabricate a fancy-dress scenario.[33]

Within the broad remit of Up Helly Aa dressing up, specifically Shetland issues were also propounded through costume. 'Lerwick Cookery Class' in 1911 referred to the large attendance at the recently instituted School Board's lessons. In the 1920s, Lerwick's new water supply and council housing were two topics brought into focus by festival squads (illus. 58).[34] They provide us with a whole category of fancy dress that, as we have seen elsewhere, was not based on people but on inanimate concepts, a stretch for fancy dress and always a cause for hilarity.

In the 1920s and '30s, there were around thirty squads with between three hundred and four hundred guizers. Across these inter-war years, favourite themes from the broader fancy-dress repository were invoked time and time again, despite the supposed veto on repetition. Making small style adjustments and inventing an original title circumvented the ban on duplication. A considerable number of variants on the Pierrot theme recur when the countrywide Harlequinade infatuation, described in Chapter Eight, was at its most intense.

59 'Scarlet Fever Microbes' at Up Helly Aa, Lerwick, photographed by R. Ramsay, 1924. Squads began to pose 'in character' from this time.

In 1920, there was 'Jazz'; in 1923, 'Toytown', 'Pierrottes' and 'Twink'; in 1924, 'Dazzle'; in 1925, 'Co-optimists'; and in 1926, 'Jazz Mania', all of them dressed in ruffs, pom-poms and conical hats derived from the archetypal melancholic.

Taking up a *tableau*-like stance for the camera became more usual in the 1920s and comedy fancy dress habitually surfaced. 'Sole Savers' in 1925 had the squad photographed in suits designed with 'hands' at the bottom and 'feet' held high in the air covering their real hands.[35] 'Scarlet Fever Microbes' posed menacingly while a 'nurse' attempted to eliminate them (illus. 59). Too frequently the comedy squads carried the taint of racism. Animal fancy dress pitched up regularly. Hiding human features behind an animal's physiognomy chimes with Shetland's masking tradition and created some of the most effective fancy dress of all. In 1909, a troupe of monkeys processed along the festival route, their masks verging on the malefic. All-covering animal fancy-dress suits, especially simian ones, were just becoming popular.

60 'The Road to the Isles' squad with men disguised as crabs at Up Helly Aa, Lerwick, photographed by R. Williamson, 1925.

61 'Nightbirds' squad at Up Helly Aa, Lerwick, photographed by T. Kay, 1936.

The theme might have been inspired by the novelty act Cambo, the Musical Monkey, which toured widely onstage and appeared as part of Imperial Animated Pictures at the beginning of the twentieth century. In 1911, frogs made an appearance in shiny suits with integral gloves for webbed hands. Their detachable heads with bulging eyes and down-turned mouths were fashioned with sharp acuity as seen in illustration 55. 'March Hares' and 'Chanticleers' materialize in 1923. The roosters are a wonderful confection of feathers and coxcombs straight out of pantomime, and the hares, wearing spats and tiny top hats, are an anthropomorphic rendering of the long-eared boxer from the tea-party scene in *Alice's Adventures in Wonderland*. In 1924, a squad was suited up as remarkably realistic penguins, huddled close together in mutual comradeship.[36] The next year 'The Road to the Isles' featured a ferry captain and model boat surrounded by other squad members disguised as crabs. They crouch beneath shells and are completely hidden except for their hands, which poke out from beneath the carapace and are fashioned as large eyes (illus. 60). In 1936, the 'Nightbirds' proved that even in the Depression years, when some Shetland fancy dress lacked the polish of more prosperous times, squads could still conjure up fantastic costumes (illus. 61).

Many of these animal and humorous rig-outs sacrificed ease of movement for effect. The discomfort must have been extreme. Fancy dress is often awkwardly shaped and unwieldy but these very qualities produce memorable and winning designs: in 1927, guizers costumed as Dalmatians were completely smothered by their black-spotted coats, a squad of handsomely sleek walruses bore the weight of heavy tusks, and men on all fours, pretending to be sheep, were stiflingly cocooned in thick woollen suits. Spotty dogs, marine mammals and outsize sheep were not prominent fancy-dress choices at this time. In the pattern books animal suits were more usually identified as children's fancy dress. Shetland men trespassed freely across gender and generational boundaries and seemed to relish their roles.

A beautiful and brilliant film produced by the newsreel company Gaumont Graphic records these 1927 Up Helly Aa animals, as well as a medley of other characters taking part in the festival that year.[37] The film catches something tangible about fancy dress and about the Shetland guizers in particular. Staying within their squads, they process in close formation: Dalmatians, walruses and sheep file past the cameraman along with 'Slantigert Tourists', 'Mossy Divots', 'Gents of the Broad Arrow', 'Town Criers', 'Michelin Men' and others. They are staging this promenade during the short hours of daylight, probably especially for the camera. Though today we may not understand some of the character intentions, the Gaumont film unveils each squad accoutred with real purpose and an understanding of the most arresting features of a costume. The film's motile magic and concentrated close-ups allow us to appreciate the perfectly crafted tricorns of the town criers, the uniformly applied arrows on the prisoners' jackets, the well-observed features of walrus flippers and tusks, the practical detailing of protective pads on sheep knees and the loops attaching spotted leggings to Dalmatian paws. The long establishment of a fancy-dress tradition within the Shetland community means that this kind of making, with an eye both to exhibition and to practicality, is an embedded credo of the families who take part. Because the same people are involved year on year, they accrue fancy-dress wisdom.

The coat of mail and winged helmet worn by James McIntosh, the Guizer Jarl in 1927, is given a new dimension by this Gaumont film as he stands against a huge Shetland sky, the wind ruffling his long hair and helmet feathers. His squad stand along the length of their dragon-prowed galley and raise their halberds in unison. The angle of photography casts them in a heroic light. They are dressed as icons of Nordic identity and are attempting to act out this status, though they do so tentatively. Performance would become an established component of Up Helly Aa in the years to come, but in 1927 it was still a novel idea. Clips from the film show the sheep being rounded up for auction, and the exceedingly realistic walruses edging their way up the beach. The sea creatures' costumes were contrived with the natural gait of the beasts in mind. However, away from the beach, when the squad walk upright in parade, the men tilt their walrussy helmets upwards to see the way ahead, and this reveals them as the humans they are. Most fancy dress is problematic in this regard and some outfits work better than others but perfect simulacrum is not the point. Whatever privations were suffered by the Shetland men inside their suits, they were expected to keep their masks on.

Though they were never mistaken for a walrus or a Michelin Man, each person's identity was submerged; in Shetland, recognition of the individual is not such an essential part of fancy dress as it sometimes is elsewhere. In the torchlight procession, the apogee of Up Helly Aa, the costumed squads sweat beneath the weight of their outfits and their 2-metre (6 ft) torches. The original flame is passed from torch to torch so that each man is illuminated in turn and his costume emerges out of the darkness into a pool of light. The Norse galley is trundled through the streets and the men fall in behind the Guizer Jarl in a double crocodile formation. Flickering light rather than total illumination picks out a fantastic hat, a shining cloak or a feathered tail and when the torches are hurled into the long ship and the vessel burns brightly a different, more concentrated light irradiates the costumes. Additionally, the Northern skies produce a heart-stopping backdrop against which this costumed spectacle is played out, and in 1938, a breathtaking display of aurora borealis appeared at the mustering of the guizers.[38] That so many ordinary men are happy to dress up is a clear reflection of this annual venture's intense allure.

Four

CARNIVALS AND RAGS

Street carnival in the British Isles provided the consummate opportunity for dressing up and showing off. Like fire festivals, its most distinguishing features are its processional nature and its *plein-air* environment. Revellers on decorated vehicles, called floats or turn-outs, are carnival's main attraction, and fancy dress is sometimes a peripheral, though necessary, supplement to the overall concept. Its more demotic idiom also aligns carnival with the celebrations described in the previous chapter, as well as with certain traditional folkloric festivals. Carnival sanctioned an outpouring of resourceful creativity and, although it shared some of the same costumed characters with balls, fancy dress for these outdoor spectacles was exaggerated and frequently worn in divergent ways with less decorum. Themes could be fleetingly topical, sometimes with a very local flavour. Carnival fancy dress often expressed fervent patriotism but also dissent. It erred on the side of caricature and was often unashamedly comic. Commercial trademarks and mascots figured prominently. Abundantly original, carnival outfits mirrored popular culture, poked fun at officialdom and stuffiness, aped and, at the same time, worshipped celebrities and film stars.

The antecedents of British carnival can be traced to several outdoor celebrations defined by dressing up. The knee breeches, tatter-coats and flower-filled hats of Morris Men and other guizing mummers undoubtedly play a significant, if ill-defined, role. Carnival also drew on May Day festivities: open-air costumed rituals enacted according to the farming year. In turn, these rites took on the character of British street carnival and the two often blended together. Seasonal fairs are also plausible forebears. The fair and carnival that grew up around the Derby, one of the most celebrated horse races in the British Isles, was known for its medley of deviant characters in unusual habiliments. Another progenitor is the processional celebration connected with the sixteenth-century Roman Catholic plotter Guy Fawkes, already discussed. Some of the disruptive elements of these originators were adopted by street carnival. Like the Christian pre-Lenten festival of Catholic lands, British carnival was a loud, peripatetic street party, although film footage from the 1920s and '30s reveals just how far British carnival was from the polished festivities of Venice and Nice.[1] Spectators were an essential component of the proceedings, with costumed paraders and high-spirited onlookers in a mutual, disorderly relationship of heady jocularity. Carnival's very public expression of fancy dress sometimes prompted a temporary relaxation of class boundaries and an enhanced sense of unity.

The processionary aspect of carnival had forebears in horse parades and, perhaps more relevant because of the fantastical costumes, in travelling circuses that advertised their presence by marching through the towns where they were to perform. More modern recreational activities, however, fuelled a fascination for dynamic carnival. Decorated bicycle parades and stunt riding together with roller- and ice-skating jamborees in the 1870s and '80s just pre-date other forms of processional carnival, though all types persisted side by side and each craze stimulated the others.

An example of this early progenitor of carnival occurred in 1876 at the Masquerade Skating Carnival that inaugurated the new ice rink

62 Miss Pickard as Empress Theodora of Byzantium and Mr Cawrse as a Musketeer at a roller carnival, Holland Park Skating Rink, London, 1884.

in Bridlington, a coastal town on the North Sea. Only those appearing in character dress or wearing masks were allowed onto the ice. The local paper reveals the extent to which fancy dress was enmeshed in Victorian life by suggesting that the rink entrepreneur 'would do well to have occasional special nights when the skaters would appear in characters illustrating, for instance, those of the sixteenth century, the Commonwealth, the Georgian or other era'.[2]

With the arrival from America of James Plimpton's Patent Roller Skates, improved four-wheelers with good manoeuvrability, roller rinks quickly opened up in Britain and the colonies. Never missing a beat, fancy dress interposed itself into this propellable world with Sunderland skating rink organizing a Masquerade Skating Carnival and Fancy Costume Ball in 1877 where new costumes could be hired from the rink manager.[3] Did the clothes make allowances for ostentatious footwork? There is no reference to what the Sunderland or Bridlington fancy dress looked like but illustrations from other roller carnivals show us that characters were interchangeable with those encountered at balls, and garments were highly embellished with skirt length sometimes taken into consideration (illus. 62). Whatever the costume, there was an expectation that everyone taking to the rink would appear in fancy dress, and notices of such events stressed this aspect as a necessary part of the proceedings. Commercial rinks could accommodate a large number of spectators on a balcony, and being seen in costume was an essential corollary to donning it. Indoor rinks were the ideal venues for winter events based around Christmas and St Valentine's Day themes. Seaside roller-skating fancy-dress jamborees often complemented the main carnival procession. Ice and roller-skating carnivals had a long life, continuing through the twentieth century.

Bicycle carnivals in the 1880s were primarily organized around speed trials and trick cycling, but as enthusiasm for them increased a variety of novelty contests involving fancy dress were added. In 1888, the Portishead Sports, an annual athletics event, closed with an amusing fancy-dress cycle handicap where 'the little manoeuvres of John Chinaman, the timidity of the college pupil, and the corner cutting of the French clown were in contrast with the steady going of the "cycling scout".'[4] By the 1890s, fancy dress and cycling were becoming closely allied, and the queen's jubilee of 1897 quickened the process. In that year, Biggleswade, a market town in eastern England, held two cycle

63 Competitors line up for the decorated bicycle parade in Market Square, Biggleswade, 1897.

events.[5] One was organized by the Biggleswade and District Cycling Club and the other was a civic celebration. The former consisted of several different types of competitive event plus a display by the Paddock Troupe of young lady trick and fancy bicyclists, a professional team of performers.[6] The other occasion included a cycle parade with prizes for the best-decorated machine. These are nowhere described in detail but the start of the parade from Market Square was captured on camera and shows the ingenious ways participants dressed up themselves and their bicycles (illus. 63).

In 1898, the Bicycle Carnival at Bury St Edmunds, another small town in the east of England, tapped into the widespread enthusiasm for cycling, coupled it with the compulsion to dress up and fed the desire to support a local charity, the Suffolk General Hospital. Novelty clothes heightened the diversionary aspect of the bicycling event, putting people in a good frame of mind to give generously to a worthy cause. This was to become standard for all carnivals. At Bury St Edmunds, Miss Hutchins took the lady's prize of a gold brooch dressed as a 'Hop Picker'. She was likely clothed in an Arcadian costume in preference to a real hop picker's workaday garments. Fancy dress frequently depicted the countryside as idyllic and Miss Hutchins probably banished any hint of the squalid living conditions of London's East End poor who annually travelled to labour in the Kent hop fields at harvest time. The gentleman's prize of a silver matchbox was awarded to a Mr Daynes, who rode his bicycle as 'The Whistling Coon'. The song of that name had been recorded a few years earlier by George Washington Johnson (1846–1914), an early African American phonograph star. Mr Daynes's get-up is an unavoidable facet of fancy dress, an example of the casual racism that pervaded Britain. Others in the procession, listed in the newspaper, were straight out of the popular fancy-dress manuals.[7] None of the characters was particularly defined by the bicycle except 'Girton Girl', new to the roster of costumes and one that thematically meshed the outfit with the machine. Both the bicycle and Girton, the pioneering Cambridge women's college, were vectors of female emancipation and we hope that 'Girton Girl' in Bury St Edmunds was seen to be acknowledging the merits of women's education. However, the lady cyclist and woman academic were not frictionless characters at the time and were frequently lampooned and resented. 'Girton Girl' was the sister to Ardern Holt's 'Graduate Girl' and was doubtless dressed in academic robes: a photograph from the Biggleswade fancy-dress cycle parade shows just such an outfit, though the character is not named (illus. 64).

In 1907, prizes were also offered as a lure to participants at the cycling carnival held in Banbury, a small town north of Oxford, and everyone 'had gone to considerable trouble in their endeavour to attract the attention of the judges'.[8] This became the typical wording in many

64 Women in fancy dress with decorated bicycles in Biggleswade, 1897. The character in academic robes and a mortarboard was sometimes called 'Girton Girl' or 'Graduate Girl'. Her bicycle is decked out with musical motifs and a violin.

accounts of carnival. By the time of the Banbury carnival, bicycles were thoroughly integrated with fancy dress, with cyclists using their machines as innovative adjuncts to their costumes. In Banbury, Mr H. Trulocke came dressed as a 'Red Indian', a mainstream character costume but here made distinctive and scooping a prize because he had transformed his bicycle into a canoe and was 'paddling' it along the street. Mrs Green skilfully negotiated the carnival route as a sixpenny bazaar. She wore a colander on her head and both she and a framework fixed over her bicycle were covered with miscellaneous wares from such a shop.[9] Bicycles gave fancy dress an extra dimension, extending the character possibilities (illus. 65). Crêpe paper played a part in cycle decoration as it did in dress. It could be stretched and wound around

65 A prize-winner posing for a studio shot with his bicycle decorated as 'The Cow with the Crumpled Horn', 1910–20.

spokes and handlebars as well as used to cover three-dimensional shapes. The descriptions of the Banbury cyclists and surviving photographs from elsewhere lead us to assume that each get-up was home-made, perhaps a communal effort by family and friends with several try-outs as to the feasibility of peddling around the town on such hazardously bedecked machines (illus. 66). Sunflowers were particular favourites of the bicycle-decorating sorority though there was some disquiet in Chesterfield in 1899 when Miss Norman was awarded first prize as a

66 A sunflower-themed costume and bicycle at Ramsgate Floral Fete, 1907.

'Sunflower' despite the fact that her bicycle was immobile.[10] Bicycles maintained a presence at carnivals, and bicycle-only parades were still popular throughout the 1920s and continued to be so in several centres after the Second World War (illus. 67 and illus. 68).

Alongside bicycle parades, there were miners' galas, regattas, Bonfire Night spectacles, May Days, Charter Days and a wide assortment of other civic and village celebrations. Many of these were transforming themselves into broader carnival attractions even as they retained some

67 'Fag Ends' stands next to a charity collector dressed as a baker, Romford Hospital Carnival, photographed by Henry Robinson, c. 1900.
68 Three prize-winners with Coronation-themed bicycles, Northampton Carnival Parade, 1953.

69 King Neptune in his shell chariot, escorted by helmeted 'Big Heads', Southsea Carnival, 1922.

of their older practices. In 1883, the *Penny Illustrated Paper* asked 'Don't we all long for the fun and frolic of Carnival sometimes? What nation needs a golden thread of gaiety to run through it more than Britain? Why shouldn't our land be made "Merrie England" once again . . .'[11] The *Penny Illustrated* was echoing a general mood: many other newspapers in the 1880s carried reports of town commissioners and parish councils debating proposals for carnivals.

In 1885, responding to this new spirit, Falmouth, a thriving port town on the Cornish coast, witnessed a carnival with floats parading through the streets instead of a waterborne regatta. The majority of these were trade exhibits, although two kinds of non-commercial floats seen at Falmouth would become the mainstay of carnivals elsewhere.

The first was King Neptune and his court. They processed along the Falmouth route in a boat rigged out as a man-of-war. The sea king and his posse would stand their ground at carnivals through the twentieth century (illus. 69). The Neptune *tableau* was a dry-land simulacrum of the Crossing the Line ceremony, the long-standing and still-current initiation rite for sailors on their maiden voyage to the Southern Ocean that is famous for aberrant fancy dress and freakish accessories. Another group at Falmouth was a band of cross-dressed locals calling themselves 'Professional Beauties'.[12] Cross-gender fancy dress would play a pivotal role in British carnivals, with women dressing as men by the early twentieth century.

Two years on from the Falmouth event, Ryde, a seaside holiday destination on the Isle of Wight, celebrated Queen Victoria's Jubilee in 1887 and this was continued the next year as a carnival. The theme was mainly kings and queens of England, although Robin Hood, Red Riding Hood (complete with performing wolf) and a group of ghosts also made an appearance.[13] They were dressed head-to-toe in white with conical caps covering their faces and had something of the grotesque about them. These figures reappeared at the 1889 Ryde carnival when the introduction of limelight, along with 3,500 lanterns and coloured fires, must have thrown the costumes into phantasmagoric shadow.[14] They can perhaps be regarded as an early prototype of carnival 'Big Heads'. These outsize sculptural figures with human merrymakers hidden inside are of various types and were designed to completely conceal the wearer, preserving some of the old notion of disguise. Their odd proportions and leering faces gave them a frightening as well as a comic aspect. These Brobdingnagian figures were moulded to represent fantasy creatures and, increasingly during the twentieth century, real people in caricature (illus. 70). They perhaps have an age-old lineage harking back to folk and fairground traditions and they would have been familiar from guy effigies. Similar structures were a feature of

70 Tennis-playing 'Big Heads' impersonate the five-time winner of Wimbledon, Suzanne Lenglen, Blackpool Carnival, 1923.

European carnivals, and the renowned parade in Nice in the south of France was much reported in the British illustrated press from the turn of the nineteenth century. Clarkson, Barnum's Carnival Novelties and Becks British Carnival Novelties, all in London, together with Metro of Hull certainly stocked these heads though many were home-made from papier mâché set over a framework and painted with gloss.

It is significant that one of the prime movers behind the Ryde carnival was Gustav Mullins (1854–1921), an island-based photographer with a Royal Warrant, who clearly understood the visual appeal of such events in coastal towns. Seaside carnivals became the bellwether of the genre and this locale is significant. The holiday atmosphere fostered a hedonism that rhymed with carnival's vital spark. Occupying the liminal space between land and sea, such resorts were ideal for carnivals.

In the 1920s and '30s, when carnival was in full swing, the transgressive environment of the seaside with its pier and fairground amusements prompted a lowering of constraints. People were emboldened to dress outrageously once they had experienced the hall of mirrors or put their head through a comic cut-out figure board. Ugliness was redefined and allowable.

A coastal venue was not, of course, essential for carnival. The annual Guy Fawkes celebration in Chard in the county of Somerset burned the arch-conspirator on a bonfire but otherwise came to reflect other carnivals that were not centred around this particular November commemoration. In 1891, thousands reportedly thronged the streets and groups of pretend sheriffs and faux policemen headed the procession along with real civic dignitaries. An assortment of entrants, both mounted and walking, followed on behind, including 'Chard Dairy Competition' (in fact, a spoof with men dressed as dairymaids churning butter), 'King of Clowns', 'Dancing Bear' (with very realistic beast), 'Lord Nelson' and 'Far-Famed Midgets' presenting 'the smallest people in the world', made no more palatable by using children dressed as Commodore Nutt, General Tom Thumb and Minnie Warren, all acclaimed small-stature entertainers.[15] This jumble of *tableaux* on several different types of carts and trolleys, as well as pedestrian masqueraders, would characterize carnival Britain, and many of the same sentiments, if not the precise themes, would feature elsewhere.

In 1900, in tune with contemporary military and imperial attitudes that were always present at carnivals, a Boer War phenomenon swept London's suburbs and towns in the south of England. In Ryde, the heart of the carnival was the evening parade, where national pride was on display, reinforcing values rather than upending them. Bands in uniforms, which we might call quasi-fancy dress, supplied martial music. The floats included a war *tableau* representing a *kopje* (the name for a small hill in South Africa) held by khaki-clad warriors surmounted by a Union Jack, 'Reminiscence of Ladysmith' and 'Sons of Empire'. Ryde was at the southernmost tip of these Boer War spectacles, which all featured model warships, guns and khaki. Fancy dress, as we mostly understand it, was rather muted. Civilians utilized khaki to rig themselves out as soldiers, and the soldier impersonator became a sort of everyman while other carnival participants mimicked the leading military figures of the day.[16] The belligerent imagery of these particular carnivals was solidly male but women were accommodated alongside them in Ryde on floats understood as 'feminine': 'Harvest', 'The Geisha', 'Lady Card Players'.[17]

By the time of the Boer War parades, street carnivals were getting into their stride in other towns in Britain. Across the north of the country the strong tradition of silver band competitions, flower shows and sports displays were being organized during the summer months so as to include outdoor carnivals. Good weather favoured the 1908 carnival in Breightmet, Greater Manchester, where there were both mounted and walking characters. Newspaper reports do not always make a clear distinction between the two. The juxtaposition of the different vehicles and pedestrians was, in any case, part of carnival's ethos. At Breightmet, characters, whether on vehicles or walking, represented the British empire, the king and queen, Joan of Arc, Prince Charles, the gipsy queen and gipsies, the Duchess of Devonshire, Bo-Peep, Red Riding Hood, Boy Blue, the nations of America, Russia and Italy, Faith, Hope and Charity, Robin Hood and his Foresters, the Queen of Hearts, the Fairy Queen and Fairies, Sleeping Beauty and Cinderella along with their princes, the Belle of New York, Snow White and the Maid of Athens. Two *tableaux* at Breightmet illustrate how fancy dress spanned national as well as neighbourhood concerns: 'Sufferers-yet' (Suffragettes) and 'Darcy Lever Bus' (Darcy Lever being a Manchester locale presumably notorious for its poor bus service).[18]

71 Several revellers dressed as Ally Sloper at Atherston Carnival, Warwickshire, 1905.

Floats were a relaxation of the static *tableaux vivants*. As a result, the informal atmosphere of carnival empowered at least some of the participants to play to the crowd lining the streets. This encouraged comic turns like 'Sufferers-yet' and 'Darcy Lever Bus', both of which were signed up to the 'humorous' category of entrants. Comedy turn-outs were an enduring facet of street carnivals. At Ryde in 1906, Mr Downer appeared as 'Ally Sloper' and Mr Wetherick as 'Farmer Giles', both at the time figures of fun in the popular canon. By 1906, 'Farmer Giles', dressed in a smock and sucking on a stalk of straw, would have been perceived by the Ryde carnival crowd as sartorially and socially out of date. Set against this country bumpkin, Ally Sloper, the eponymous central character of the weekly comic paper *Ally Sloper's Half-Holiday*, was the converse of the rural ignoramus and an ideal subject for fancy dress because of his distinctive nose, shabby tailcoat, battered top hat, umbrella and bottle of drink in a back pocket. He was recognized as a representative of metropolitan working-class conservatism. Although he was a scheming conniver and ridiculed foreigners, he was loyal to

72 A woman dressed as 'Paris' and a smiling girl with a flower-decorated pram, 1923. 'Sunshine and Roses' won second prize in her class.

the monarch and to the empire. His presence was not confined to the comic strip, however. He endorsed specific brands, and was the subject of music-hall sketches. He was even an outsize carnival effigy.[19] For most of the twentieth century, multiple Ally Slopers appeared at carnivals throughout the land, attesting to the character's wholehearted adoption by revellers (illus. 71). His appearance in Ryde, juxtaposed with that of 'Farmer Giles', is a telling visual comment by means of dress on the changing social landscape of the British Isles. Carnival fancy dressers tapped into popular feeling even as they looked back with some nostalgia to a more rural and hierarchical society.

Though a vehicle was not necessary, bicycles, wheelbarrows, horse carts, prams, lorries and cars were pressed into service over the years and opened up the possibilities of ingenious decoration (illus. 72). They accentuated carnival's peripatetic quality. When the full potential of large vehicles as stage sets was realized, fancy dress was on very public show as never before. Ornamental or theatricalized backdrops elevated the participants above the bystanders. Friends and relatives were recognized, cheered and applauded. Patriotic themes persisted. Topical subjects made an appearance, many based on music-hall turns. For example, 'I Wouldn't Leave My Little Wooden Hut for You', a float in the Ryde carnival of 1906, was a visual rendering of a music-hall song popularized by Daisy Dormer (1883–1947) but, as at Breightmet,

73 'Little Red Riding Hood', a children's float at Wilmslow Carnival, Cheshire, 1910. Grandma sits in the centre, flanked by Red Riding Hood, a wolf in a frilly nightcap and several fairies.

more traditional subjects were also represented. Fairy stories, nursery rhymes and folkloric themes surfaced regularly right through our period (illus. 73).

Decorated tradesmen's lorries and narrative floats vied with entries representing branded commodities. These began to appear regularly at carnivals and, as early as the 1906 Ryde parade, the 'Bovril ox' pedalled a bicycle rigged out with the distinctive swollen jars of the famous meat extract. This was free publicity from an amateur but 'The Home of the Jamaican Banana' was entered by the famous fruit shippers Elders & Fyffes, who had extended their operations to the Caribbean island at the end of the nineteenth century. We do not know how this sometimes risibly portrayed yellow fruit was presented in Ryde or whether anyone actually dressed up as a banana, though we know it became a favourite costume in the years to come.[20]

In 1906, the Ryde carnival razzmatazz on the Isle of Wight was attractive enough to tempt sightseers from across the water. Special ferries and tickets were advertised, for example, in the *Portsmouth Evening News*, a mainland paper, on 11 September 1906, and this became the norm, with local town parades drawing in visitors from outside the district. Southend-on-Sea, an Essex resort town within easy reach of the East End of London and, like Ryde, an attractive destination for holidaymakers and day trippers alike, began staging carnivals from 1906. They grew in popularity and stature over the years with floats becoming the cornerstone of the festivities. At the 1911 Southend carnival, bedecked vehicles, not necessarily with passengers, were entered into eleven different classes and judged purely on aesthetic grounds.[21] Firms and stores, sports and social clubs took up the challenge of disguising or prettifying workaday vehicles as once they had tricked out horses at ploughing matches. As elsewhere, the opportunity to populate a vehicle with characters in relevant costume eventually proved irresistible. In the first half of the 1920s, the Southend brewery Lukers, for example, entered their motorized lorry annually in competition. The meticulously executed decorations, picking out the name of the firm and covering the cab and wheels in individual paper flowers, made a striking rostrum for costumed participants. One year, the men dressed as pink-coated, horn-blowing huntsmen and posed against a pub sign with a jovial landlord in attendance. Another year, they dressed as pirates and as actual bottles of beer with their arms pushed idiotically out at the side. These 'beer bottles' walked beside the float to collect money from the crowd.[22]

Vehicles were certainly a blessing to others wearing clumsy suits and may even have encouraged new characters that might otherwise have been unmanageable. Despite their slinky allure, mermaids had not been very regular fancy-dress recruits. Perhaps they had something of the disagreeable fairground freak show about them. It could be something more practical: the scaly ladies' near immobility made the outfit very unsuitable for dancing, but carnival floats provided a much easier way of coping with the costume. In 1930, the oceanic Neptune *tableau* at Southend featured a female posse of watery creatures resting their tails on the lorry cab.[23]

Another example of an unmanoeuvrable costume is provided by a surprising 1931 float (illus. 74). A group of young women in unwieldy garb were required only to stand, smile and wave as they were drawn along the parade route on a horse-drawn wagon. Each was dressed as the Portland Vase, an unexpected infiltrator into popular culture.[24] The vase, a precious Roman glass amphora, was famously copied by Josiah Wedgwood in the eighteenth century and both the original and the pottery copy had an eventful history before and after that time. Given its classical pedigree, the vase does not seem an obvious theme for carnival fancy dress but the vessel was rarely out of the news. In 1929, this unique treasure was withdrawn from the British Museum and put up for auction by its owners, the aristocratic Portland family. Its

74 'The Portland Vase' interpreted by young women in fancy dress at Norwich Carnival, 1931.

spectacular failure to make the reserve in the grim economic climate of the times made the headlines and rekindled the object's notoriety. The firm of Wedgwood did not hesitate to take advantage of the high-profile publicity, arranging a morale-boosting bicentenary pageant for pottery staff in Stoke-on-Trent and dressing a phalanx of employees' daughters as the Portland Vase. In subsequent years, it was these vase costumes that went the rounds of several carnivals, Southend and Norwich among them. The costumes were most original, with high hats for the neck of the vase and wired skirts for its swelling base. The mythical figures realized in white cameo on the original vase are beautifully interpreted in fancy dress. It is a clever rendering. Among the 'vases' is an eighteenth-century costumed flunky, referencing the Wedgwood version rather than the Roman vase, and the placard confirms this.

75 A Dutch theme at Chipping Norton Carnival, Oxfordshire, 1931.

Multifarious *tableaux* appeared at carnivals up and down the country. Some were painstakingly elaborate, some more modest (illus. 75). Many were instantly recognizable at the time and still are so today: the Loch Ness Monster, ever a favourite, was supposedly sighted and photographed in 1934 and appeared as a float at Hebden Bridge Carnival that year. Other floats at the same carnival – 'Wheezy Anna' and 'Another Trunk Mystery' – are still to be unravelled. We know nothing about their costuming. Fancy dress on a float at Williton in Somerset seems to have been secondary to the set, as was often the case. 'Old-Age Pensions – Before and After' featured shivering old-timers in a workhouse yard juxtaposed with an elderly couple inside their comfortable cottage: the modern state pension had just been introduced in 1908, the year of the carnival. Williton, like Breightmet and others, also tackled issues nearer to home with 'The Watchet Hatepayers Association'. Here, true to its Guy Fawkes roots, eight carnival participants dressed up as recognizable parochial leaders engaged in a ratepayers' debate. The carnival 'actors' must have scrutinized their subjects closely for distinctive facial features and modes of dress. Other carnivals celebrated the special attributes of their locality, with Wells in Somerset presenting a float in 1933 that depicted this cathedral town's famous bell-ringing swans being fed by young women in crinolines.[25]

Many of the costumes in smaller carnivals were makeshift, utilizing contemporary everyday clothing. Hatherleigh, the smallest town in Devon, where we have seen Mr Moxon as a regular parader, was typical. In 1922, 'Nurse Cavell's Last Hours', depicting the selfless heroine's execution by German firing squad in 1915, seems grim for a carnival but fairly easy to put together in terms of dress, and 'Triplets This Time' would not have needed anything much out of the ordinary.[26] While many towns held processional carnivals, smaller villages unable to mount floats were, nonetheless, steadfast in their allegiance to fancy-dress competitions at village fêtes and shows.

Individual competitors, who were the essential components of small-scale parish events, still had a part to play in larger carnivals. In truth, in the early days of carnival, single participants were more focused on fancy dress than the vehicle entries. In Southend in 1911, a clear distinction was made between 'walking' competitors and the rest, and the list of 'walking' prize-winners was a typical miscellany of figures for a carnival in the teens of the twentieth century. It included 'Gainsborough costume', 'John Bull in naval uniform', 'cigarettes', 'Bubbles', 'Caught bathing at Thorpe Bay', 'Eton Boy' (comic ladies category) and 'Harem Skirt' (comic men category). Nearly two decades later, in 1930, the listed 'walking' prize-winners at Southend included some newer characters: 'Jazz Time', 'Ukulele Twins' and 'Rio Rita' (a spectacular 1929 Hollywood film featuring a song of the same title).

Dedicated children's parades became a well-established facet of the carnival experience by the end of the 1920s and can be viewed as a more democratized substitute for earlier juvenile costume balls. Children did not always walk the main route if there were large vehicles in the parade but carnival very much embraced them, laying on attractions that both they, their parents and grandparents could enjoy together. Young competitors promenaded in front of judges in a nearby park and their glad rags and improbable vehicular concoctions were just as amazing as their adult counterparts. Despite the awkwardness, inanimate objects were popular with children or, at least, their parents. In 1929, the Southend Tiny Tots parade featured Douglas Reed's toy car decorated as the prototype airship R101, a Panglossian venture by Britain to traverse the long-distance routes of the British empire. The airship crashed on its maiden voyage the following year and understandably was not seen on the fancy-dress circuit again. Along with Douglas's airship, in Southend in 1929, prizes went to competitors dressed as a dustbin and a bandstand respectively.[27] In 1930, among the children's prize-winners were Bruce and John Lupton for 'Capital and Labour', a 'concept' costume that was corporealized by the two boys, one in a top hat, the other in a flat cap. Was this their parents' choice or had their sons picked it out from a fancy-dress pattern book? These serious adult concerns crossed generations time and again. Children giving them physical form perhaps offered an effective way to mock the establishment. Everyone surely loved young Joyce Morris imitating the aviatrix Amy Johnson (1903–1941).[28] Only a few months before the 1930 Southend carnival, Johnson had made her solo record-breaking flight to Australia. The rapidity with which the famous flyer's identity was seized upon for fancy dress is understandable. Miss Johnson's sartorial sense was distinctive but effortless to copy, and her heroic role-model status made others keen to impersonate her. Aviation, a magical metaphor for modernity, was a recurring theme for fancy dress throughout the twentieth century.

In the early days of street carnival, fancy dressers still patronized professional photography studios, as happened at the Tottenham

76 Mrs Bowell dressed as a masked highwaywoman, posing for a studio photograph by William Atkinson Jr. The costume won prizes in three different competitions at Tottenham Prince of Wales Hospital Carnival, London, 1909.

77 A typical line-up of prize-winners at Southam Workers' Union Fete, Warwickshire, 1924. The characters include Pierrot, Little Bo Peep, a bear, a baker, a gypsy and Little Boy Blue with his horn.

carnival in aid of the local hospital in 1909 (illus. 76). During the decades of carnival's popularity, single studio shots gave way to less formal line-ups out in the open and these have a different kind of appeal (illus. 77). Whether inside or out, the camera was always attentive to the various carnival activities and, certainly from the 1930s, newspapers sent a photographer along to record the festivities. Newsprint images are often indistinct but people enjoyed spotting themselves, their family and friends. Although the camera does not pick out the minutiae of the costumes, many outfits appear to have been contrived without a pattern. Carnival costumes were not necessarily perfectly finished models of dressmaking. Rather, existing clothes were altered and embellished with cut-outs. British street carnival always preserved a touch of the homespun and there is a sense that the *idea* behind a costume or theme sometimes ran ahead of the mechanics of actually making it: written signboards became an integral part of many ensembles as a way of elucidating them.

Parades and competitions were not the only chances to wear fancy dress during carnival. Right from its early days, designated charity collectors wore matching, specially made costumes (illus. 78). In 1930, the *Daily Herald* reported that dozens of Southend women acted as hospital fund collectors along the route. Their 'Victorian' outfits, made for the occasion by dressmakers across the town, were jettisoned at the last minute in favour of cooler, hastily made bright-coloured beach pyjamas and light frocks, such was the skill of the town's sewing circles.[29] Three carnival balls, advertising themselves as fancy-dress dances in the 1930 Carnival Programme, rounded off the Southend festivities, and smaller towns also organized end-of-carnival costume parties.[30] Even bystanders in the crowd, frequently rattling what the novelty trade termed 'noise articles', festooned themselves in party hats and stuck on false noses. The carnival queen, too, was a conspicuous presence, though the role of temporary monarch was not an outlet for creative dressing. As she was in a line of descent from the May Queen of folklore, she was usually dressed in white. Historicism was never far away and many images of successive carnival queens show quasi-medieval laced bodices, crinolines of uncertain period or stiff Tudorbethan collars. Increasingly, the queen became a living advertisement for dresses and hair-dos supplied by local firms and this sponsorship of queenly clothing reflects the broader commercialization of carnivals after the Second World War.

Across Britain, the carnival phenomenon was slowed, though not permanently ousted, by the Second World War. In 1939, at the last Southend carnival before war was declared, 'National Service' was one of the themes and a new topical costume appeared: young Peter Heal was photographed leaping into the air disguised as Chamberlain's umbrella.[31] This quotidian object took on a symbolic life of its own after Neville Chamberlain, the British Prime Minister from 1937 to 1940,

78 A young fundraiser dressed as an elf, Ilford Hospital Carnival, Essex, *c.* 1906. The same costumes were reused and resized at subsequent Ilford carnivals.

returned from Munich holding his umbrella in one hand and carrying Hitler's signed and, as it proved to be, worthless piece of paper in the other.[32] In the early 1940s, many men and women found themselves in uniform, forsaking everyday dress and fancy dress as well.

At the end of the war, victory celebrations, discussed in Chapter Five, helped to revitalize fancy dress and this in turn fostered the idea of reinstating carnivals, often smaller in scale than previously. Fancy dress remained a constant with Randalstown in Northern Ireland not alone in entirely relinquishing decorated floats owing to petrol rationing. At their Fancy Dress Parade, following the pattern set by pre-war carnivals, topical and local-interest characters rubbed shoulders with the clichéd but dependable: 'Gipsies' alongside 'Colorado Beetle Exterminator', the beetle in question being a pest of potato crops that spread alarmingly during the Second World War.[33]

At this period, there was also a significant number of carnival cancellations and a lack of entries for competitions, but the carnival at Southend, along with other seaside towns, returned to full vigour in 1947. Rollicking impersonations were provided by 'King Cole' and the 'Carnival Queen of 1847' dressed in black robes. They shared their old-fashioned chariot with a group of young women whose blackened faces and miners' caps marked them out as coal labourers. Their placard read 'Why not Bevin girls?' referring, perhaps provocatively, to the all-male Bevin Boys who kept the mines operating during the war.[34] Distinctions between male and female had not melted away in the war years despite a loosening of attitudes towards women in the workforce. Were these pretend miners making a plea for a reconfiguration of gender roles? From this distance in time we cannot know. What we can know, however, is the extent to which war impacted, and continued to impact, on ordinary people's lives. Years after the end of hostilities, war-related fancy dress was common throughout the British Isles.

Student rags provide another instance of outdoor fancy dress. Rags have an affinity with carnival in that they became part of the British cultural landscape around the first years of the twentieth century and, like carnival, their arena of activity was a public space, catching the attention of people in the street. Also, money was solicited by costumed collectors who played up to the crowd as they mingled with it. Though there is usually a processional aspect to rags, there are also more sporadic outbreaks of activity and various comings-and-goings of a performative kind. In consequence, bystanders might be taken unawares by the fancy-dress uproar. Rags, like Guy Fawkes celebrations, had their roots in disorderly student behaviour, sometimes of a truly cruel nature. This ragging, as it is called, did not disappear when the more well-intentioned student rags, later sometimes glossed as 'Raise and Give', took to the streets, and although weird clothing was a notable feature of both types of event, the coercive dressing up involved in ignominious ragging is not fancy dress. There was plenty of rowdy conduct, however, even where decking out was voluntary, with medical students particularly quick to put on ludicrous duds. In 1912, the annual cup-tie football match between two London hospitals was an unsightly affair with some students wearing black face paint and others dressed as mock policemen and costermongers all crowding the railway platforms on the way to the match. Under cover of fancy dress these students were publicly vilifying people they despised. Significantly, the Chelsea Arts Club Ball had taken place the evening before this match and the difficulty of telling the two groups apart was noted in the newspaper.[35]

Good humour prevailed and philanthropy was to the fore at many carnivalesque student rags, however. Their costumes might be slapdash and rudimentary but were vital to the students' distinctness as charity collectors. In Durham, the rag was often themed around the idea of 'Invasion' and in 1914, it took the form of a welcome to 'Imperator Caesar' as he landed on the British coast.[36] In 1922, the students seem to be dressed as Anglo-Saxons, though it is hard to tell. This imprecision was typical of rags. Newsreel footage shows how the Durham students had corralled together miscellaneous items to serve as vestigial costumes.[37]

Along with animal suits, which figured prominently in rags, another trend that remained a particular fixture of many student jamborees was the appropriation of handcarts, wheelbarrows and especially prams piled high with a hotchpotch of stuff. These conveyances often transported daftly dressed students, attracting attention as much by their precarious locomotion as by the bizarre fancy dress of both driver and passenger. The omnipresent baby in a pram may have had its origins at rags raising money specifically for children's charities but, whatever its beginnings, the pantomime duo of badly dressed mother and Herculean baby in a bonnet invariably took to the streets in student processions. Men frequently dressed as women, not just babies and little girls, and the unequal ratio of men to women in higher education meant that the student rag remained predominantly a male affair until after the Second World War. Men were allowed, even expected, to behave mawkishly and dress foolishly and a male carnival queen was not unusual. In 1927, the Bradford Technical College 'queen' wore lace curtaining and carried a bouquet of radishes. Fairies were the nonpareil of cross-dressing at rags with a Mr Davies, a medical student, setting the record by appearing in a ballet dress for six years running. His tall figure and bony anatomy made a mockery of the tutu fairy outfit and this out-of-kilter juxtaposition of body and frock made a first-rate fancy dress. The body shape worked against the costume in other instances of cross-dressing. Men were quick to pick up on this idea and exaggerated the possibilities. In 1948, a Mae West imitator in Bristol, defined by a crown of pretend blonde hair and very long eyelashes, immoderately padded out his chest and bottom, overemphasizing both, and making a caricature of the silky film star. The ensemble itself was only half-realized because it was worn with thick socks and masculine lace-up shoes, a recurrent detail seen in much male-to-female fancy dress, increasing the comic effect but also presenting women in a derogatory light.[38]

Many press accounts of rags simply described the togs as fantastic, quaint, singular, awful, weird, wonderful or comic without further details. Specific characters were either unrecognizable or not even attempted. Students threw together ensembles from mismatched oddments, teaming them with a *mésalliance* of accessories. Hats were knocked into strange shapes and scarves knotted in peculiar ways. The humble umbrella was frequently co-opted. Sometimes shredded, sometimes festooned with streamers, it was brandished and twirled around, adding to the perpetual motion characteristic of these happenings. In whatever way rag duds were assembled, the resulting attire was doubtless more astonishing than the grainy black-and-white newspaper images allow. Where specific characters are mentioned, through the decades of the twentieth century, 'King Neptune', 'pirates', 'crusaders', 'skeletons', 'cowboys', 'Indians' and 'cavemen' turn up in most years (illus. 79). Members of the Ku Klux Klan were extensively impersonated as well. It is hard to believe that this unacceptable organization should feature, not only in student rags, but in the pattern books put out by Weldons in the 1920s where the conical hat and enveloping robes are put forward as a fancy-dress suggestion for eight- to sixteen-year-old boys. Commonly held values of the day are revealed by fancy dress and we should remember that students as a body could often be conservative, racist and anti-union. Their fancy-dress choices sometimes reflected these concerns.

Most rag outfits were acquired haphazardly, though one exception was newsworthy. Jim Oxley was an especially fortunate student because he was lent the futuristic suit worn by the actor Raymond Massey in *Things to Come*, the Wellsian science-fiction film that had just been released at the time of the rag.[39] Art students could be creative with

79 Mac Beardell, Doug Frazer and Dennis Wright, students at Westminster College, dressed in animal skins for a London rag carnival, from *The Sketch*, Wednesday, 29 March 1950. While 'caveman' was a stock character for rag day stunts, this float represented the aftermath of H-bomb warfare.

little monetary outlay. The medieval theme, complete with ornately caparisoned 'horses', staged by London's Goldsmiths' College in 1949 was a marvel of clever construction. In 1950, bulls, matador masks and hats crafted by the same college were masterworks of cut and curled paper. Film footage reveals the expert handiwork involved.[40]

A more likely channel for student fancy dress was the novelty shop. These businesses had sprung up or expanded in response to the public's preoccupation with carnival and rag between the wars and some, like Metro in Hull, carried on trading beyond the Second World War. With a large showroom in Manor Street, Metro took out advertisement space in the Hull newspaper just prior to the university rag week there in 1950:

> Our serious students will mask their mugs, hoist hysterical hats, fix false noses, and shake rattles till the welkin rings . . . Giant paper mache [*sic*] heads will bob on youthful shoulders. Rattlers, squeakers, ticklers, trumpets will ensure the carnival atmosphere. We take our modest share in this addition to the gaiety of nations . . . These aids to fun have been supplied by us including novelties never seen before in Hull.[41]

Metro tapped into the need for something new and jokey each year. The emphasis in their advertisement is on accoutrements and accessories, with counterfeit body parts and crackpot millinery having the capacity to alter a person's looks considerably. Costumes, in the strict sense of garments, were not always needed and Metro was not a costumier as such. Along with other types of suppliers and makers, however, it was in the business of transformation.

Five

CORONATIONS AND CELEBRATIONS

National celebrations presented further golden opportunities for dressing up. Coronations, jubilees and royal weddings provided a break from routine, while peace parties and victory parades were a heartfelt manifestation of relief at the cessation of war. All these events induced an outpouring of patriotism. Appropriate festive clothing contributed to the celebratory atmosphere. The galas organized for Queen Victoria's crowning in 1838 do not appear to have included much fancy dress: military and trade uniforms, masonic and civic robes along with ecclesiastical vestments were the sort of attire seen on the streets, with costume confined to coronation balls. At the very beginning of Victoria's reign, fancy dress had not yet fanned out into the widespread craze it would become, and the effect of the queen's own championing of dressing up had still to be felt. The popular success of the 1838 coronation events, however, encouraged national and civic leaders to institute celebratory holidays for similar occasions and, by the time of Victoria's two jubilees in 1887 and 1897, patriotic fancy dress was evidently being espoused by some (illus. 80). At this stage, the most elaborate decorations were reserved for buildings and vehicles rather than people. Here is how Bishop's Waltham, a small town in Hampshire, celebrated the Queen's Golden Jubilee in 1887:

80 Emmeline Bayer dressed as 'Union Jack' for the Children's Fancy Dress Ball, Adelaide, photographed by the firm of Wivell, 1887.

> The town was literally bedecked from end to end. The railway engine, which conveys visitors from the main line to the town, was embowered with evergreens . . . The railway premises were adorned with considerable care, and the platform transformed into a mass of greenery, and made quite garden-like in appearance. The old Palace ruins bore loyal sentiments, and the town itself never presented a gayer, livelier, and prettier appearance. In the High-street bunting reached from side to side the whole length of the thoroughfare. Many of the houses were completely hidden from view by a covering of branches of trees, shrubs, and flowers. Flags were utilised everywhere, and there were many instances of well -executed devices, mottoes, sentiments, and loyal expressions, showing a general desire on the part of the population to honour the festival, and a commendable rivalry in the production of the gayest and most suitable display . . . In the evening there were some very fair illuminations, gas-jet devices, transparencies, Japanese and Chinese lanterns, variegated oil lamps, and other means being adopted to ensure a brilliant scene.[1]

Shortly afterwards, at the turn of the twentieth century, fancy dress came to play an increasingly important part in these illuminated empire-wide jubilations. By the time of Edward VII's coronation in 1902, the fad for dressing up had gained considerable momentum by way of street carnivals. Ordinary people's experience of costume balls was still limited and anxieties about the correct etiquette lingered, as related in the *Dundee Courier* concerning the 1902 coronation programme of events at Cupar:

> The day's festivities will be terminated by a grand ball . . . Fancy dress is optional. This is somewhat of a novelty in

> Cupar and district, and we believe there is some little misapprehension as to what is exactly to take place on that festive occasion. The Convener of the Town Council Committee authorises us to state that no invitations have been or will be issued. The function is entirely a public one, and any members of the public will be entitled to go to the ball on purchasing a ticket, the cost being *7s 6d* for gentlemen and *2s* for ladies. With regard to the question of fancy dress, the committee desire that the ball should be in keeping with the fetes of the day, and should not proceed on the ordinary orthodox lines of a full dress dance. The function is really a continuation of the carnival of the day, and accordingly the committee desire as many as possible to appear in fancy dress . . . A considerable number of those who are taking an interest in the function will appear in fancy dress.[2]

The advice to view the Cupar ball as an extension of carnival would ring true for many townsfolk who consequently would have understood the costume implications. A fancy-dress outfit might be within their financial reach whereas full formal evening dress might not. National holidays were to be inclusive, fostering loyalty and a sense of belonging, and, while coronation balls and parties continued for both adults and children, fancy-dress cycle parades and comedy cricket and football matches were widely reported as part of larger community celebrations. Fraserburgh was typical in announcing 'A Fancy Dress Football Match (Dan Leno style) between Fraserburgh Cricket Club and Fraserburgh Cycle Club to be played on the Links on the Coronation Day'.[3] Melbourn in Cambridgeshire was not alone in laying on a comedy match between 'ladies' and gentlemen with the dresses of the 'lady' cricketers showing a variety of taste.[4]

While men dressed up as women in coronation holiday mood across Britain, the ruling class sparkled for the king across the empire, nowhere more so than in India. The State Ball held in Delhi, as part of the imperious Durbar, could well have been mistaken for a fancy-dress extravaganza, such was its sartorial overkill. In fact, the real fancy dress happened in another Indian city, Calcutta (today's Kolkata), where the arrangements for Establishment balls were upheld, and guests were asked to wear the clothes of a hundred years before: Viceroy Curzon (1859–1925) assumed the persona of one of his predecessors, Lord Wellesley, thus cementing the line of succession, and his wife, Mary Curzon (1870–1906), wore a dress that incorporated Benares embroidery, a not unusual appropriation for British upper-class women.[5]

There was dazzling pageantry too for the next coronation, that of George V in 1911. The Royal Botanic Gardens staged a Coronation Costume Ball on a majestic scale where the privileged guests were all required to be in fancy dress. Every one of the Dominions and every phase of Britain's national history was supposedly to be represented.[6] Britain's colonies were also on display in quite a different fancy-dress context but one nonetheless connected to the 1911 coronation. Vote-seeking participants in the Women's Coronation Procession dressed up to draw attention to their urgent demand for suffrage within the coronation year. Aware that costume was a potent and direct way of getting their message across, they portrayed famous women from history and were led by that striving and suffering heroine, the peasant girl turned military leader Joan of Arc. They viewed their London parade as a demonstration of loyalty to the king, with one magnificent float bearing personifications of the countries of the empire.[7]

Activist dressing-up aside, the exclusive nature of several coronation events in 1911 came in for some criticism, and in Evesham in Worcestershire dissatisfaction with a fancy-dress ball paid for out of public funds resulted in a disquieting fracas, with a jeering crowd

81 Children's Coronation Fancy Dress Ball, Port Sunlight, Merseyside, 1902. Lord Nelson is on the left and other characters represented are King Charles II, 'Ping Pong Up-to-Date', 'Starlight Soap', Kate Greenaway, and a diminutive King Edward VII with the figure of 'Peace' in the group picture.

greeting alarmed costumed guests.[8] More inclusive that year were the variety of entertainments offered at the Edinburgh Marine Park and Zoological Gardens billed as 'A Wonderland of Pleasure Palaces by the Sea'. Tickets to the Coronation Fancy Dress Ball there were cheap, and masks and hats were on sale on the night.[9] Port Sunlight, the model village built and nurtured by William Hesketh Lever (1851–1925) and his brother James to house the workers of their soap-manufacturing business, witnessed three coronation balls for children, one in 1902 and two in 1911 (illus. 81). Called 'Calico Balls' because of the stipulation that guests were to wear garments fashioned from inexpensive material, they were to be affordable for the families involved, 'the child of the most humble parent in the village standing an equal chance with the children of more highly remunerated officials'.[10] At the 1902 Port Sunlight party, one child impersonated the industrialist and banker John Pierpont Morgan (1837–1913), an unusual encroacher into the domain of fancy dress, but Britannia and John Bull, a well-established incarnation of England with his Union Jack waistcoat and shallow-crowned hat, were present in some numbers.

Even at annual carnivals not associated with national celebrations, Britannia, stamped on British coins, was rarely absent (illus. 82).

82 *England's Pride and Glory*, a float at Dolton Carnival, Devon, 1913.

Poseidon's trident and the Union Jack shield were Victorian additions to the helmeted lady's livery, ensuring she never went unrecognized. She was, in fact, so well liked that it was possible to rent the outfit and be photographed wearing it at The Fancy Dress Studio in London (illus. 83). This company, which kept a stock of other popular character costumes, had branches in Oxford Street and Tottenham Court Road and offered six free postcards of the resulting image.[11] While Britannia appeared at many different fancy-dress celebrations, one float that was

83 A young woman dressed as Britannia, The Fancy Dress Studio, 37 Oxford Street, London, 1900–1920.

84 A floral coronation coach for King George v, Collingham, Yorkshire, 1911.

specific to coronations and became a favourite from 1911 was a mock coronation coach with royal passengers. Some were very good facsimiles of the real thing.[12] Elsewhere the carriage was more of a fantasy (illus. 84).

The necessarily ritualized nature of the Westminster Abbey crowning ceremony itself, elements of which do have continuity with the rituals of remote history, are interestingly paralleled by the invented traditions of popular coronation festivities, which show a remarkable similarity across all four celebrations in 1902, 1911, 1937 and 1953. Certainly from 1911, fancy dress was an unshakeable presence alongside church services, bell-ringing, patriotic addresses, the National Anthem, tree-planting, mug and medal distribution, communal teas and bonfires. The union flag and the colours red, white and blue, always in evidence at coronations, were also worked into other annual carnivals and festivals, both as embellishments for vehicles and buildings, and as fancy dress.

Empire Day was one such celebration that adopted the tri-coloured theme. The timings of coronations were not predictable, but Empire Day, established gradually at the beginning of the twentieth century and celebrated annually, can arguably be seen as rectifying the infrequency of nationwide festivals of patriotism. Children wore ribbons, waved flags and sometimes dressed in costume to remind them of the parts of the globe that were pink. In 1927, at one Chelsea school – Empire Day was essentially an educational tool – the imperial sentiment could not be plainer. A Pathé newsreel shows children in different national costumes taking their turn to shake hands with a pint-sized John Bull, impressively kitted out.[13] In the same decade – the 1920s – infants from Studley Council School in Warwickshire dressed up for Empire Day and the majority of boys wore service uniforms (illus. 85). Despite its politicization and a growing resistance to its increasingly militaristic

85 Studley Council School infants in costume for Empire Day, Warwickshire, 1920s. Most of the boys are in service uniforms.

turn, several childhood reminiscences and biographies relate people's enjoyment of the day's vibrant symbolism.[14]

Some of the emblematic devices that marked these royal and patriotic ceremonials also appeared in times of war and at its ending. Fancy dress, while muted, did not cease as a practice during the First World War and was co-opted into fund-raising efforts.[15] The uncharacteristically long title of *Weldon's 350 Ideas for Fancy Dresses for Ladies, Children and Men: Practical Designs for Red Cross Entertainments, Private Theatricals, Garden Fêtes, Tableaux, School Plays, Pageants, Bicycle Gymnkhanas, Minuets, Historical Plays, Shakespearean Characters, Great Britain and Her Allies* of 1917 attests to fancy dress's continued, if differently inflected, presence during the war, and in that year the council school in Feltham, a West London suburb, was the modest venue for a fancy-dress party. Prizes were awarded for the most handsome, the most original and the most comical costumes after a parade around the hall and a vote by non-competitors. There are no detailed descriptions of the outfits but most make clear reference to the national events that impinged on everyone's life: 'War Bride', 'Lloyd George's Baby', 'War Loan', 'Women's Land Army'.[16]

In the Second World War, with London venues sandbagged against bombs, fancy-dress events continued elsewhere both as morale boosters and as a way to solicit funds for the war effort. The canteen of the enormous Butterley Ironworks in Ripley, Derbyshire, was given over to a fancy-dress ball in 1942 as a respite from the manufacture of Bofors gun platforms and pontoons for the D-Day landings.[17] Prisoners of war and troops on active service turned to dressing up for solace and out of boredom. Sergeant Sharrocks, a Wigan professional rugby player wounded in North Africa and a prisoner in Germany in 1942, told his local paper they had fancy-dress balls every Friday night in his camp: 'It was amazing what they managed to make out of old blankets and odds and ends and if anyone was able to produce an odd piece of silk they felt it was a grand ball. The prizes, which went to the "best lady" and the "best gentleman", were always cigarettes.'[18]

Images of peace celebrations across Britain and her colonies carry a melancholy charge but they also speak of hope after the darkness of war. Many communities decorated their neighbourhoods in red, white and blue and adorned themselves in fancy costumes in 1919, the year of the Versailles Treaty. Street parties were becoming widespread at this time and perhaps we can be allowed a symbolic interpretation here of coming out into the light after four years of trench warfare and brutal mechanized hostilities. An image of Heath Street Peace Tea in Dagenham in East London poignantly records little girls dressed as 'long ago children' in mob caps and flowery hats (illus. 86). Their every-day clothes can be seen beneath the carefully cut-out crêpe paper frocks. Britannia too sits by the tea table, a solemn girl in a crêpe paper sash and plumed crêpe helmet, flimsy but unmistakeable as the monumental

86 Heath Street Peace Tea, Dagenham, East London, 1919.

87 Patriotic costumes at the victory celebration after the First World War, Canungra, Queensland, 1919.

maiden's armoured headgear. Imaginative renderings of Britannia's helmet, resourcefully fashioned from assorted materials, appear in many victory fancy-dress entertainments as they did at coronations. The allegorical female figure was brought to life by the women who 'kept the home fires burning'.

Several thousand miles away, in Canungra, a small township on Australia's Queensland coast, boys and girls line up for a photograph dressed in something more elaborate (illus. 87). Right across the colonies and dominions, people shared the same sovereign and fought the same wars, and this was reflected in their fancy dress. British settlers living in different parts of the world frequently chose costumes indicative of what they saw as the embodiment of empire, and amateur dressmakers borrowed from a bank of conventional characters to both express pride in their own 'young' country and nostalgia for the 'old' one. It is often overseas, outside of the British Isles, that the components of these characters become highly developed and often exaggerated. At the end of the First World War, in which Australians were heavily involved, Canungra, like many other places in Australia, dressed up its children in celebration of peace. In the photograph we see them wearing what the caption terms 'patriotic costumes'. Britannia is there and we can pick out John Bull, a figure used on recruiting posters. Liberty wears the conspicuous rayed crown of the famous statue in New York harbour, a gift to the Americans from the people of France, and America shines out in stars and stripes. There are other characters as well, and two small clowns with conical hats and painted faces sit on the ground in front of the cart. These last recur in First World War victory images and may represent the clownish Kaiser. The children in Australia were not allowed to forget their ties to Britain or who their allies were. Children, a paradigm for a peaceful future, were an essential part of victory celebrations wherever they were held.

Though there are many records of local fancy-dress parties like those described, it was another form of dressing up that became central to some other end-of-war celebrations, affirming the hopeful confidence of the nation in 1919. The pageant, a costumed re-enactment of historic events, focused attention on the perceived long past of a given community, stressing its stability and its resoluteness in the face of adversity, and presenting it in a national and even sometimes international context. For the first half of the twentieth century, these staged chronicles were a significant part of civic life, accommodating an almost infinite number of amateur actors.[19] Strange to our sensibilities today, certain so-called peace pageants seem in reality to have been pageants of war, reminiscent of the Boer War carnivals of 1900 we looked at in Chapter Four. The participants, some of them veterans of the trenches, re-enacted battles in muddy fields and their unrelieved khaki is far away from our notion of fancy dress.[20] In Nottingham in 1919, there was a shortage of men willing to dress up as soldiers for this graphic portrayal of war and a call went out for volunteers even as rehearsals were under way. Women came forward, however, and children, who might otherwise have been difficult to place in such a hostile scenario but were vital to these commemorations, were marshalled into the formation of a living Union Jack.[21] A few peace pageants were wordless but mostly they were more akin to spoken theatre and are not part of our fancy-dress narrative in this book. We acknowledge that the relationship between the two is close, especially so at victory jubilees when the term 'pageant' is often used loosely.

Whether they were true pageants or not, parading in historic costume or national dress of the Allies formed part of many peace celebrations. In Wood Green, now in the London Borough of Haringey, hundreds of schoolchildren took part in the peace pageant there, ostensibly celebrating the history of the area but in fact embracing 'British history' as taught at that period, a common theme of victory festivities. The large number of children to be dressed for this North London pageant meant appropriating costumes and characters from a whole range of periods. Phalanxes of 'Ancient Britons', 'Saxons', 'Plantagenets', 'Stuarts', 'Georgians' and 'Elizabethans' were co-opted as well as 'gypsies'.[22] One of the gypsy outfits survives today, complete with tambourine. It belonged to Grace Boyce (1889–1950), possibly a young teacher at the school, and it stands as a tribute to those who dressed the children of Haringey for this festival of peace.[23]

In these celebrations, reality and myth often collided, with many a 'Lord Nelson' and 'Florence Nightingale' parading alongside 'Robin Hood' and 'Maid Marian'. Miss Gladys Mann as Lady Godiva attracted attention countrywide when she rode through Coventry on a caparisoned white horse as part of the peace pageant there. The annual Godiva parade in this Midlands industrial town is famous for the risqué lady's near-naked ride but in 1919, chary of criticism in sombre times, she was beautifully clothed. 'Coventry will never desire to return to the customary pink-fleshings-and-chiffon notion which savoured so much of the circus,' ventured the local correspondent. Important in Coventry, as in all other peace festivities, was the prominent part played by children. They were the focus of attention in their fancy-dress outfits. Twenty thousand Coventry schoolchildren took part in the celebrations 'and a more beautiful scene was never witnessed in the ancient city . . . The general scheme was to take British Empire and Allied Colours and carry them out in the dresses of the children of the city.' The drabness of the surroundings was noted but 'this served to accentuate the beautiful colour effects, while the overlooking lofty twin towers of St Michael and Trinity formed a background than which scarcely anything could have been more impressive.'[24]

Grown-ups seem to have dressed up less than children at victory parties but that may be because children drew the camera's gaze more than adults. The overriding truth is that so many men are missing from the frame because of death and injury and, in the light of this, we can understand why children feature so consistently in photographs. What does emerge from these images is how much children dress up as adults, how they repeatedly stand in for them, and how regularly their costumes are pint-sized facsimiles of uniforms. Since the mid-nineteenth century, children had dressed in sailor suits, both as everyday dress and as fancy dress, so this miniaturization was not new. During the First World War, however, it became much more explicit. We know that Gamages department store had child-size military uniforms on sale from at least 1915. Some of these were assimilated into the war effort: Jeannie Jackson, the daughter of a miner from Burnley in Lancashire, collected £1,100 for the war fund and became a celebrity in her diminutive officer's uniform with photographs in all the newspapers.[25] Children everywhere donned uniforms for peace parades, as at Camberwell (illus. 88). In Masterton, New Zealand, the procession included a float rigged out as HMS *New*

88 Children dressed as service personnel, Camberwell Peace Carnival, South London, June 1919.

Zealand. Both girls and boys dressed in naval uniform stand on the mock battle cruiser's deck.[26] Masterton and Camberwell were by no means unique in portraying children as small-scale service personnel on war duty. The visual imagery of the First World War was noticeable in fancy dress well after 1919. Its echoes reverberated through the ensuing decades. Boys frequently lined up in military uniform and very visibly carried toy weapons.

Moving images give us a greater sense of how fancy dress fitted into the overall picture of First World War peace parades despite shaky camera work, rudimentary editing and a lack of textual documentation. The event staged in Galashiels, a textile town in the Scottish Borders, is emblematic of the way many districts welcomed peace.[27]

Such countrywide occasions were marked by grief as well as jubilation, and the separate elements that comprised an entire peace observance were thus a blend of solemnity, remembrance, honour, celebration and rejoicing. The Galashiels Historical Peace Pageant, as the film footage is titled, comprises several ceremonies which are assimilated into the whole and, whatever precise form these took, dress – mayoral robes, military and service uniforms and fancy dress – was seen as a crucial ingredient of the proceedings. After the wreath-laying, the Galashiels procession takes a more animated turn, becoming almost carnival-like with decorated carts, costumes and music. Peace, a young woman with streaming hair and a flowing white dress, holds an olive branch and stands smiling under an arch of flowers on a cart pulled by a white horse. A brass band follows on behind and heralds something darker, though in a jocular vein: a wagon carrying a life-size model of Kaiser Wilhelm II (1859–1941), the last emperor of Germany, wedged upright and wearing his unmistakeable cipher, a *Pickelhaube* or spiked helmet, routinely used in cartoons and anti-German propaganda. Here is the villain being trundled through the streets of Galashiels but we can see that it is merely a dressed-up dummy and not a real person in evil guise. Nobody wants to take on the appearance of the Kaiser. The celebrations in the Australian town of Kaniva included a mock funeral for Kaiser Wilhelm and there are recorded instances of his effigy being strung up or stuck with a bayonet. Regional newspapers printed photographs of British soldiers with captured *Pickelhauben*, trophies of war, though they are not shown wearing them.[28] The Kaiser's uniform and helmet were not, therefore, a very public form of fancy dress at this time. In this Scottish parade, two clowns as mocking buffoons mounted on the same horse follow the swinish cart. As in Canungra above, they were used to stand in for the Kaiser character. The procession then continues: two girls as First World War despatch riders in goggles and caps precede Mary, Queen of Scots, the long-imprisoned and subsequently beheaded queen rarely absent from Scottish fancy dress.[29] Britannia and a May Queen bearing a pole topped with a flowery crown follow on. Next come a cavalcade of children decked out in a medley of costumes. Many are proven favourites: Little Bo Peep, Pierrot, Dutch girls, Native Americans, cowboys, a Chinese lady. Some are topical for the time: 'Mr Vim', for instance, copying the brand mascot for the bleach-laden scouring powder. We can pick out some of the Allies: the personification of Japan by her kimono and Serbia indicated by the broad stripes on the full skirt of her peasant-style dress. We are alerted in the film to a more delinquent aspect of fancy dress by a number of male adults, members of a brass band, who are clothed in a ragbag of assorted suits, patched and mismatched, with hats awry. One impersonates a clergyman and another pretends to be a policeman. There is a grown-up baby and several men dressed as women. Feasibly, this pantomime has been enacted before, and the rough-and-tumble band was the Earlston Clown Band, a permanent feature of the area's folkloric culture.[30] We see similar slapstick musicians in carnivals elsewhere.

At first unnoticed in the carnival crowd but then clearly understood for what they are, a considerable number of girls in Galashiels pass by dressed as men. It is only when we remember the date, 1919, that this public show of cross-dressing takes us a little by surprise and leads us to question the implications. The majority of these young women wear replicas of service uniforms complete with trousers. Both 'soldiers' and 'sailors' intermingle with the other characters. Many are arm-in-arm with a friend, their long hair escaping from military caps or sailor hats. The film shows their broad smiles, evidence of their palpable joy at dressing this way, and the waving crowds lining the route appear equally elated. From the film footage, there is no sense of unease or opprobrium at these girls in trousers. Here on the cusp of modernity these Galashiels girls are using fancy dress as a cover for putting on a garment associated with men.

So, a word about women in trousers is not inappropriate here. While trousers of varying cut were worn by women in several cultures across the globe, the skirt prevailed in large tracts of the world. Throughout history there have always been women who have crossed sartorial boundaries, whether donning trousers or dressing like men in other ways, but they are the exception. The chronicle of cross-dressed women is sometimes one of outrage and scandal and sometimes one of bemused tolerance. In the years before the First World War, trousers, though they are not always called that, made an appearance as women's attire in the form of pantaloons or pantalettes, bloomers, knickerbockers and the *jupes-culotte* or harem trousers of the Paris fashion designer Paul Poiret (1879–1944). Health, horse riding and other sports, together with a period orientalist sensibility, all helped to bring trousers into the female domain.[31] Progress was slow, perhaps less slow in the case of fancy dress. Despite men-to-women dissimulation being more widespread than vice versa, well before the First World War young women certainly went out guizing at New Year dressed as men.[32] When artificial lighting, particularly flash photography, became available to amateurs, women may have been more emboldened to wear male clothing in front of a relative or friend's camera at home, though early professional studio shots of cross-dressing women also survive, as with Elizabeth Robertson's picture referred to below. The large numbers of young women cross-dressers in Galashiels, however, warrant our close attention. Although we know that uniformed women's auxiliary forces were formed at this time, they did not wear trousers. Photographs held by the Imperial War Museum in London do show other women who contributed to the war effort clad in them: female RAF despatch riders in jodhpurs, Women's Land Army recruits and horse trainers in breeches, construction workers, munitions workers, shipyard workers and coal heavers in boiler suits all took on occupations traditionally held by men. These women are not portrayed by the Galashiels fancy dressers for there is a twist to this story of dressing up. As we have seen with children, the iconography of war penetrated many facets of life, not least the music hall.

Music hall embraced the soldierly look most notably in the form of Vesta Tilley (1864–1952), the enthusiastically received performer who meticulously prepared for her male stage roles and whose image in a variety of military and naval disguises was clearly copied by the girls of Galashiels. We know that some of Vesta Tilley's most ardent fans were young, single women and, though this male impersonator toured round Britain in person, photographic postcards of her, on sale everywhere, would probably have provided the models for fancy dress (illus. 89). Did dressing up as a man become more acceptable if you impersonated a woman dressed as a man? Nobody in Galashiels would miss the references to this renowned star. The girls wear either Tilley's famous recruiting sergeant's khaki uniform with swagger stick or her white sailor suit.[33] The uniformed cavalcaders in Galashiels are playing with gender identity, though this particular costume, suppressing femininity, may have been rendered acceptable by Tilley's very conscious female clothing offstage.[34]

89 Postcard of the stage star Vesta Tilley in military uniform, 1914–18.

Because there were so many Vestas in Galashiels, there was safety in numbers. Word must have gone round that a Vesta Tilley lookalike was admissible as fancy dress for a victory parade, though some men might have felt the character troubling rather than entertaining.[35] Perhaps a local tailor, conversant with the techniques of sewing uniforms, made all of them. From afar, they look accomplished and professional and, in this town where many people had been employed in textile manufacturing, we might expect a high level of competence in handling and sewing fabric. We should not discount the possibility that Galashiels may well present a typical example, rather than its opposite, of the range of fancy dress and of the increased acceptability of women's trousers. There is certainly other evidence for women being photographed as Vesta during the war. One example was Elizabeth Ann Robertson (b. 1899), who dressed up as 'England's greatest recruiting sergeant' for a party in Edinburgh in 1918. Women were also photographed in their soldier husbands' uniforms, though perhaps this is not strictly fancy dress.[36] However, as yet, there is nothing similar to the comprehensive outbreak of transvestism seen among these youthful Galashiels revellers.

Records of fancy dress on Victory in Europe Day and Victory over Japan Day (VE and VJ Day) following on from the Second World War are numerous and diverse. As we saw with the Kaiser, a quarter of a century later it was unusual, though not unknown, for people to masquerade in public as the enemy. Ratings on navy ships and soldiers on active service, away from the public gaze but often caught on camera, postured as Adolf Hitler.[37] His toothbrush moustache, slicked-down hair and terrible gesture were all too easy to copy. 'Hitler' appears in the victory parade in Henlow, Bedfordshire, with a sign that reads 'Who Said He's Dead'. A more reassuring imitation makes an appearance in Hull, where two Führers, convincingly recognized by the moustache, hold up their hands in surrender. It is noticeable how seldom named war heroes are commemorated in fancy dress at this time. Peace celebrations, following on very swiftly from the war's end, may have been too early for such recognition. In the Sutton district of the town of

St Helens, between Liverpool and Manchester, a party does include a Churchill lookalike, a portly man in a top hat smoking a cigar. He stands out as the only person dressed up and consequently became the focus of the photographer's lens. In Dumbarton, a Scottish shipbuilding town on the north bank of the River Clyde, we see a fake Winston Churchill, a pretend 'Monty' (Field Marshal Montgomery, 1887–1976) and an imitation Harry S. Truman, the president of the United States from 1945 to 1953. We recognize the first by his owl spectacles and cigar, the second by his military uniform and distinctive moustache, and the third only by context and the stars and stripes above his head.[38]

For the most part, VE Day and VJ Day followed much the same pattern as earlier celebrations. The termination of war was broadcast to the British people late on 7 May 1945, and the next day, VE Day, was declared a national holiday, leaving very little time for perfecting preparations. The spontaneous gathering of crowds of people in the capital and other cities was caught on camera by both amateur and professional photographers: a sea of uniforms interspersed with men and women in what seem to be their everyday or office clothes.[39] Fancy dress, when it appeared at all, manifested itself in paper hats, an obligingly transforming and humorous article of dress that went on to be a mainstay of other neighbourhood and national public celebrations held later in the following months. In Worthing on the south coast, cone-shaped paper hats in red, white and blue left over from the May VE Day were worn by children at the Orme Road Victory Street Tea in August. In Edmonton in Hazel Close, a London street of interwar semi-detached houses, people have turned out in festive hats as well as some semblance of full fancy dress. There is a clown, a Dutch girl and a conjuror, this last only deciphered for us in a recollection by Tom Wallace, who remembered it from his boyhood. A paper top hat and a crêpe paper fan seem to comprise Tom's entire outfit, which he wears with his own short trousers and long socks falling round his ankles.[40]

90 VE Day crowds with children in fancy dress, Wilkins Road, Cowley, Oxford, 1945. A boy in the front row appears to have a 'Hitler' moustache and a board that reads 'Never Again'.

Fancy dress at these victory parties was of necessity sometimes makeshift. Pulled together quickly with available materials, it was neither polished nor wide-ranging in theme (illus. 90). Characters are perfunctory and many people simply festooned themselves in red, white and blue. The niceties of authenticity and the detailing of earlier balls and parties are irrelevant here. Hundreds of photographs of street parties, many lacking any substantial fancy dress, exist in newspapers and family albums across Britain. There are some magical exceptions among the mostly run-of-the-mill pictures. One such is the captivating image of 'The Allies' taken by the photographer of Sussex rural life George Garland (1900–1978) (illus. 91). The children, standing companionably in an English field, are dressed to represent Britain, China, the Soviet Union, the United States of America and France. These are not habitual personifications but thoughtful representative costumes, immediately recognizable. Alongside routine fancy dress, some people wore unique, victory-themed outfits and these are anything but sketchy. Pamela Andrews in Essex, for example, was dressed in a white frock with red buttons, the skirt banded in blue and red and the bodice embroidered with the names of the Allied nations and notable war leaders. The dress was a collaboration between Pamela's mother and grandmother.[41]

91 Children pose as 'The Allies' dressed to represent Britain, China, the Soviet Union, the USA and France, photographed by George Garland at the Pulborough Victory Revels, Sussex, 1946.

Children in London and other cities throughout Britain survived enemy aerial raids to dress up for peace. The consequences of the Hull Blitz provided the stark background to a professionally made film documenting the peace celebrations there and, because of its clarity and completeness, this footage provides us with a microcosm of what might have gone on elsewhere as regards fancy dress.[42] As in other places, the Hull celebration presents evidence for both stock fancy-dress characters and some aberrations. The speed with which everything had to be pulled together for 3,000 children makes for repetition, but it was natural that the themes of victory should be uppermost in people's minds. The Union Jack, with its strong geometric parallels and diagonals, stands out everywhere along the column of parading children and frequently serves as the costume itself, draped and pinned around small bodies or fashioned into aprons, collars and trousers. Whether the material for these provisional, patriotic costumes was included in the Board of Trade's relaxation of rationing for red, white and blue bunting is unclear but flag-makers like Turtle & Pearce and Tutill must have readied themselves for this time. Among the many flag frocks, there are some unmistakeable portrayals of Britannia. Victory, Liberty and France are simulated by rudimentary but recognizable costumes. The services are represented by children in facsimile small uniforms, as we have seen before, some more accurate than others. A smartly turned-out small boy, carrying a model destroyer, wears a replica naval captain's outfit with brass-buttoned jacket and white cap. Another boy is in full Highland regimental dress while a third is an air-raid warden. At least two small guardsmen in red tunics and busbies march in the parade. Although women were not drafted into combat roles during the Second World War, they took a much greater part in military, naval and air force operations than in the First. These servicewomen are negligible in the fancy-dress record and in Hull we see just one or two dressed up that way. Other uniforms and outfits associated with less soldierly war service were more popular choices for girls in Second World War victory festivities. Parading alongside one of the several Britannias is a Land Girl in a junior version of the Women's Land Army outfit of breeches, jersey and soft felt hat, but perhaps a quarter of all the girls taking part in the Hull parade are dressed as nurses.

92 Jean Alder and her brother, Michael, at Beckingham Road fancy dress party, Westborough School, Guildford, in September 1945. Jean is dressed as a nurse. Michael wears a Home Guard hat and a blue suit made by his grandmother. He was supposed to represent a wounded soldier, a recurrent character at this time.

The uniformed nursing sister approached cult status among young girls and as fancy dress it attained new heights during the celebrations after the Second World War (illus. 92). It had reached a peak of popularity in the First World War when professionally made postcards of child nurses tending small boys in uniform were freely on sale. As part of a commercial transaction, fancy dress had been appropriated for the national cause. Girls continued to dress up as nurses in their own homes and were often photographed there or in a studio. A nurse's uniform worn as costume accords well with two of fancy dress's precepts: it is simple to make and instantly identifiable. In addition, it provided girls with a wholly acceptable character that was particular to their gender and was emphatically of this world rather than the world of 'fairie'. Nursing is fantasy in a different key, a dream of being grown-up, responsible, caring and needed. The nurse remained an immoveable component of dressing up and, at this stage, had not been downgraded to the tacky and jokey adult outfit it would later become.

While nurses, along with allegorical figures, can be seen as a leitmotif distributed across the moving column of Hull children, costumes of real flair punctuate this parade. 'LIGHT AFTER DARK' is the heartfelt message picked out in appliqué lettering sewn across the bodice of one dress with 'EUROPE CELEBRATION' on the skirt. A pocket-sized Pearly King, a figure of working-class culture in London, perhaps acknowledges the Blitz in the capital. Other costumes reflect the concerns of war: the wounded with arms in slings and legs in splints, refugees in ragged clothes pushing barrows and a girl dressed for factory work in dungarees and a bandana-style knotted headscarf. This image of a working woman took on iconic status when a 1942 painting by Laura Knight, *Ruby Loftus Screwing a Breech Ring*, was published in eight British newspapers, shown on newsreel film and reproduced as a poster. It depicts a young woman working at an industrial lathe in the Royal Ordnance Factory in South Wales.[43]

The Ruby Loftus portrayal, today popularly linked with the cult of 'vintage', is specific to the Second World War, and other character imitations seen on VE Day and VJ Day were also explicitly of their period and have since fallen out of the repertoire of dressing up. Several of them accord with a new cultural idiom that came across the Atlantic from America. Cigarette girls, film stars and Hawaiian beauties provided a tonic for bombed-out Hull. Carmen Miranda (Maria do Carmo Miranda da Cunha, 1909–1955) is there. A winning samba singer and film star from Brazil, she was a favourite of British cinema-goers with her Latin-accented songs and her audacious costumes. She was a gift to masqueraders, though parading through the streets of Hull might have been a precarious business in platform shoes and 'Tutti-Frutti' hat. This fruit turban became Carmen Miranda's trademark logo and her most famous film, *The Gang's All Here* of 1943, used an optical trick to magnify the daring coiffure. Pretend Carmen Mirandas were not as poised as the real thing, though they were unmistakeable as to character, one of the tenets of successful fancy dress. Towards the end of her career, this much-loved star, and portrayals of her, were criticized as stereotyping Hispanic Americans.[44]

Another example in the same vein, one that carried on after the war and persists today, is the American-inflected 'hula dance girl' also seen in Hull and already gaining popularity in Britain before the Second World War. A skirt of raffia strands secured to an elastic waistband and a necklace of crêpe-paper flowers recreated the hula look without need for a pattern or too much expertise. The hula ensemble, as controversial as that of Carmen Miranda, has been re-evaluated in Hawaii, and the layers of misuse and misinterpretation that have accumulated around this dress have been peeled back in an attempt to arrive at some sort of historical accuracy.[45] In the 1930s, however, Hollywood had contributed to a stereotype of the style by releasing a series of photographs featuring the curly-headed child star Shirley Temple (1928–2014) wearing a hula outfit when she visited Hawaii in 1935. The grass skirt was popularized by her and in part owes its ubiquity to the presence of American service personnel in Hawaii, a staging post for the war in the Pacific.[46] Along with nylons and chewing gum, it was transferred to Britain and translated effortlessly into fancy dress.

Fancy-dress ideas from previous eras were recycled in Hull. A Japanese girl dressed in kimono and holding an unfurled parasol defies the concerns of war by depicting an adversary, though the outfit is not worn to provoke trouble. Its appearance serves to point up the distance between reality and fantasy. The kimono here in no way equates with the nation that Britain and the United States were still fighting at this point in 1945 and the outfit may well have been understood as 'Chinese' anyway, such was the lack of awareness of foreign dress. There are some animal impersonations in the parade – a bird, a lion, a cat. The all-enveloping nature of a suit with a wayward tail, aberrant beak or shaggy mane had tremendous appeal, and the tempting opportunity to act out the relevant bestial qualities was seductive. This category of fancy dress, unusual at the beginning of our period, gradually evolved into a staple of dressing up.

It is axiomatic that both peace celebrations and fancy dress are provisional, outside of the everyday, and dressing up is an appropriate response to heightened emotions. There is also a sense that changing your appearance, becoming somebody else, albeit only superficially, accords with the greater change from war to peace. This transitional moment, perhaps at first overwhelming, could best be comprehended and brought about by something as easy as dressing up. The young remained at the core of the celebrations. Costumed children can be understood as a salve against loss and, as they paraded and partied up and down the country, they represented the positive and joyful aspects of a realignment to peace.

Six

THE BUSINESS OF FANCY DRESS: THE NINETEENTH CENTURY

This chapter and the one that follows take a chronological view of the practicalities involved in acquiring fancy dress. The years after the First World War are examined in the next chapter while those from Queen Victoria's accession to 1914 are discussed here.

In the mid-nineteenth century, independent professional dress-makers or costumiers were the two main conduits for fancy dress. Several costumiers whose names come up repeatedly throughout this book had been in business for fifty years or more since the high days of masquerade. In the 1850s, if not before, they benefited from the upswing of theatrical entrepreneurship that saw the stage transformed into a respectable and much appreciated popular pursuit for actors and audiences alike. The sum and substance of their business revolved around a nimble response both to contemporary trends and to the practical turnarounds necessary for limited production runs. They were therefore in a good position to ride the wave of fancy dress's popularity. They took advantage of the proliferation of regional newspapers to advertise their stock, and they benefited from the expansion of the railway network to transport it across the British Isles and beyond. One newspaper page out of many captures how they operated. In 1845, seven suppliers of fancy dress and associated accessories put notices on the front page of the *Manchester Courier and Lancashire General Advertiser* in connection with a charity ball in the city. Mr Grundy at 4 Exchange Street announced that he had just received a consignment of historical and other costumes adapted for fancy dress, and Varley & Ollivant next door had outfits, including costumes of all nations, from Simmons, a leading London costume-maker. Franklin advertised trimmings and Mendelson promoted jewellery. The showiest notices were submitted by the grand London costumiers who had a presence in Manchester for the ball's duration. Hart of Regent Street took spacious rooms in Manchester's St Anne's Square, and Nathans, one of the most prominent costumiers of the time and a name that will recur, posted this advertisement for the same Manchester ball:

> MESSRS. NATHANS, from London, beg most respectfully to inform the Nobility and Gentry of Manchester and its vicinity, that owing to the great demand for DRESSES, they will receive on Monday next, from their Establishment in London, upwards of TWO HUNDRED COSTLY COSTUMES of all Nations and Characters, too numerous to mention, on SALE OF HIRE. The above are NOW OPEN for INSPECTION at Mr. WATTS', 21, King-street. Any Lady or Gentleman wishing for any particular Costume can have it made to order without any extra charge.[1]

Although smaller towns could not support as many costumiers as Manchester, notices like these appeared in many local newspapers when a fancy-dress ball was imminent. While the London firms of Nathans, Hart, Simmons and Clarkson dominate the newspaper columns throughout Britain during the second half of the nineteenth century, Burkinshaw of Liverpool had a high profile too, and habitually took out advertisement space in *The Stage*.[2] Other regional establishments also supplied fancy dress: Burnell in Plymouth and Lionel Graham in Portsmouth, both naval towns where balls had long been part of the social calendar, and Melville's Drapery Establishment in Dundee, where 'ladies need have no fear of seeing any time their dresses duplicated.'[3]

Tailors and dressmakers provided ball costumes alongside other styles of clothing; Mesdames Brown of Worthing specialized in cycling costumes and made fancy dress as well.[4] A few private individuals took the opportunity to hire out or sell on their own costumes, taking space in the small advertisement columns of a relevant newspaper. A 'most beautiful Circassian fancy dress; white and pink satin, magnificently embroidered in natural flowers and gold' was offered at the time of the Lord Mayor's Ball in Liverpool in 1883.[5]

Frequently, a firm like Nathans was contracted by the ball organizers to supply the costumes, as happened at Weymouth, a resort on the south coast, in 1856.[6] Similarly, Harrison Brothers, who started trading in 1840 and had an establishment at 31 Bow Street in London's Covent Garden, was the exclusive supplier of costumes for a grand masquerade, garden party and fancy-dress ball held at North Woolwich Gardens on the bank of the River Thames in East London in June 1887. Admission was one shilling and ticket-holders could hire costumes at a reduced price by making prior arrangements with Harrison, who would then deliver them to the gardens on the night. In the eighteenth century, pleasure gardens had defined London's nightlife and some continued to operate in the next century. The Woolwich extravaganza seems to have embraced both masking and character costume, a sign that masquerade in its earlier incarnation had not entirely died out. The thousands of lamps and Japanese lanterns promised at Woolwich also echoed the ambience of its precursors and gave promise, like them, of shadowy corners and even illicit assignations. These nineteenth-century commercial enterprises were sustained by go-ahead costumiers like Harrison and perhaps more so by the suburban railway companies that laid on special trains to convey working-class party-goers to and from the venue: 'The Proprietor of the Gardens has secured a special train back to Liverpool St., at 2.45 a.m., and a special boat to South Woolwich at 2.45 a.m.' would have been welcome information for prospective carousers of limited means who, courtesy of Harrison, did not need to carry or, perhaps embarrassingly, wear their costumes on public transport.[7]

Deciding on a character, acquiring the costume, trying it on and then finally getting dressed up on the day were part of a longer chain of fancy-dress production and consumption. The exacting work of costumiers in transforming ordinary men and women into illusory beings is not well documented and evidence for behind-the-scenes preparation for costume balls, parties and carnivals is piecemeal. Cutting, basting and sewing, ironing and steaming, packing and transporting – the mechanics of the trade – are mostly hidden from view and accomplished offstage, as it were. We know that Clarkson was taken to court for the Sunday employment of women at his factory in Kennington, south of the River Thames, on Boxing Day 1898, so we can assume his business had more than enough work, and that such enterprises were financially worthwhile.[8]

Fancy-dress manufacture often ran alongside, or derived from, ancillary tailoring operations that complemented each other. Nathans, established in London in 1790 and a name we have already seen in connection with the Manchester ball, supplied fancy dress along with professional theatre costumes and seem only to have started making the latter when some sort of historical accuracy became paramount on the nineteenth-century stage. Previously, actors had been expected to supply their own costumes for contemporary dress roles so the manufacture of fancy dress must have formed a sizeable slice of the Nathans organization and generated a large skilled workforce.[9] In an advertisement at the back of Ardern Holt's *Gentlemen's Fancy Dress: How to*

Choose It of 1882, Nathans styles itself as 'Court Costumiers', reminding us of another, in fact original, undertaking of the business. With experience in theatrical costume, court dress and a further speciality, military dress uniforms, we can see how Nathans was ideally suited for fancy-dress production. Many gentlemen attending fancy-dress balls considered their soldierly apparel as suitable for such occasions, calling into question the idea of fancy dress as a bounded entity. What we might deduce from its permeable borders is that many people, particularly those from the ruling class, were well used to dealing with costumiers and, furthermore, were familiar with a daily cycle of changing clothes to suit the time and occasion. They were adept at managing the minutiae of complex attire and employed servants who understood the correct procedures. The tailors and seamstresses who worked for Nathans fashioned a multiplicity of styles but all of them – uniforms, court dress, theatre costumes and fancy dress – had one thing in common in that they were destined for public display.

Several other establishments, like Nathans, had additional interests that enhanced the effectiveness of their fancy-dress operations. The London store Debenham & Freebody diversified into publishing books about fancy dress and also into making it, as detailed below. Redmayne, with premises in London's New Bond Street and Conduit Street, were silk mercers as well as costumiers supplying silks, satins, velvets, plush and brocades along with ribbon for regimental medals and decorations. Although they did not advertise themselves as costumiers, Spence, a large and well-stocked draper at St Paul's Churchyard, among a superabundance of cloth recommended their best French cotton sateen in over a hundred colours as the most effective material for fancy dress. Moreover, they not only supplied the material but sent their expert representatives to give advice about what they termed 'getting up costumes for Fancy Dress Balls and Fancy Fairs', a sort of halfway house between a costumier and home production that was perhaps not as cheap as the latter but arguably more satisfying. A business such as that run by George Kenning offered an Aladdin's cave of desirable fancy-dress goods for the professional costumier and domestic dressmaker alike. One of his advertisements lists forty or more special trimmings, laces and accessories that he stocked especially for costume balls. This multitude of fanciful adornments includes rosettes, anklets, ruffles, 'guilles', butterflies, bats, serpents, gold and silver dust, and Concave's frost. Other suppliers, like Robert White at 30 Bow Street and James White at No. 21, carried similar, though slightly different, stock to tempt the buyer: imitation gold and silver braid, fringing, gimps, bullion fringes, tassels, pearls, frosting and gilt sequins, frosting armlets and wristlets with or without chains, stars, crescents, folly bells, silver bells, cockle shells, jewelled crowns, diadems, daggers, collars, belts and more. Kenning hoped to reach a wider buying public by operating three branches in London and three outside the capital in Manchester, Glasgow and Liverpool. Placed in Marie Schild's 1884 guide to men's costume, the George Kenning advertisement gives no hint of the firm's other, perhaps principal, interest, that of Masonic paraphernalia. The ribbons and regalia of this predominantly male organization are, arguably, as 'fancy' as fancy dress and Kenning's involvement in both areas of bodily ornamentation, plus yet another line in military and naval buttons, was not unusual. His clientele likely had an interest in more than one type of merchandise. Kenning's business acumen encouraged shoppers to become habitués because he provided the indispensable accoutrements for the institutions and practices of upper- and middle-class life.

In addition, specialist wigmakers, boot and shoemakers, and purveyors of paste jewellery and make-up, grew up alongside costumiers, and many were clustered around London's Covent Garden in a mutually beneficial relationship. Clarkson, as we saw in the Introduction, was purportedly in the business of disguise and, ever a successful self-promoter, claimed to be one of the few correct historical coiffeurs for fancy-dress balls. He, like several others, also supplied a teeming array of transforming appendages. His business offered whiskers, mutton chops and 'red hot pokers', moustaches for those without facial hair, and skin moustache masks for those who had. He stocked a selection of make-up, including face patches for powder costumes, and a string of prerequisites such as wig paste, both English and German, and curling irons. In line with the firm's specialist skills of mutating the face and head, Clarkson carried a variety of masks, giant heads, moveable foreheads, ears, eyes, eyelashes and mouths, demons, yokels and death's heads, and dominos (eye masks and all-enveloping capes for disguise). As was the usual practice, Clarkson provided private fitting rooms at his premises. There, his dual role of wig-maker to the balding, and face-changer and perruquier to bacchants, might have caused some consternation to his clients, the one rather far away in spirit from the other. Like most big firms, Clarkson offered post-free lists and catalogues and this system was predicated on an efficient postal system, as was the mailing and transport of the artefacts themselves. The firm were wholesalers and exporters as well as retailers and their services extended to attending customers in their own homes. His agents, technicians of transmutation, travelled throughout Britain.

A few suppliers specialized in one type of accessory. Monsieur M. Armand was a theatrical bootmaker and Thomas Holland made coloured silk or satin shoes to match any costume in one of four heel heights. The London Glove Company, while not claiming to be in the fancy-dress business, certainly carried a large assortment suitable for dress and evening wear. Even though they did not necessarily accord with the character, throughout the nineteenth century gloves or mittens were considered essential at balls to cover perspiring hands. Jewellers, too, supplied accessories specific to fancy dress though they might also have traded in other types of jewellery. Thornhill, a London firm with royal patronage established in 1734, advertised 'jewellery, ornaments, belts & appendages appropriately designed to suit any fancy or theatrical costume'. The 'little secrets' offered by the cosmetics firm of Piesse & Lubin, situated further along New Bond Street from Thornhill, were also in the business of deception. They stocked an assortment of make-up, and for fancy-dress balls they recommended 'Powder Bloom' as well as gold, silver and diamond hair powders and *mouches* (face patches) in black velvet. All these suppliers were based in London and most offered a mail-order service. Some branded products were advertised as being available in shops countrywide and the extensive reach of fancy dress across Britain supported appropriate stockists in provincial towns and cities.

Among these many purveyors of fancy-dress consumables, an exhortation from a vendor in Hastings on the south coast of England commands our attention on several counts. His lack of a London or large city address is unusual and his caricatural name, M. Smout, is satisfyingly Dickensian. Today an air of humorous improbability surrounds Mr Smout who, in the Victorian era, despatched real seaweed suitable for draping and trimming the costumes of sea nymphs, undines and water sprites from his premises at 17 Trinity Street. His advertisement assured buyers of the elegance and natural appearance of his products and proclaimed, 'they give a "chic" to the wearer by reason of their novelty.' This was a business opportunity unmatched in fancy-dress narratives, and Mr Smout, the kelp king, surmising that his very specialist avocation would appeal to those masquerading as peris of the ocean, took out advertising space in Marie Schild's book alongside all the grand London dealers.[10]

Costumiers, among them many women and some with French names, continued to flourish and to adapt their practices to a new class of clientele as the nineteenth century progressed. The lists and catalogues produced by these purveyors of artifice, if they exist at all, have yet to be investigated but what certainly has survived are a number of fancy-dress guides which were designed to steer the reader through the plethora of costume choices and to give hints on their hiring, buying or making. These late nineteenth- and early twentieth-century volumes are different in flavour from the later pattern books of the interwar years considered in the next chapter. Prior to the First World War, foremost among the authors of book-length manuals were Charles Harrison – whose 1882 guide, *Theatricals and Tableaux Vivants for Amateurs*, we have already encountered – Ardern Holt, Marie Schild and Eliza Aria. Weldons and Butterick, two firms in the forefront of fashion publishing and paper-pattern manufacture, also produced books penned anonymously, though we know that Jennie Taylor Wandle compiled the Butterick publication and a 'Marie Bayer', likely an invented French-sounding name for a young journalist at Weldons, Louisa Patterson, the former.[11] These volumes, spanning nearly thirty years from Holt's earliest in 1879 to Aria's 1906 contribution, not only helped readers with costuming but counselled them on etiquette. The information was frequently contradictory, often opinionated and, to our modern ear, a bit toffee-nosed, but their words of advice signal real anxieties that the authors seemed keen to dispel. Advertisements, embedded in the text and as separate entities, blurred the division between practical guidance and promotion, a situation that was also prevalent in manuals for amateur photographers.

The books by Ardern Holt appear to have reigned supreme during the last years of the nineteenth century and their continued influence can be discerned in the next century despite the appearance of new styles of publication. Holt's *Fancy Dresses Described or What to Wear at Fancy Balls* ran to six editions between 1879 and 1896 and survives today in some quantity. The number of pages increased with each edition, a testament to its serviceability, so that by 1896 it had expanded to 312 pages from its original 92 in 1879. Most of the second-hand volumes listed for sale today and many of the volumes consulted in libraries show signs of active readership; these titles were well used, passed from hand to hand, seriously consulted. We know that the Hon. Secretary of the Literary Institute of Walsall, a town in the West Midlands, obtained Ardern Holt's book and *Weldon's Practical Fancy Dress for Ladies* for members to consult in connection with a children's fancy-dress ball in 1887 and this must have been a common practice.[12] Ardern Holt also published *Gentlemen's Fancy Dress: How to Choose It* in 1882. Fittingly for a supremo of disguise, the author hides behind an ambiguously gendered pen name. A contemporary review of the fifth edition of 1887 calls the author 'Mr'.[13] A popular London shopping guide, compiled by Charles Eyre Pascoe in his *London of Today: An Illustrated Handbook for the Season*, published regularly throughout the 1880s and '90s, gives the name as 'Mistress Ardern Holt', and in all likelihood the name was a pseudonym for several successive journalists. As royal correspondent for *The Queen*, Holt wrote regularly about the monarch's household and this same magazine routinely featured fancy dress in its correspondence columns and gave recommendations and tips. It also included some hand-coloured engravings. There was a huge appetite for this type of material and we have seen how interest in Queen Victoria and her family went hand in hand with an interest in fancy dress. Royal participation endorsed dressing up and tempered its potentially anarchic side. Ardern Holt's books ensured that fancy dress became tractable and safe.

93 'Wastepaper Basket', from Ardern Holt, *Fancy Dresses Described or What to Wear at Fancy Balls* (1896).

The content of both *Fancy Dresses Described*, with an appendix for children in later issues, and *Gentlemen's Fancy Dress*, a separate Holt volume, follow the same arrangement in each of the editions. The Introduction to the ladies' volume guides those new to fancy dress through some tricky points of protocol and touches on the question of authenticity. With historic and national dress, we might expect authenticity to be a recurring watchword in Holt's instructions to readers, but this proves not to be the case. It is certainly a concern, with the author acknowledging the 'lamentably incorrect' historic dress of past balls, and national costumes unrecognized by 'the peasantry they were intended to portray'.[14] Complete accuracy is thought unrealistic, however, but there is enough guidance throughout the book for a party-goer to at least make an attempt at credibility. Other books published around the same time all took the same line. Opinions about authenticity, or the lack of it, are outweighed by other kinds of advice touching on personal presentation. Holt instructs women 'who really desire to look well to study what is individually becoming to themselves . . . if they wish their costumes to be really a success'.[15] Comeliness is emphasized though some of the suggested characters push at the limits of allure. 'Ostrich', 'Penwiper' ('everywhere edged with steel pens') and 'Wastepaper Basket' seem clumsily unattractive, though we remember that at this period abstract and animal costumes were distilled into graceful frocks with relevant ciphers applied to them (illus. 93).[16] Holt's Introduction varies little from edition to edition, with lists for costumes suitable for brunettes and those best for blondes. Suggestions for elderly ladies follow, 'My Grandmother', 'Night', 'Puritan' and 'Quakeress' among them. Under the heading 'Sisters', Holt recommended, for example, 'Music and Painting', 'Cinderella's two sisters', 'Salt and Fresh Water', 'A Circassian Princess and Slave'. The author then continues with a selection of children's characters, a paragraph on correct shoes and gloves, and a section on hairdressing and powdering.

72 FANCY DRESSES DESCRIBED; OR,

caught up with narcissus; hair powdered; silver wreath of narcissus; shoes and stockings embroidered with crystal beads. *See* WINTER.

ICE MAIDEN. White gauze dress and veil fastened with wreath of icicles; long gloves of the same high up the arm; bracelets and chains of icicles; girdle of falling icicles.

ICELANDIC BRIDE. High black cloth dress, with long sleeves; the stomacher embroidered in fine gold-work; high white horn-shaped cap, with gold embroidered band; lace veil; large silver belt.

INCROYABLE (1798). Short red, white, and blue skirt; blue satin coat with tails, and revers at throat; the lappet and waistcoat of old brocade, red, blue, and black bow, with long ends on one shoulder; gold buttons; cravat of old lace; gendarme hat, with tricolour rosette; black shoes and buckles, blue stockings. Old-fashioned gold-headed cane; eyeglass. Coloured Illustration Plate XV. Or striped satin skirt, red, white, and blue; gold satin tunic, looped up with red roses; handsome long-tailed coat of blue satin, lined gold, and large gold buttons, and bouquet of roses in buttonhole at right; high frill and jabot at throat; *chapeau à la claque*, trimmed gold and brocade, tricolour at side; blue silk stockings, worked gold, and patent shoes; eyeglass, and elaborate jewellery.

IDYLLS OF THE KING. *See* ELAINE, ENID, &c.

IMOGEN. A long robe of soft white silk, made high to the throat, but without sleeves; the full bodice girded in at the waist with a dead-gold band, and from thence the skirt flowing evenly to the feet; a gold band round the neck, and a circlet of the same, or a chaplet of pearls, on the hair, which might be left flowing; on the right arm one bracelet, a thick band of beaten gold is best; shoes of white wash-leather; no gloves.

INDIAN DRESSES should come veritably from that country, and are of great variety. North American Indian Queen for fancy dress wears a brown satin cuirass and skirt bordered with cut leather fringe; sandals; a diadem of coloured feathers, bird's wings in front, and a great many beads for jewellery. *See also* RANEE.

INDIAN GIRL, LUTI. (In Mrs. Browning's poem, *A Romance of the Ganges.*) For a dark girl with smooth black

94 Double-page spread from the 1882 edition of Ardern Holt, *Fancy Dresses Described or What to Wear at Fancy Balls*, showing the alphabetic layout and a colour illustration of an *incroyable*.

Holt is disparaging of clever names for character costumes: 'Bounding Ball of Babylon' and 'Petite Sole à la Normandie' are dismissed as very mediocre costumes. Popular plays and operas are lauded as inspiration, as are Kate Greenaway illustrations and what Holt calls 'artistic dressing'. The Introduction ends on a positive note: 'There are few occasions when a woman has a better opportunity of showing her charms to advantage than at a Fancy Ball.' Holt's book for gentlemen is more practical; it itemizes those costumes that can serve as a guide to many others in the book. In a long paragraph, Holt addresses the problem of historic facial hair, clearly an anxiety for gentlemen fancy

95 *Incroyable* costume of trimmed satin made by a professional dressmaker, *c.* 1890. An *incroyable* was the name given to a French male dandy of the 1790s. This is a feminized version, a close copy of the coloured illustration in Ardern Holt's 1882 *Fancy Dresses Described or What to Wear at Fancy Balls*.

dressers, and then continues: 'people at Fancy Balls often render themselves ridiculous because they assume characters in every way opposed to their own personality.'[17] Just a few years later, the nascent carnival scene would encourage good-time men and women to do just that, casting Holt somewhat in the role of spoilsport.

The main body of each of Holt's books is taken up with an alphabetical listing of the characters and there are hundreds of them. The 1896 edition of *Fancy Dresses Described*, for example, begins with 'Abbess' and follows with 'Abigail', 'Abruzzi Peasant', 'Academical Dress', 'Aida', 'Adrienne Lecouvreur', 'Africa', 'Agnes Sorel', 'Agriculture', 'Air', 'Albanian', 'period of Albert Durer', 'Alcestes', 'Costume of Aldgate School', 'Alcestis', 'Algerian Costume', 'Alice Bridgenorth', 'Alice in Wonderland', 'Alice Lee', 'Aline', 'All is not Gold that Glitters', 'Almanack' down to 'Azucena' when 'Babes in the Wood' take over followed by 'Babet', 'Babolin', 'Baby', 'Baby Bunting', 'Baccarat', 'Bacchante', 'Backgammon' and on through each letter, with 'Zenobia', 'Zerlina', 'Zingari', 'Zitella' and 'Zurich' rounding off this exacting directory (illus. 94 and illus. 95). The gentlemen's shorter volume starts with 'Abbe', 'Captain Absolute', 'Afghan Chief' and 'Aladdin' and ends with 'Wind', 'Windsor Uniform', 'Winter', 'Yankee' and finally 'Zouave'. Later editions of the men's volume have additional suggestions suitable for boys: characters from Gilbert and Sullivan's *Ruddygore* (later renamed *Ruddigore*) are included at the end of the 1898 publication. The operas of Gilbert and Sullivan were performed across the British empire, and the specific Holt edition consulted here comes with an early Indian bookseller's stamp from Bombay (today's Mumbai). Arguably, men's fancy dress in the early part of our period was further from their everyday clothing than that for women. Knee breeches, trunks and Tudor hose must have been quite a sartorial departure, whereas a woman's fancy-dress silhouette was closer to her ordinary wear with perhaps a shorter hemline.

Today we can wander through Holt's pages and enjoy the rambling connections between the characters refracted from the worlds of theatre, literature and history. Pausing to reflect on this dizzying list, there are some surprising omissions: 'the boy Mozart', for example, and indeed composers of any stripe do not feature. Figures from mythology, national, folk and popular culture, the natural world and the sciences are all included in a jumbled confusion and we presume that most of them were well understood by Holt's readers, though many are not recognized today. French operetta which transferred across the Channel is an apposite example. The leading ladies of *La Fille de Madame Angot*, *La Marjolaine*, *Les Noces d'Olivette* and others had an all-too-brief moment in the fancy-dress limelight. 'Madame Barnabé' in her 'short skirt of sky-blue Cashmere' lapsed into obscurity and is not remembered by many people in the twenty-first century as a character from *La Timbale d'argent* by Léon Vasseur (1844–1917).[18] This operetta, his only successful venture, played to audiences around Britain in 1876. It was adapted and produced by Richard D'Oyly Carte (1844–1901), whose collaboration with Gilbert and Sullivan would provide much more lasting resonances in the cultural life of Britain generally and in dressing up more specifically. While we cannot gauge the relative popularity of any of these costumes at the time Holt was writing, abstruse references like these remind us that popular culture is a fickle thing.

Over the lifetime of Holt's six editions not many characters are retired from the lists though plenty are added. There are nine pages of characters beginning with 'A' in the 1882 edition and seventeen pages in 1896, for example. New entrants in 1887 include 'Shuttlecock', 'Academical Dress', 'Masher' and 'Masherette' (illus. 96), with 'Targets' 'Lady Speaker' and 'New Woman' appearing in 1896.[19] All these are suggestive of Victorian women's increasing visibility in sport as well as their aspirations in other areas of public life. Outnumbering these, however, were whimsical newcomers: 'She Went into the Garden to Cut

96 Geraldine Hargrave dressed as a 'Masherette' at the Children's Fancy Dress Ball, Adelaide, photographed by the firm of Wivell, 1887. She is the feminine equivalent of a 'Masher', an impeccably suited man-about-town who, in some contexts, was seen as a predatory dandy.

a Cabbage Leaf', a recruit to the 1896 edition, was a costume based on an eighteenth-century memory test, relaunched in 1885 as a poem in a Randolph Caldecott picture book, *The Great Panjandrum Himself*. Since Holt's final edition, this and many costume options have atrophied, never to be reanimated. But, as we shall see, a surprising number *did* linger on in permutations more pertinent to their times.

In Holt's fancy-dress bible, each character has a textual description of the garments and accessories relevant to that role:

> JUTLAND PEASANT GIRL. Green, black, and red striped petticoat; large black and green apron with border; green velvet bodice, tight sleeves trimmed with band of embroidery across front to imitate square bodice; red and black handkerchief about head, with revers of lace turning up from ears.
> SUEZ CANAL. Long flowing robe of cloth-of-gold, with waves of blue satin bordered with pearls, underskirt of red satin embroidered with Egyptian designs. A gold key at the girdle; Egyptian head-dress of pearls, turquoise, and diamonds; girdle of roses and lilies.[20]

Few entries are shorter but others run to considerably more words. Not many are illustrated and so, for the majority without pictures, the text was important. In some measure, however, the written word conjured up things already known about from other publications, performances and exhibitions of all persuasions. The world was becoming increasingly imbued with images and impressions.

Among the descriptions, and following on the more general advice in the Introduction, there are reminders about vestiary precision: the correct bodice for a 'Normandy Peasant' is plain if worn over a linen chemisette, but laced across the front if worn with a muslin fichu. Other entries peel away layers of knowledge that underwrite the costume.

A succinct description of an outfit may be followed by variations and alternatives as well as snippets of information about other wearers or originators, thereby validating it. For example, the costume description for Portia from *The Merchant of Venice* – Shakespeare's heroines were always in favour during the lifespan of Holt's books – goes into some detail about two separate outfits worn onstage by the renowned actress Ellen Terry (1847–1928). Attenders at past grand balls are sometimes named in Holt's lists and their garments are recorded, as in the case of Lady Villiers, who attended the Queen's ball in May 1842 as Donna Vittoria Colonna, a Renaissance noblewoman and poet.[21]

In Holt's dictionary-like checklist the obscure keep company with the familiar: 'Elizabeth, Queen of England' is followed by 'Eizler Berenger', about whom we know nothing.[22] For today's readers, there is a delightful eccentricity in the listings, a certain arbitrary oddness familiar to those who surf the Internet, and maybe the accidental juxtapositions were part of the book's appeal at the time. One early colonial commentator in Australia succinctly noted the 'strange intermingling of different climes and times which constitute the pleasing perplexity of a fancy ball'.[23]

This congeries of characters derives from several different starting points and the inconsistencies throughout Holt's books have much to do with the diverse original sources and the way the editions were put together. We have little firm evidence from the author about the matter though we can immediately see that the work is a compilation. Holt, as a correspondent and journalist, would have known where to look for ideas. Several seminal eighteenth-century works which brought together engravings depicting dress of all kinds would doubtless have been known to the author.[24] Back numbers of *The Queen* must have provided the cornerstone of Holt's book-length work and the author would have had access to printed matter of many kinds beyond the reach of ordinary readers. Other periodical publications were useful here, and

97 A fancy-dress design for 'Eve and the Serpent' by Léon Sault, 1860s.

The World of Fashion, a monthly magazine which ran from 1824 to 1891, provides us with one example that, like *The Queen*, included a few colour plates, as well as black-and-white ones, of fashionable dress along with the occasional foreign or historic dress.[25] These illustrations were a distinctive feature of an otherwise sparsely illustrated early Victorian press. The influential *History of British Costume* by Planché (1834), and, for later editions of Holt, Racinet's entrancingly illustrated *Le Costume historique* (1888), may have been consulted. There was a plethora of other expensively produced volumes on clothing and customs produced in the 1880s and *National Types and Costumes* (1885) was one of a growing number illustrated with photographs. Though none of these were aimed specifically at fancy dressers, their contents were mined by authors like Holt who filtered their contents down to a different and wider audience in an affordable form.

Holt must also have been familiar with an array of other costume fashion plates. One example is provided by Léon Sault's series of captivating fancy-dress designs, many of which were tailored by the House of Worth in Paris for a moneyed clientele (illus. 97).[26] Sault later published the designs in a lavish four-volume *L'Art du travestissement* (The Art of Fancy Dress) around 1880. On Saturday 5 November 1887, *The Era*, a newspaper famed for its theatrical coverage and one perhaps combed for inspiration by Holt, carried a claim on page seven, by the costumier John Simmons of Covent Garden, that he was the sole agent for Léon Sault's 'most exquisite' designs for costumes. This is a doubtful boast given the lack of stringent copyright regulations at the time, but the laxity worked in fancy dress's favour because fashion and fancy-dress plates from France – Paris being the polestar of extravagant dressing up – and, increasingly, from America quickly found their way into British publications, adding new characters to the repertoire. Costumes worn at the Liverpool Fancy Ball commemorating the visit of the Channel Fleet to the Mersey in 1863, some sixteen years prior to Holt's first edition, have been shown to replicate hand-coloured prints from the *Galerie dramatique.*[27] Liverpool was not exceptional: party-goers across the empire were already dressing up as characters that only later appeared in Holt's books.[28] We do not know if Holt had access to the vast reference libraries amassed by costumiers. By the 1930s, Nathans, for example, had assembled between five and six hundred costume books as well as their own invaluable back catalogue of original designs.

Even after its publication, Holt's directory did not always replace earlier sources. In 1888, the mayor of Blackburn's son, Joseph Appleby, celebrated his coming-of-age with a costume ball for four hundred guests. Staff at the Free Library there were apparently rushed off their feet by researchers requesting Planché as well as Kretschmer and Rohrbach's equally useful *Costume of All Nations* (1882).[29] Ball invitees were not only library borrowers. They were enthusiastic theatre-goers, circus aficionados, avid museum and art gallery visitors, devotees of the novel and browsers of the new spate of illustrated journals. All of these provided inspiration for fancy dress. However, the fact that Ardern Holt's book compressed such an array of original sources into one volume was much in its favour.

Holt's copious and tantalizing costume options were definitely part of each manual's appeal but, more than that, Holt linked up with Debenham & Freebody, a department store known for its range of clothing styles, to simplify the process of acquiring a costume. The famous emporium undertook to supply any outfit featured in the book, and sent out sketches, descriptions and samples of material post-free to party-going customers. The partnership of a well-known correspondent and a leading London shop was an astute business move. To help ensure some sort of proprietorship over the designs itemized by Ardern Holt, *Fancy Dresses Described* did not carry advertisements for other suppliers though the store did take out advertising space in similar publications to maximize its chances of competing for this lucrative market. Each edition of Holt's book for women's costume carried the Debenham & Freebody notice for made-to-order outfits as well as for material for home dressmaking. The enlarged final edition gave information about their Country Agency, outlining their facilities for provincial houses of business.[30]

Marie Schild was another author who wrote extensively about fancy dress. She was the editor of the *Brighton Courier of Fashion*, the *Millinery Journal* and the monthly *Journal of Parisian Dress Patterns and Needlework*, and she came to the subject with a practical knowledge of tailoring. From 1868, forerunners of today's paper patterns were included in her magazines.[31] Like Holt, she formed an advantageous partnership to further her business. She collaborated with the London print publisher Samuel Miller to produce her *Album of Fancy Costumes* (1881), *Old English Costumes* (1883), *Children's Fancy Costumes* (1884) and, though her name did not appear on it, *Male Character Costumes* (1884). Attesting to their appeal, all these books ran to several editions, their titles and subtitles not always tallying and changing over the years. In the introduction to the first title she tells us that her descriptions were based on Miller's own publications, together with his collection of French theatrical, national and allegorical costume prints, reinforcing the view of many at the time concerning the French derivation of one strand of British fancy dress. Schild's books are less wide-ranging than Holt's. There is still plenty of choice, however, with 44 varieties of 'Louis' (women's historic costume always referenced the reigning male monarch) included in the *Album of Fancy Costumes*. Weighted towards historic and national dress, Schild, like Holt, set out her fancy-dress books alphabetically, though her spin-off volume, *Old English Costumes* of 1883, is in narrative form and moves chronologically through the eras from ancient Britons to the nineteenth century, with details of the garments and specific historic characters set out at the end. This volume,

98 A page of illustrations from Marie Schild, *Male Character Costumes for Fancy Dress Balls and Private Theatricals* (1884). 'Playing Cards' showed off a gentleman's legs as did the now mostly forgotten 'Jean de Nivelle', a 15th-century French nobleman, the subject of an 1880 opera by Léo Delibes.

a foil to the overly French stance of her previous publication, tells us that the source was Knight's *British Costume* published by Bell & Sons. This is a less well-known provenance than Planché, for instance, but these kinds of books are a reminder of the intense interest the Victorians took in their past, even to the extent of dressing up as their forebears.

Moving on to the more practical aspects of making costumes, for one shilling and sixpence customers could acquire a coloured picture

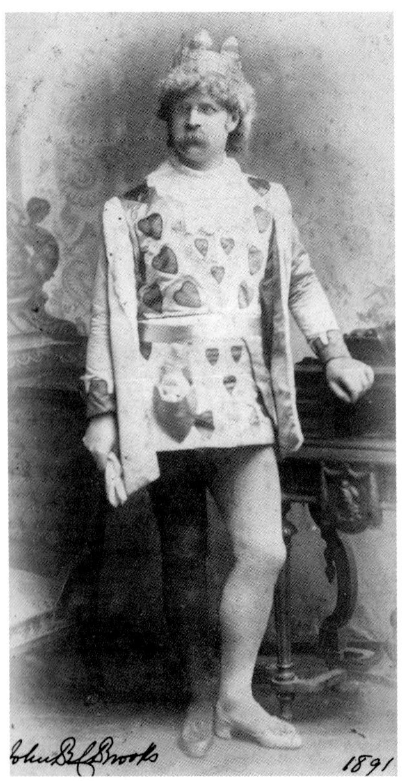

99 John Brooks dressed as the 'King of Hearts', photographed by Monsieur Sauvy of King Street, Manchester, 1891. The costume closely follows Marie Schild's suggestion with a heart-shaped pouch at the waist.

of most of the characters described in Schild's handbook for men.[32] This was a great advantage, though there were some accompanying illustrations (illus. 98 and illus. 99). Building on her magazine experience, her books on women's fancy dress and on English costume were even more obliging in providing proto-paper patterns for domestic production, whether by the prospective wearer, her servants or a local seamstress. Schild's 'paper models', as she called them, cost six shillings and sixpence and consisted of two parts: an exact representation of the costume made in coloured paper and a flat pattern in plain paper. This could be cut to fit the wearer and Schild recommended sending nine named measurements when ordering. In the absence of an illustrated wrapper for the paper pattern – these would become standard later – readers were advised to buy the relevant coloured print from Samuel Miller. Loose costume prints, the majority by unnamed artists, had been an affordable alternative to books from the seventeenth century, if not earlier. It seems amazing that two hundred to three hundred such plates could be sent out at any one time from Miller's London publishing establishment provided a guinea's worth was retained by the customer. From this we can perhaps presume a shared endeavour, with groups of party-goers clubbing together to view a selection of characters in anticipation of a ball. Miller's prints reached Australia courtesy of W. Watson, Schild's agent in Melbourne, who ensured that dressing up flourished in the Antipodes as it did in Britain.[33]

Plainly, pictures play an important part in how a costume is understood. Surviving fancy-dress garments and archive photographs of people wearing them tell us that dressmakers frequently copied the illustrations closely. But even as colour plates and more black-and-white images were added to later editions, the majority of dresses in Holt and Schild are not illustrated at all. All the illustrations are akin to fashion plates and in every respect represent an ideal. They are aspirational, designed to enhance the party-goer's refinement. They are also very much of their time, with body shapes altered over the decades according to prevailing fashion: evocations of bustles and hourglass silhouettes in the late 1870s and '80s giving way to flaring hemlines and leg-of-mutton sleeves in the 1890s, whatever the period or nationality of the costume. The pose of the illustrated figures communicates polished self-assurance, and this applies even where the costume does not naturally lend itself to elegance. 'The Hornet', for example, in high-heeled shoes with yellow bows, is as fashionably tasteful as any other outfit in *Fancy Dresses Described*.[34]

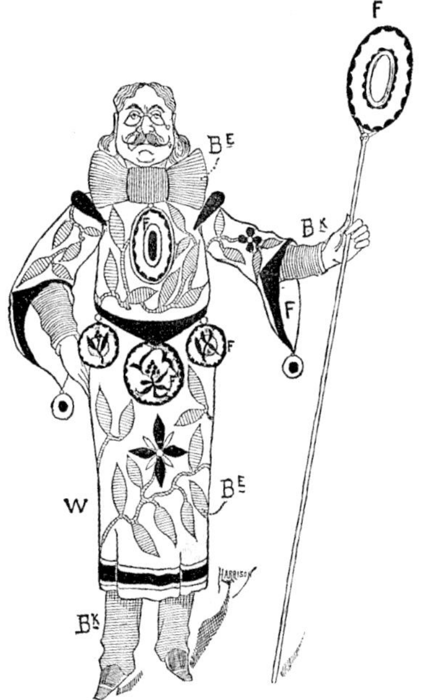

100 The 'China Maniac' from Charles Harrison, *Theatricals and Tableaux Vivants for Amateurs* (1882). Cardboard cut-out plates are suspended from the costume, which is designed to fit over an ordinary dress suit. The colour coding can be reversed to give the effect of Wedgwood china.

By contrast, Charles Harrison's own inventions in the 'Fancy Designs' section of his guide, *Theatricals and Tableaux Vivants for Amateurs*, published in London like all the other manuals, are much more robust and off-centre and 'can be made at home, and with a certain amount of novelty and effect'. He calls one of his characters the 'China Maniac' (illus. 100). Harrison's editorship of *Moonshine*, an illustrated comic paper, is germane to his mode of fancy-dress designs. Other

101 'The Willow Pattern Plate, or Blue China' from *Weldon's Fancy Dress for Ladies* (First Series), *c.* 1888. Linen bedspreads printed with the willow pattern were widely available and recommended for this costume.

waggish togs conceived by him were 'Woman's Rights', 'Poetaster', 'Combination of Ancient and Modern', 'Modern Mephistopheles' and 'Modern Sphinx'. As early as 1882, when Harrison published his book, we sense a move away from the discriminating refinement of Holt's outfits and a gesture towards street carnival and burlesque.

Weldon's Practical Fancy Dress for Ladies and *Weldon's Practical Fancy Dress for Children* ran to two series in the late 1880s and early 1900s, overlapping with Holt and Schild in both time and content. Like them they were reprinted and slightly changed over the years, sometimes omitting the term 'practical', and they flourished in a magazine-type format later in the twentieth century. The Weldons manuals, essentially catalogues of their own paper patterns, certainly improved on Holt's and Schild's arrangements. Every outfit is illustrated and the images still radiate a fashionable composure, with even 'the Willow Pattern Plate or Blue China' looking utterly unlike tableware and definitely nothing like Harrison's 'China Maniac' (illus. 101). As with Miller and Schild, Weldons operated out of premises off the Strand in Southampton Street and launched a mail-order service for their paper patterns. They embedded helpful details and making hints in the main descriptive text as well as giving the required yardage for each costume plus the price of a flat pattern. For three times that price, in addition to the flat pattern, Weldons offered a ready tacked one demonstrating how the garment pieces fitted together. Despite the paper pattern and the punctilious suggestions, attempting many of the costumes, for instance 'Magpie', was not for the faint-hearted. For some readers today this entry reads like a foreign language, with words such as 'kilting up', 'bertha', 'sarcanet' and 'bretelle' dimly understood at best (illus. 102).

Masquerade and Carnival: Their Customs and Costumes, a newcomer from across the Atlantic, was published in 1892 by Butterick. Like Weldons, they were early exponents of paper patterns, in fact pioneers of improvements to the technology though not the very first to devise such a boon to home dressmakers.[35] As with many other fancy-dress books, the illustrations show stylishly posed models in an array of outfits. Unlike most of its contemporaries, the Butterick book features men and women characters together on the same page, and the images are rounded and detailed (illus. 103). As with *Weldon's Practical Fancy Dress*, *Masquerade and Carnival* had more illustrations than either Holt or Schild, with the images close to the text. The thematic, rather than alphabetic, layout of this Butterick publication was to be followed by others in the twentieth century. *Masquerade and Carnival* reveals its transatlantic origins, with sections such as 'Martha Washington Balls and Tea-Parties' indicative of America's slightly different perspective on fancy dress.[36] 'Bat' was first included in the final edition of Ardern Holt in 1896 and, though it had appeared in the 1870s in *La Mode Illustrée*, Holt's bat was perhaps copied from *Masquerade and Carnival* as were several other Halloween and American-inspired outfits. This flying mammal would become very popular in Britain.

102 'Magpie' from *Weldon's Practical Fancy Dress for Ladies* (Second Series), *c.* 1889. The paper pattern does not include the magpie on the shoulder.

Mrs Aria's book, *Costume: Fanciful, Historical, Theatrical* of 1906, straddled several genres, as evidenced by the title. It included

THEIR CUSTOMS AND COSTUMES. 45

FIGURE No. 39.—TURK.—This costume is gorgeous in coloring and elaborate in detail. The robe is of bright yellow silk, figured with green and lined with red, and bordered with white fur.

FIGURE No. 39.—TURK.

The mantle is of gray woolen goods lined with red silk and bordered with black or brown fur, and is fastened at the back so that it will not slip off. The long stockings are turquoise-blue, and the shoes are of yellow kid decorated with small bright-red masks. The girdle is blue silk of the same tint as the stockings, and has an immense imitation ruby or carbuncle at the center. The turban is of blue gauze made a la Turk, and is heavily decorated with plumes of red, yellow, gray, green and blue, together with strings of glass beads which imitate jewels.

FIGURE No. 40.—HOLLAND PEASANT COSTUME.—Round full skirt of brown or gray woolen goods, with sleeveless bodice of the same decorated with fancy braid or ribbon in some bright contrasting tint. The neck is only slightly low at the back where it is of oval shape. The skirt may also be trimmed with rows of braid or ribbon. Shirt waist or blouse of soft white muslin, with neck and wristbands embroidered with red. Long white apron of white or blue woolen, trimmed with a gay bordering of printed material or embroidery.

The cotton bonnet is made of a very thick cordonette, starched and ironed, and then skilfully folded as represented, and held in shape by long, silver-headed pins. These caps are worn by the peasants of Norway, Finland and the northern part of Holland.

FIGURE No. 40.—HOLLAND PEASANT COSTUME

103 A page from *Masquerade and Carnival: Their Customs and Costumes* (1892), with illustrations and descriptive text for 'Turk' and 'Holland Peasant Costume'. This Butterick publication contains detailed drawings for every entry.

some images, both coloured and monochrome, spread throughout the text. Her illustrator, Percy Anderson (1851–1928), was a notable stage designer who worked for all the high-profile companies. Eliza Davis Aria (1866–1931) herself was steeped in the theatrical world, and her family connections linked her to the literary and artistic luminaries of the day.[37] She launched her own fashion monthly, *The World of Dress*, and as a gossip columnist and an editor of fashion pages her words appeared as privileged information. Hers was not a book to turn to for an extended list of possible roles. The greater part of it is taken up with a chronological history of dress, certainly useful for some ball attendees, and only one chapter, 'On Fancy Dress', pinpoints party wear. Mrs Aria's words, sometimes verging on the rhapsodic, are much more descriptive than Holt's or Schild's:

> A good idea for a fancy-dress ball, if not one based perhaps upon the truest spirit of poetry, is 'Greens'; chiffon or silk of many shades of green, with a head-dress in the shape of a cabbage. Very successful, though not inexpensive, is the Oyster dress, composed of a very thin white satin lined with pink satin, adorned at discretion with fringes of pearls, while

104 A young woman dressed in cabbage leaves, Hellidon, Northamptonshire, 1896–1920.

> a pink chiffon chemisette is gauged to admiration upon the draped white satin bodice, and the coiffure of the wearer is surmounted by a coronet of oyster shells set on a bandeau of pale-pink chiffon, with a floating veil of a deeper pink.[38]

The cabbage costume worn by a fancy dresser at Hellidon, Northamptonshire, was perhaps not what Mrs Aria had in mind (illus. 104). However, she did suggest other idiosyncratic characters including 'Gooseberry-Fool', 'Flames', 'The Imaginative Man', 'Wallflower' and 'The Seville Orange', each evaluated for suitability and effect (illus. 105).[39] Giving counsel and passing judgement were an innate part of all these fancy-dress guides and Mrs Aria was no exception:

> In deciding upon a costume . . . the first thought of the reveller should be to secure the becoming and the suitable, and to be successful the choice should be mainly influenced by his or her personality. I quite realise the problem to be a difficult one, since happily we have not the gift given to us to see ourselves as others see us, else should we never meet a podgy Mephistopheles bulging out of his clothes, nor an attenuated Juno . . . Visits to the National Gallery, and an afternoon spent at the Wallace Collection, will prove themselves at once a profit and a pleasure, and an easy guide towards the selection of the appropriate dress. It is advisable on such occasions to be accompanied by the kind friend who, without fear to risk a reproach, will counsel with all wisdom, and temper your ambitions to your personality.[40]

We might expect originality to be a foundational tenet of fancy dress but few of these guides comment wholly in its favour. Aria summed up the prevailing attitude: 'At a fancy-dress ball the costume

105 'The Seville Orange' from Mrs Aria, *Costume: Fanciful, Historical, Theatrical* (1906). Velvet streamers and padded oranges are applied to the silk dress and used to bind up the hair.

which is merely original and not pretty should be condemned except when the novelty prize is the desideratum of the occasion.'[41]

Aria's book, six years on from *Weldon's*, carries no commercial advertising or mail-order facility but includes practical suggestions to 'obviate some difficulties of those who fret their hour on the stage or at the fancy-dress ball'.[42] Her main contribution to the viability of construction revolves around suitable materials. She recommends Japanese crêpe for a rainbow and she is a great exponent of draped and

106 'Sir Walter Raleigh', the gentleman's winner of the Fancy Dress Photo Competition run by the popular magazine *Pick-Me-Up*, 27 January 1894. There was a special mention for Mr Will Sibley of Southampton for his '*Pick-Me-Up* costume', presumably a paper outfit made from the magazine itself.

wound chiffon.[43] This light-as-air material was not confined to fancy dress and even appeared in the title of a book on fashion, *The Cult of Chiffon* (1902) by Mrs Eric Pritchard (Marian Elizabeth Pritchard, 1869–1945). The fabric's soft and delicate feel was thought to be commensurate with womanly charm, and much female fancy dress of the time aspired to emulate this virtue. Wearing costumes with grace was deemed imperative for certain costume balls even as the grotesque and the comic came into play. This emphasis on decorous attractiveness permeated society, with fancy dress just one of the domains where this precept held sway. Germane to fancy dress, if not specifically about it, earlier books such as *Dress as a Fine Art* (1854) by Mrs Merrifield (Mary Philadelphia Merrifield), and two books by Mrs Haweis (Mary Eliza Haweis), *The Art of Beauty* (1878) and *The Art of Dress* (1879), reinforced these concepts and left an imprint on the work of later women writers like Aria and Pritchard.[44]

We have seen that, by the early years of the twentieth century, street carnival was as popular as the costume party. The books described above were initially aimed at the latter but could be adapted for the former and, partly as a result of carnival's prevalence, home costume-making became routine during the lifetime of these pre-First World War guides. They were by no means the only publications to cover fancy dress. By the early 1880s, *The Ladies Treasury* published a supplement on original fancy-dress-ball costumes which was less staid than Holt.[45] Other serial magazines about dressing fashionably on a budget regularly incorporated fancy dress that could be adapted to several kinds of occasions. *Fashions for All: The Ladies' Journal of Practical Fashions*, for example, had a particularly long life (it appeared from April 1908 until 1937, continuing in production during the First World War) and so offers a good vantage point from which to view the dress concerns of the day. This affordable and informative magazine consistently offered fancy-dress ideas and patterns.[46] Another publication, *Pick-Me-Up*, a weekly that ran from 1888 to 1909, dealt in lightweight social and political comment and also held several fancy-dress photography competitions. Readers were asked to send in pictures of themselves in character costume, though there was no suggestion that these should be home-made. In 1894, Miss Phyllis Marlowe, posing flamboyantly as 'The Dancing Girl', secured the Ladies' Prize and Mr Cottrell, looking serious and moody as 'Sir Walter Raleigh', won Best Gentleman (illus. 106).[47] Cottrell's outfit certainly looks professionally made.

Domestic production did not entirely supplant the work of the costumier and tailor. We know that paper patterns and sewing machines were originally designed for professionals who, as a result of these technical innovations, were able to produce more styles at a cheaper price than previously. As a wider cross-section of the population followed the craze for dressing up, several once-exclusive theatrical firms broadened their appeal so that, by the end of the nineteenth century, buying or hiring from a costumier was not solely for the well off. Creating a fancy dress at home, however, could undoubtedly be a less expensive option depending on the materials used. Even using a commercial paper pattern, home-made garments could be unique in colour and detailing. As we saw above, suppliers of all sorts both generated and fed this increasing demand for fantasy creations, and there was a near-miraculous cornucopia of stuff to tempt any dressmaker. People of limited means were no longer shaded out by wealthy merrymakers.

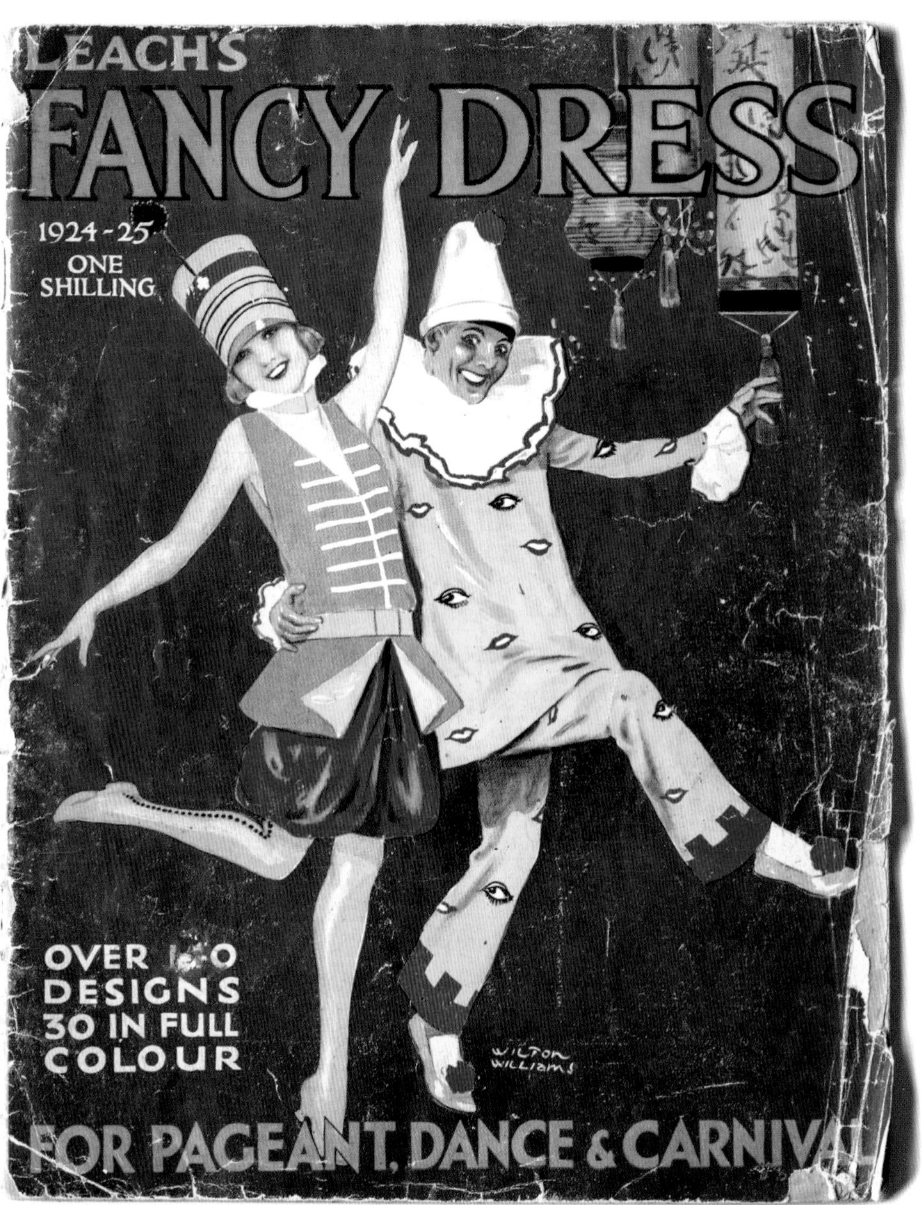

107 A 'Glad Eye Pierrot' and a young woman as a fanciful hussar on the front cover of *Leach's Fancy Dress* (1924–5).

Seven

THE BUSINESS OF FANCY DRESS: THE TWENTIETH CENTURY

The First World War marks an inexact watershed in the history of fancy dress. Celebrations at the end of hostilities were sometimes hastily put together and many costumes were piecemeal and dreamed up with whatever was close to hand. Despite this, victory kindled a renewed desire to dress up, and fancy dress, while retaining much that was deemed traditional, took on new features and embraced a modernity that was commensurate with the Jazz Age and the spirit of voguish contemporaneity. The way people chose and acquired their costumes changed. It became much more acceptable to improvise a perfunctory disguise. It did not necessarily have to be beautifully constructed or finished in every detail. Guides to fancy dress were no longer primarily in book form but were magazines, larger in format. Wordy texts gave way to illustrations, now with more colour, so that by the 1920s images were paramount in helping revellers shape their ideas about party attire. Moreover, the publishers of these titles produced their own paper patterns of all the styles illustrated. The magazines were full of joyful, costumed party-goers and the covers epitomized the change in tone (illus. 107). Models were young and lithe. Many of their costumes have low necklines, though the flat-chested female figures – the *garçonne* look – are boyishly devoid of any cleavage.[1] Clothes are much more revealing and worn with some abandon. Among a number of such magazines – the market was a crowded one – *The Lady Book of Fancy Dresses*, *Leach's Fancy Dress* and *Weldon's Fancy Dress* were popular imprints. Not all of them are dated or paginated, though they seem to have been issued at least annually.

The Lady magazine, founded in 1885 and perceived today as rather starchy, published its sixpenny fancy-dress supplements during the 1920s. It included sections for children's costume but only the occasional man's outfit. Leach-Way and Weldons both published magazines (the *Lady's Companion* and *Weldon's Ladies' Journal* respectively) with an emphasis on fashion, and they, too, produced specialist fancy-dress publications. Both businesses were best known for their paper patterns. *Leach's Fancy Dress* and *Leach's Fancy Dress for Children* ran from the early 1920s to the mid-1930s and were snappy, even racy, by comparison with *The Lady*. Its possible predecessor, *Mrs Leach's Fancy Ball Costumes for Children and Young Ladies*, was published in the mid-1880s. Also building on the success of earlier decades, *Weldon's* catalogues had varying titles, less explanatory text than previously, and boasted around three hundred designs in each issue. All these publications are attractive, with words and pictures differently juxtaposed across the page (illus. 108).

Although the design of these catalogues is as far away from Ardern Holt as it is possible to be, many of the characters are recognizable from way back and reflect an unchanging attachment to a set of dependable outfits. Others are definitely new, while some *seem* to be new but are largely reimagined or renamed for the times and given a fresh shine. The many variations of Pierrot and the insistent inclusion of the character throughout all these pattern magazines in the 1920s and '30s is astonishing and the phenomenon warrants separate comment in Chapter

Eight. Along with the ever-present Pierrot, the decades after the First World War witnessed a different genus of costume encroaching on the *poudré* outfits, the orientalist fantasies and the pristine peasant frocks. We saw that in the nineteenth century, French-flavoured fashions held a particularly emotive draw for readers of Ardern Holt and Marie Schild, and in the 1920s, France again set the tone with new patterns that were encapsulated in the word 'bohemian'. The universal and abiding appeal of Puccini's opera *La Bohème*, first staged in Britain at Manchester's Theatre Royal in 1897, continued to buoy up people's notion of the unconventional and marginalized. It is worth noting that by 1913, Kalderash gypsies from Eastern Europe were encamped across the British Isles, viewed with suspicion but also seen as persuasively exotic with their sweeping long skirts and gold-coin jewellery.[2] So, 'Gypsy' continued to hold a fascination, and 'French art student', 'French artist', 'French workman', 'Quartier Latin', 'Montmartre' and 'Apache Dance' all make an appearance as fancy dress for both genders, women now wearing trousers that were no longer Eastern fantasies but uncompromising in their masculine cut.

In 1924, ever up-to-the-minute, *Leach's Fancy Dress* featured a trouser-wearing character called 'Miss Bohemia' who was retitled 'Madcap' the following year, accentuating its affinity with the dynamism of the Roaring Twenties. By the same token, 'Apache Dance' also typified the era. Originally from the Parisian underworld, this brutal and electrifying dance involved dramatic gestures and fight-like moves. A version formulated by French professional dancers was being performed in London by 1908.[3] Its magnetic appeal continued into the mid-century and couples clothed as 'Apache dancers' were quickly enlisted into the ranks of fancy dress. In the *Leach's* version, the man sports checked trousers, an orange shirt (orange was the keynote colour for fancy dress in the interwar period) and a peaked cap worn askew. The girl has tousled hair and wears a knee-length skirt. Young women

108 Page from *Leach's Fancy Dress* (1927–30), with 'Chinese Pagoda', 'June Rose,' 'Pierrette de la Lune' and 'Harvest Maid'.

NEW FANCY DRESSES

AN APACHE
Patt. No. 37,973

PATTERN No. 37,973.—What girl can ever resist the allurement of the apache? The trousers and cap require $3\frac{1}{4}$ yards of 27-inch-wide black velvet, while the plain white blouse takes $1\frac{1}{8}$ yards of 38-inch-wide silk. A highly coloured silk handkerchief is tied around the neck.

PATTERN No. 37,975.—Here is an ideal fancy dress for the fluffy type of girl. The bodice and top of the skirt require $1\frac{1}{2}$ yards of 36-inch wide yellow taffetas and the pleated head-dress-frill and skirt take $2\frac{3}{4}$ yards of 36-inch-wide flounce lace.

THE FAN
Patt. No. 37,975

AN EASTERN PRINCESS
Patt. No. 37,965

PATTERN No. 37,965.—The Eastern Princess is always a favourite at a carnival dance, and small wonder, considering her charm. She wears a gold tissue bodice and pale yellow silk trousers over which are arranged loops of gold and green ribbon. A swathed gold and green cap forms a magnificent headdress. Allow $2\frac{1}{2}$ yards of 31-inch-wide silk, and $1\frac{3}{8}$ yards of 20-inch-wide gold tissue with $\frac{1}{4}$ yard each of 40-inch green and gold materials for head-dress.

PATTERN No. 37,968.—This early Victorian posy should adorn the dark-haired and lustrous-eyed girl. The demure pantaloons and bodice take $2\frac{1}{4}$ yards of 38-inch-wide silver sateen. The standout skirt of book-muslin covered with flowers is edged with silver lace of which 7 yards 8 inches wide, are wanted for entire trimming.

AN EARLY VICTORIAN POSY
Patt. No. 37,968

PATTERN No. 37,969.—Perhaps the most original idea is the Stumpy Umbrella. Her skirt is made of black sateen, lined with another material for stiffness, and is caught at top on to a slip of brown sateen to represent a stick. A broad band is topped by umbrella spikes. Allow 5 yards of 38-inch-wide black sateen and the same of another colour.

Paper Patterns of these designs are cut in 36-inch bust sizes only.

Particulars of prices will be found on the last page of this issue.

AN UMBRELLA
Patt. No. 37.969

109 The 'Apache' outfit appears alongside 'Fan', 'Umbrella', 'Early Victorian Posy' and 'Eastern Princess' in *Fashions for All: The Ladies' Journal of Practical Fashions*, December 1925.

could appear as an 'Apache' without a male partner, dressed in trousers and a gamine cap over bobbed hair (illus. 109). The cigarette, previously a stand-alone abstract costume promoted in Holt's 1896 guide, was now used as a chic appendage of interwar modernity, adding lustre to 'Apache' and several other fancy-dress characters.

As well as androgynous outfits, scanty and body-hugging clothes were also more to the fore in this period. 'Eve' and 'Devil Fish' were provocative choices for *The Lady Book of Fancy Dresses* from the 1920s and '30s. 'Eve' wears a flesh-coloured bodice and 'Devil Fish', an octopus with tentacled skirt, is attired in a strappy top with a pair of titillating eyes painted right over the nipple area (illus. 110). This audacious many-armed mollusc was up against stiff competition. From the 1930s, provocative garments with barely there skirts and shorts were conspicuous in pattern books. Even a character called 'Dinner at Eight' was an excuse for a sleeveless tailcoat and tight-fitting shorts.[4]

110 'Devil Fish' alongside 'Pierrot' in *The Lady Book of Fancy Dresses* (c. 1924).

These new-style publications were upbeat with plenty of variety in the way the pages were presented. The short text is chatty and exhortatory: 'Dress to express your temperament!', 'Doesn't the dull girl become positively scintillating when she can get right out of her (apparently) dull self?'[5] Matching or complementary pairs became a particular feature, perhaps designed to get reluctant men into costume. More wide-ranging than Holt's 'Sisters', *Leach's* featured 'Two's Company' and 'Partners Please', for

111 'Querette and Pierre-Oh!', a version of 'Question and Answer', was popular in the 1920s along with the Pierrot craze. Some versions had an exclamation mark as well as a question mark.

example, and a typical colour spread from 1924 showed 'A Rodeo Couple', 'A Pair of Puppets', 'Harlequin and Columbine' and 'Question and Answer'. This last costume was later recycled as 'Querette and Pierre-Oh!' (illus. 111). Renaming and reusing were common, as was arranging characters in groups: 'Four Fascinating Ways of Being Quite Different' and 'Feminine Costumes with Bunchy Skirts'.[6] These groups

112 George Johnson as the 'Striding Man', the brand image of Johnnie Walker whisky, Shanghai, *c*. 1925.

were the successors to the quadrilles of an earlier era though the classifications are mostly meaningless. The illustrations of costumed young people clustered together on the page projected a highly charged camaraderie, sending out the message that fancy dress was a sociable and fun activity.

Another theme, not new to post-First World War costume but now more overt and widespread, was the addition of outfits directly sponsored by commercial firms. George Johnson, a British architect living in Shanghai, kitted himself out as the impeccable 'Striding Man', the brand image of Johnnie Walker whisky (illus. 112). Children and

113 Costume designs for Chivers Marmalade, Odol toothpaste, Ovaltine, OK Sauce and Yardley's Perfumes from *Weldon's Fancy Dress for Children*, 1940s.

young women were notably implicated in this kind of fancy dress, with some costumes being particularly cumbersome. 'Heinz 57', dressed in a crinoline and wearing a cucumber on her head, was the most bizarre of all from *Weldon's* in the 1930s and, over the years, *Leach's* and *Weldon's* included several pages of such brand costumes (illus. 113). Manufacturers frequently took out separate advertising space in the magazines and offered patterns, material or stencils free of charge. Fancy dress was ambushed by contemporary economic life and thrived on competition.

Prizes were not unknown at early balls and parties and became commonplace with the coming of carnival, but they were elevated to a more urgent level when business sponsorship increased. Suppliers of fancy dress picked up on 'Costumes That Will Win Prizes' and recommended outfits of all kinds, not just advertising brand names, that might come first in competition. Virgie Grais, a theatrical and general costumier, claimed to have provided 41 first prizes from 41 hirings and 32 second prizes from 28 hirings, proving their customers used the same costume several times over before returning it.[7] An advertisement for the costumier Charles Fox included a recommendation from a satisfied customer: 'I ordered Eastern Dancer. I was more than surprised at the cut, originality, delightful blending of colours and quality of materials used. I secured three firsts, and two second prizes out of seven dances.'[8] Mr Coatesworth of Staircross near Barnsley in South Yorkshire was a fancy-dress addict, winning two hundred prizes across several different counties for the same 'Red Indian Chief' ensemble.[9]

Coatesworth's 'Red Indian' was a tried-and-tested fancy-dress wardrobe favourite but alongside this a desire to be different and audacious characterized the era. Novelty notion costumes were plentiful and attempted to copy real objects more closely than before. Fancy dressers posed for the camera with tolerable finesse despite ungainly outfits and top-heavy hats (illus. 114). *Leach's* pattern book reflects this with oddball confections like 'Sugar Stick', 'Crème de Menthe', by Leach's own admission 'an elegant absurdity in green satin', and 'Cherry Brandy', 'a coquettish costume', all from 1927 (illus. 115). A 1930 article confirmed the tendency to discard personality costumes in favour of inanimate things and mentions British industries, railway trains and their destinations, jewels of the empire and eclipse.[10]

We have no statistics about the take-up of these magazines' paper patterns but we should entertain the idea that the publications might at least have encouraged party-goers, who now came from a range of

114 A young girl dressed as HP Sauce, 1920s. The costume alludes to the manufacturer's slogan, 'Mary had a little lamb with lots of HP Sauce'.

115 'Crème de Menthe', 'Cherry Brandy', 'Sugar Stick' and 'Gondolier' from *Leach's Fancy Dress* (1927).

classes, to be bold in their costume choices even if they did not follow the pictured suggestions. Charles Fox's prize-winning 'Eastern Dancer' and Mr Coatesworth's 'Red Indian Chief' show us that perennial favourites were still very much in play and newspaper reports of fancy-dress affairs, both metropolitan and parochial, continued to list time-honoured standards as prize-winners. The absurd and zany intermixed with the conventional, this jumbled combination more than ever one of the most recognizable characteristics of fancy dress.

As with the early guides, fancy dress followed the fads and fashions of the day with straight styles, dropped waists and shorter skirts in the 1920s. When Coco Chanel allegedly invented the suntan on a cruise in 1923, a fancy dress named 'Sun Bathing' followed in *Leach's* in 1931. Fancy dress in the next decade was inflected with a Hollywood slinkiness and several character costumes imitated celluloid stars, as we saw in Chapter Five. An outfit called 'Film Fan' adopted the cinema theme, with postcards of the stars trimming the hem of a pyjama suit and making a play on words with a fan attached at the waist.[11] *Weldon's* included designs chosen and modelled by famous film stars themselves. Clara Bow (1905–1965), the original 'It Girl' with sex appeal, was photographed wearing her favourite white satin 'Folly' dress: 'I love the cheeky ruffle of crisp tarlatan, the impish black pompoms, and pert clown's hat,' she is quoted as saying.[12]

Despite the pairing of designs with paper patterns, home-made costumes did not entirely oust hiring and buying, and firms offering ready-made fancy dress continued to flourish. One of these was John Barran of Leeds, credited with inventing ready-to-wear at the end of the nineteenth century. Children's fancy dress was one of their specialities, and the firm seems to have gone on making it at least until the Second World War.[13] General outfitters at the cheaper end of the clothing market also offered fancy dress at reasonable prices. By 1923, Gamages, a much-favoured London store on the edge of the City of London away from the classier Oxford Street shops, claimed to have the largest stock of fancy dress in England. Those living outside London could use its legendary mail-order service.[14] Burkinshaw, perhaps the biggest theatrical tailor and costumier elsewhere, operated in Liverpool from 1870 to 1939. Their advertisements in *The Lady Book of Fancy Dresses* in the mid-1920s listed a selection of the firm's many lines: armlets and wristlets, braid, coins for gypsy costumes, crooks with silver-plated top sticks, light and dark grapes, Harlequin and Jazz prints, hoop earrings, hose, large black felt hats, icicles, jewels to sew on, leno for Columbine frocks, gold and silver leaves, mittens, velvet and silk patches, poke bonnets, pompoms, ruffs, Russian boots, sabots, skullcaps, sashing, spangled trimming, sandals, snake bracelets, tinsel gauze, Jazz and Shock wigs. Multifarious pompoms and assorted wings of every pattern are the most frequently mentioned fancy-dress peripherals in stockists' advertisements but 'Harold Lloyd spectacles' come close behind, proof again of the reach of Hollywood – Lloyd (1893–1971) was a notable silent film comedian – and of the transformative effect of one appendage.

The tendency to publicize the adjuncts to fancy dress rather than the actual clothes was in step with a more do-it-yourself approach, though the prevalence of home dressmaking generally as a practice at this time poses some statistical challenges and the numbers engaged in it are by no means clear. Fancy dressers, carried along in the slipstream of such a liberality of materials, could buy relevant accessories but sometimes needed help and encouragement to create the actual garments. Making them was potentially enjoyable though we cannot assume that home-made items always brought pleasure to either the maker or wearer.[15] Many publications recognize this dilemma and *The Lady Book of Fancy Dresses*, mindful of the criticism levelled at some home-made items regarding fit, proffered costume patterns cut to special measurements as well as patterns made up to the customer's own design. The gentle reminders, and in some cases quite detailed instructions, dispersed throughout each issue of *The Lady* fancy-dress magazine helped to minimize mistakes when using the pattern, and confirm that at least some women were not confident in their abilities to turn material into clothing, even fancy costumes. As an acknowledgement of the work involved, 'best homemade costume' appeared regularly as a judging category: at the Steyning Cricket Club Carnival in 1932 the winners of that section were Miss M. Banfield as 'harvest' and Mr B. Hughes as 'Indian chief'. The runners-up were 'brigand', 'shepherdess', 'things of the past' and 'bear tamer'.[16]

Though eccentric and short-term fabrications might plausibly bypass stringent tailoring operations, the level of skill required for some of the costumes, with their tiers and frills and picot hems, was considerable. To meet the challenge of women who were increasingly juggling work outside the home with domestic duties, *Leach's* offered ready-cut-out Pierrot and Pierrette costumes several times in the mid-1930s. In 1933, impromptu costumes which did not need paper patterns at all were featured. In the same issue, a punchy paragraph enjoined readers to contrive a striking and becoming dress for half-a-crown, utilizing cast-off clothing, a rag bag of scraps and cheap white cotton and crêpe dyed to the required colour. Other quickly put-together outfits were suggested in 1922: 'Dinner Table' is improvised with a napkin as a headdress, two tablecloths and cutlery from a penny bazaar, while 'Restless Night' is portrayed as a man in pyjamas with a doll and a feeding bottle.[17] And into this economy drive steps Sigmund Freud, whose ideas on the interior self, like fancy dress, were quickly popularized. A section on spur-of-the-moment fancy dress in *The Lady Book of Fancy Dresses* admits that 'let's pretend' is a theme for the psychoanalyst but goes on to recommend the humble bath towel for dressing up in Eastern disguise on a wet day at a seaside boarding house.[18]

The little economies and labour-saving strategies can be seen as part of a much bigger picture of industrial and financial decline following on the Wall Street Crash of 1929. The Depression years adversely affected the publishing trade, and all magazines were reduced in format and carried less colour. *Leach's*, perhaps more so than the other publications, offers up a chronicle of changing times. Pressing issues of the day were confronted head on. Fancy dress was adjusted to include portrayals of the negative, external forces at work in society during the 1930s: 'Tariff Wall' (a red dress with white tape lines for bricks), 'Sacked' (a brown dress gathered in at the neck), 'Smash and Grab' (a white dress with black sateen 'holes' filled with cut-out pictures of watches and jewellery), 'Pawnshop' (cheap jewellery tacked onto an everyday dress and a hat of three golden balls) and 'Gangster' (flashy jewellery and a toy pistol).[19] A common-sense approach for the less affluent who wanted to dress up is captured around the same time in a Bournemouth newspaper. It urged readers to stipulate economy on party invitations by limiting expenditure to a named sum or asking friends to wear a fancy headdress with ordinary evening clothes.[20]

Though the theme of economic restriction cannot be missed in *Leach's* pattern books and newspaper articles, there is never any suggestion that fancy dress itself is inappropriate for straitened times. In 1930, a column called 'Earning a Living' by Constance Coventry recommended a costumier business as a profitable venture for artistic women, and in 1933, *The Sphere*, perhaps over-optimistically, even suggested that the popularity of fancy dress was a sign of returning prosperity.[21]

Books, whose main subject was general dressmaking and housekeeping, frequently included fancy dress and offered advice on making it inexpensively. This was particularly true where children were concerned. Agnes M. Miall, an author of over fifty novels, plays, etiquette and needlework books, and even a volume on fortune-telling, made sure to include fancy dress in her *Making Clothes for Children*, published in 1934 by a firm associated with many teach-yourself titles, Pitman. Minimal expenditure is stressed and, despite the availability of paper

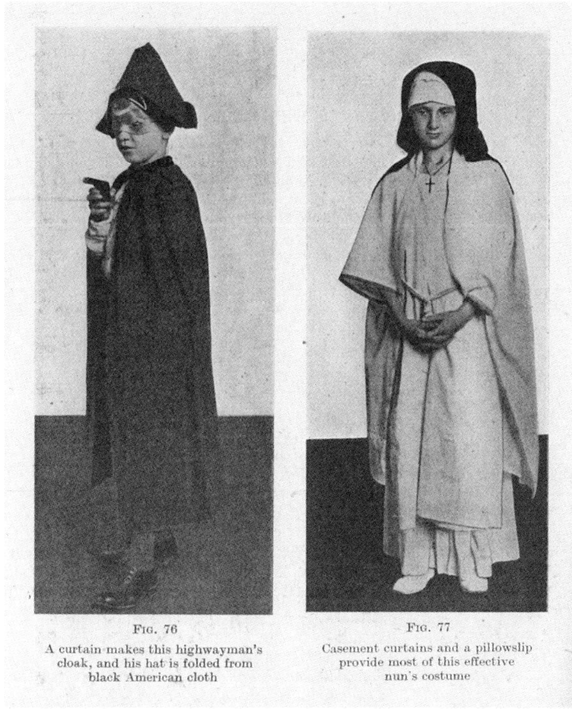

116 Curtains and pillowslips are recommended for making costumes in Agnes M. Miall, *Making Clothes for Children* (1934).

patterns at this period, Agnes Miall sees the creation of fancy dress as a matter of flair, with the resourceful reader's prior dressmaking knowledge coming to the fore to improvise costumes without a pattern (illus. 116). She gives lots of examples of what she terms 'costume trunk conversions': white summer frocks cut economically into aprons, fichus, mob caps and blouses for peasant costume, plus faded and worn curtains for skirts, cloaks and period dress. She writes:

> Silver foil saved from cigarette and chocolate boxes may be pasted over buckram to make glittering armour and crowns, or wrapped round wooden swords and fairies' wands . . . balls

> of string or macramé may be knitted into chain armour and painted with aluminium paint.[22]

An illustrated article in *Wife and Home* in 1933 gives us another insight into the resourcefulness of amateur fancy-dress fabricators in hard times. 'Let the Kiddies Dress Up' stresses the ease with which attractive outfits can be produced with just a small outlay of money: simple tacking stitches and a hot iron transform cretonne left over from curtains into a pirate's outfit, and scarlet crêpe paper pleated onto a tape waistband makes a gypsy skirt, though clearly some dexterity is involved. Although the article does include some bona fide dress-making, not all of it very simple, its recommendations for a bride, for instance, relies on gathering together and recasting things from around the house. Reiterating the racist attitude towards non-white subjects of the British empire, 'the bride's' brother, it is suggested, could be dressed as an 'Indian student' with the sideboard runner twisted into a turban.[23]

The catchword of all these publications is ingenuity. The concept is inseparable from fancy dress and, in the interwar period, the term can be seen as a cover for financial hardship. Working people, especially those living in the northern parts of the British Isles, were most affected by the economic slump, but a lingering affluence among the upper class was disclosed by uninterrupted glittering fancy-dress balls which kept the genre in the public eye. Elite balls certainly still made the news, and regional newspapers carried copy about them from their London correspondents. The *Western Morning News,* reporting on the Galaxy Ball of 1929, thought the event provided new ideas for the provincial dress-maker, who was, of course, described as 'ingenious'. 'New Moon', 'The Evening Star' and 'The Sun' were singled out as adaptable examples.[24]

Cecil Beaton, the renowned chronicler of twentieth-century fashion and one of the prime movers behind many of these *beau monde* balls, worked with a rich clientele who partied on apparently regardless of economic hard times. Beaton himself took to fancy dress like a duck to water and is pictured in several guises over the years. As a man unlikely to subscribe to *Leach's* or to need tips from a local newspaper, he nonetheless utilized commonplace materials to enwrap his society sitters. His sister, Nancy, posing as a 'Shooting Star' for the Galaxy Ball, sparkles in scrunched-up cellophane and foil. Likewise, another sister, Baba, and two beautiful companions effervesce as a trio of soapsuds surrounded by balloons for the Living Poster Ball of 1930 (illus. 117).[25] Elsewhere he even utilized wood shavings, and in his 'Suggestions for Fancy Dress', published in British *Vogue* in 1937, he wrote:

> Nowadays an effective grandeur can only be legitimately achieved with everyday utensils, and materials being used for purposes for which they were not meant. Steel wool pot-cleaners, egg-beaters, egg-separators, dish-cloths, tin moulds and patent hangers all make excellent costume trimming.[26]

The transformative power of these slightly tongue-in-cheek recommendations is uncertain, though the consummate designing skills of Cecil Beaton could no doubt have conjured up something spellbinding with them.

At a less stellar level of society, others were certainly inventive in their use of the everyday. The material most associated with fancy dress is crêpe paper, humble and inexpensive. Cecil Beaton might have used it more had it caught the light in his lens, but others found its matte surface in a kaleidoscope of colours ideal for costume-making. Its story is worth telling, for fancy dress and crêpe paper, manufactured from sized and crinkled tissue, have an almost symbiotic relationship (illus. 118). From its inception as a viable craft material – it was cut and shaped into artificial flowers and paper napkins, and used to festoon halls,

117 Baba Beaton, Wanda Baillie-Hamilton and Lady Bridget Poulett photographed by Cecil Beaton as the Soapsuds Group at the Living Poster Ball, 1930.

118 A group of girls in crêpe paper frocks with cut filigree hems, Horsham, Surrey, 1920s.

homes, bicycles and cars – crêpe has had a close connection with artifice and with celebration, two sentiments that can certainly be applied to fancy dress. Backtracking a little here to 1895, the Lancashire paper-manufacturing firm of James R. Crompton added 'crepe and crinkled tissue in 24 art shades' to their list of specialized papers.[27] This date accords with Ardern Holt's first very brief mention of crêpe paper in the sixth and final edition of *Fancy Dresses Described*, published a year later. It was perhaps too recent a product in 1896 to feature extensively in Holt's alphabetical compendium of costume but by the twentieth century, crêpe paper was becoming one of the mainstays of British fancy-dress production, taking its cue from the United States.

The paper's many advantages as a material for decorations of all kinds, not just costumes, were commended in a bountiful selection of magazines, catalogues, explanatory pamphlets and instruction books produced by the American firm Dennison, whose crêpe paper rolls, products and publications made significant inroads into Britain. The market was well primed for this colourful crêpe and, after a gestation

119 A young woman dressed as a rose, her skirt made from crêpe paper stiffened with wire, photographed by A. C. Clarkson, Birkenhead, 1925–35.

period, its flat packages became a familiar commodity in stationers' shops, its eminent suitability for fancy dress established. A paper-clad wearer might experience some ticklish moments: crêpe tears if a line of stitching is too near the edge and it wilts in a rainstorm, but the rustle of crêpe flounces and the fluttering of crêpe ribbons gave the costumes great appeal.[28] Crêpe paper's tractable surfaces could be sculpted into all manner of curved contours and snipped to render picot or filigree effects. Stretched across wire or cardboard, with only a few dabs of glue to hold it over the framework, crêpe paper mutated into wings for angels, ears for bats, beaks for blackbirds or petals for flower skirts (illus. 119). None of the edges needed hemming, and creasing or fluting the paper against the grain gave a ruffled finish.

By the early 1900s, Dennison was keen to make its name synonymous with crêpe paper. In 1909, one of its greatest marketing opportunities came on the opening day of Harry Gordon Selfridge's grand Oxford Street department store. Miss Elizabeth Bissell, one of two women sent from Dennison Art Department to design and oversee a Dennison's window display for Selfridges, records how the British public are 'crazy about the paper work' and 'the thing is undoubtedly a success'.[29] Dennison's *Art and Decoration in Crepe and Tissue Paper*, a title that would run into 23 editions and must have been on sale at Selfridges, was followed by other Dennison booklets devoted to particular themes.

120 Page from Dennison's booklet, *How to Make Crepe Paper Costumes* (1925).

Aware, and perhaps even apprehensive, that consumers might not understand how best to transform crêpe paper into three-dimensional garments, *How to Make Crepe Paper Costumes* combines directions for making with character suggestions. The choice was rather conventional but the finished results as shown in the booklet were ornate in the extreme. The only concessions to modernity in the 1925 edition were 'Mr Radio Man' and 'Jazz Music', the sole male outfits described (illus. 120).[30] Throughout, the illustrations take us to a highly embellished world of layering, pleating and fringing, each one a fantasy confection of pieced shapes, many scattered with cut-out motifs. The seeming impossibility of fashioning such cloud cuckoo visions is tempered by instructions beside each set of costumes, and there are more general tuition sections later in the book on handling the paper and configuring garments. Dennison describes two construction methods to process flat paper into costumes: a slip-over model, worn like an apron, and a more complicated one comprising a top layer of decorative crêpe fastened to a cloth under-structure. There is clarification on using the sewing machine with crêpe and guidance on successful cutting with or against the grain to create fluted edges, petals in several styles, fringes and pompoms. Wire wrapping is explained and there are further directions for intricate manipulation of the crêpe for particular effects. Accessories are singled out for special guidance: wings, wigs, shepherds' crooks and hats reflect the kinds of popular, traditional costume pictured throughout the book.

Fashioning raw material into a wearable shape is not a straightforward process, which must be why the Dennison's booklet ran in parallel with their free face-to-face lessons. We know that two English saleswomen were taught to make crêpe paper flowers by Dennison's staff at the time of Selfridges' opening, setting the scene for future displays and demonstrations of crêpe costume-making throughout Britain.

The years between 1920 and 1955 were the heyday of crêpe-paper fancy dress and these were the years when Dennison was actively promoting the product in the British Isles. They took out advertising space in most issues of *Leach's Fancy Dress* from 1920 to 1936 and varied the text each time to keep the information fresh. In 1922, their advertisement in *Leach's* informed would-be fancy-dress creators to call in at Dennison's London showroom for a free lesson. By 1925, if not before, these lessons were being offered in the capital on a daily basis at

Dennison's British headquarters in Kingsway, a major thoroughfare in central London close to all the other paper-pattern suppliers.[31] As well as lessons, they offered free advice and undertook to design complete sets of original costumes for a nominal charge.[32]

Dennison made a point of ensuring that their products spanned the country. They advertised in provincial newspapers, and local suppliers plugged Dennison in their promotions. Slade's of Abington Street, Northampton, a major shoe-manufacturing town in the centre of the country and an early promoter of a revived carnival, was one such retailer who mounted a display of Dennison crêpe-paper items at its premises in 1925.[33] Moreover, from at least 1922, specially trained Dennison's agents gave demonstrations of crêpe paper dressmaking, ensuring that this sometimes intractable material was used to good effect and its full potential realized. In that year, two weeks before the British Legion Masked Fancy Dress Dance, Harold Moore, who ran a stationery business in Belfast, offered a three-hour session of fancy costume-making with Dennison crêpe. With a growing emphasis on competitive fancy dress in the 1920s, several Belfast firms offered prizes at the dance, among them Harold Moore himself, for the most effective dress in Dennison paper.[34]

The many demonstrations up and down the country throughout the 1920s provided work for women in years of financial uncertainty and kept the Dennison name uppermost in people's minds. They did not have a monopoly, because there were several British firms making crêpe, but Dennison's clever campaigns must have ensured that it was a strong contender in the market. In 1931, in dire economic times, Dennison themselves offered valuable cash prizes for the best decorated vehicles and fancy crêpe-paper costumes nationwide. The competition was open to everyone participating in any carnival or fête throughout the country.[35] Around the same period, the Wimbledon Palais de Danse, boasting the largest sprung dance floor in the world, hosted a

PARTY FUN

Fig. 85.
This costume owes its success to the colouring. The rose, with bodice as stem, and the rosebud hat, complete a neat costume.

Fig. 86.
The beauty of this dress is suited to the shy wearer. Unless the wearer has charm the crinoline costume ought not to be worn.

121 The possibilities of crêpe paper are illustrated by these flounced skirts from Hazel Hurst's *Crepe-Craft in the Home: A Hint Book for Modern Women* (1935).

'Dennison Crepe Night', with the lure of prizes. A limit of five shillings was put on the cost of costumes, suggesting the undated poster comes from a period of monetary constraint in the 1930s or '40s.[36] In 1938, Chelmsford Co-Operative Society members utilized over 2 miles (3.2 km) of crêpe paper to create fancy dress for their children, who paraded through the town dressed as products of the Co-Operative Wholesale Society.[37]

Crêpe paper was established as a viable alternative to textile material and its survival rate in the form of existing garments is surprisingly high. Home dressmakers tapped into their reserves of making know-how to create flights of fancy in crêpe, and some truly wonderful concoctions were captured on a Pathé newsreel item of 1933, 'Carnival Costumes in Paper'.[38] In the hands of experienced practitioners, certain effects can be realized in paper more readily than in textile. In truth, there is a tendency for crêpe costumes to look excessively frilly because manifold flounces are almost as easy to produce as single ones. It was the ideal material for multi-layered crinolines, outsize bonnets and exaggerated Pierrot ruffles. Fancy dress is all about overemphasis, and Hazel Hurst, a professional window dresser, demonstrated her skills in this regard by creating some dramatic pieces to illustrate her book on crêpe craft (illus. 121).[39]

Dennison was still in operation after the Second World War and images of victory celebrations in 1945 and coronation parties in 1953 show how closely fancy dress and crêpe were interrelated. While crêpe paper had become cognate with celebratory and carnival costume, a quite different type of organization from Dennison has bequeathed us another apposite and surprisingly informative view of the logistics of acquiring and wearing costumes of different lands, a persistent theme for fancy dress. As with crêpe paper, we need to go back in time to fully comprehend the part played by Christian missions in dressing up. Since 1880, missionary exhibitions displaying and explicating foreign peoples and their countries had flourished alongside other exhibitionary formats, and both should be seen in a context of competing spectacles, vying for audiences alongside other mass entertainments. While not overlooking the serious concerns of fundraising and missionary endeavour, it has to be the case that these Christian extravaganzas – they were resolutely *not* church bazaars – fostered the idea of dressing up.

In 1908, 'The Orient in London: A Great Missionary Exhibition', held in the Royal Agricultural Hall in Islington, North London, had 25,000 exhibits laid out in twenty courts. A redoubtable lady from Streatham, Miss E. Forster, organized the replication of indigenous dress for nine hundred volunteer stewards. Specimen garments, genuine articles brought back or sent from missionary postings abroad, were loaned out to participating churches in turn. A copy of each outfit was quickly

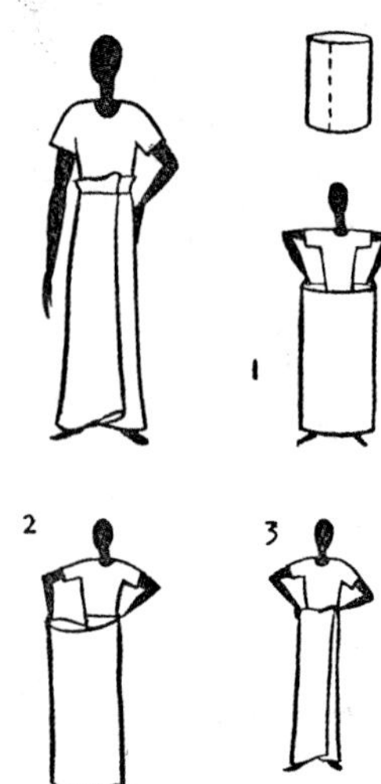

122 Instructions for tying a Sri Lankan sarong from *Let's Dress Up! Dressing Up with Costumes of Many Countries*, first published in 1949 by the United Council for Missionary Education. This image is taken from the 1964 fourth impression.

made to serve as a model for further copies while the originals moved on to the next church. In the following year, 1909, there was no need for such handiwork because six hundred foreign costumes had been acquired from 'mission lands' to clothe the lecturers and stewards at 'Africa and the East', another large missionary exhibition held at the same Islington venue.[40] Can we really call this fancy dress? Now seen as a problematic, even unacceptable, form of cultural appropriation, this kind of dressing up was a tactic designed to impart an understanding of how non-Christian people lived. Wearing their clothes, it was thought, had educational immediacy. For some this strategy must have seemed like an opportunity for fancy-dress jollity. The authorities sensed an incipient waywardness in this regard when, in 1927, the London Missionary Society felt it necessary to place restrictions on the hiring out of their materials, stipulating that they could only be used for missionary education.[41]

The correct use of these genuine garments is stressed in *Let's Dress Up! Dressing Up with Costumes of Many Countries*, first published in 1949 and reprinted several times by the United Council for Missionary Education. The book is not out on the far edge of our concerns about ways to assemble fancy dress because common sense, coupled with a proclivity for efficiency and thrift, situate it alongside other publications we have already described. This is why it is included here. The first section, 'Dressing Up with Borrowed Costumes', sets the tone for the whole: where possible, authentic dress from the country concerned is to be favoured over anything else. Each missionary society kept a store of 'overseas costumes' which, as we have seen, could be lent or hired out. Turning to the niceties of correct appearance, readers are advised that a bulky look is to be avoided and wearing a swimsuit beneath the costume is suggested. No watches, wedding rings or spectacles are allowed, and girls should be dissuaded from rearranging their hair to look, as they think, more attractive. It only spoils the character effect. The book proceeds by continent, then by country, then by region. Distinction is made, for instance, between clothes from different parts of India and Pakistan: Kashmir, the Northwest Frontier, Muslim areas, North and South India and Hindu regions. Instructions are given for tying a turban, for securing a Japanese obi, and for putting on a sari from India and a sarong from Sri Lanka. Each entry is illustrated in the text with a small ink drawing (illus. 122).[42] All this punctilious information presupposes a knowledge of the clothes gained from close observation, handling and even wearing. In places, the book reads more like an anthropological study than a guide to fancy dress.

Improvisation, a characteristic sign of fancy dress across its several manifestations, is the theme of the entire second section of *Let's Dress Up!*

> Now that so many countries have adopted modern Western dress, particularly in the case of boys and men, improvisation of costumes has become easier. It is entirely correct, for instance . . . for schoolboys in every country to wear shirts and shorts and for schoolgirls in many countries to wear a simple dress.[43]

There is not much mileage here for true fancy-dress devotees. 'A pair of old pyjamas dyed to the right butcher-blue colour' for a Chinese peasant, though not hugely appealing, is better than school uniform, which, nonetheless, is employed several times more: 'A uniform coat with all the badges removed' is recommended for a Sun Yat-sen jacket of the Chinese middle class, for example. Scarves, towels, sheets and curtains can all be utilized and, acknowledging ongoing rationing, butter muslin and surgical gauze can be home-dyed and used for veils and waistbands. Cardboard can be fashioned into jewellery, metallic paper used for crowns with Rowntrees Clear Gums in red and green standing in for rubies and emeralds.[44] The labour, mess, inconvenience and awkwardness involved in this creativity is airily overlooked. As with all fancy-dress making, an implicit proficiency in the heterogeneous technical processes involved is taken for granted.

While missionary dress up might seem tangential to fancy dress, holiday-camp larks are right on target. Handy tips and hearty encouragement for fancy dress are to the fore in a book published at the same time as the missionary publication towards the end of our period. *The Butlin Holiday Book, 1949–50* covered some of the same ground as *Let's Dress Up!* with plenty of pointers to getting by on a budget. Its style was much more free-and-easy, with fun as its mantra. The 265-page annual was put out by the highly successful holiday camp enterprise run by the doyen of working-class leisure Sir William 'Billy' Butlin (1899–1980). Well before the *Holiday Book* and even before the opening of his first camp at Skegness in 1936, Butlin was wise to the allure of fancy dress. He was instrumental in organizing a hospital charity carnival in the town from 1931, and in 1932, he provided every incentive for carnival aspirants to dress up, securing 150 costumes, which were put on view at Crofts, a local family store. Materials and advice were also available, dressing rooms were provided at Butlin's Amusement Park and a skilled make-up artist was on hand. Additionally, copying other successful carnivals elsewhere, the indefatigable entrepreneur arranged for Pathé to record the event. He enticed people into costume by inviting them to be filmed and then seeing themselves at the local picture house. The newsreel was subsequently shown in cinemas across the country.[45] Dressing up continued as part of holiday camp life, and working-class British families of modest means and limited time took their vacation in these self-contained resorts at seaside locations around Britain.[46]

The weeks spent at Barry Island, Clacton or Skegness were anticipated from year to year, and old hands knew that the highly organized structure of the campers' day was frequently punctuated by races, matches and games of all sorts as well as fancy-dress competitions, which dovetailed with the combative mindset of the holiday camp.

123 An illustration from Mary Essex, 'Fancy Dress for Nothing', *The Butlin Holiday Book, 1949–50*. The character of 'Chance' has an age-old fancy-dress history, while the artist exemplifies the continuing appeal of everything French.

You were sensible to come prepared, and this is where Mary Essex, the loquacious author of 'Fancy Dress for Nothing', an article in the annual, comes to the aid of campers. This chapter, as implied by the title, gives instructions, satisfactorily precise in many instances, for a myriad of different low-cost costumes of an improvisatory sort. The costumes shown in the accompanying illustrations are probably more polished than those assembled by campers but the carefree attitude of those pictured in the line drawings hits the right note (illus. 123). The costumes described in the text are not, however, rustled up in a moment. Many campers would have gathered likely props together before setting off on holiday. Essex has a breezy tone and sounds just the sort of person to have bits and bobs of felt and hessian, drifts of net and balls of knitting cotton to hand ready to be fashioned into a first-prize costume at Butlin's. These are among the numerous examples of everyday materials she recommends. Cotton wool is high on her list for conversion to powdered wigs, Bo-Peep's lambs or the White Rabbit's tail. Crêpe paper comes up, mostly for outlandish wigs. Essex is mindful that crêpe tears easily, so although a textile lining, as recommended by Dennison, is ideal for crêpe paper frocks, this was difficult in 1949 because coupons were still needed to purchase cloth. Ever alive to price and rationing, Essex reminds her readers, for example, that tinsel is not rationed and does well for fairy wings. Perhaps because of the privations engendered by post-war shortages, she counsels would-be fancy dressers with a variety of pithy exhortations urging holidaymakers to go for the prizes with ingenious costumes. Most of her examples are not remotely original but she recommends clichéd characters with such flair as to make them seem sure-fire winners:

> I have known a whole family turn out as a cowboy family with great success. And with this, *don't* forget the baby because the baby gets all the publicity and steals the thunder. The men wore flannel trousers to which slip mats (the fluffier kind) had been attached; the inevitable safety-pin and straps round knees and ankles was all that was asked. Scarlet or any loud-coloured shirts, with sleeves rolled up. All the pistols they could beg, borrow or steal stuck into important-looking belts (incidentally cartridge paper is a good idea), the washing-line looped round their necks, and slouch hats made of stiffish brown paper . . . For the women light, tan-brown paper skirts to look like leather and wide hats to match . . . For the baby, the slouch hat, no shirt, tiny trousers with furry fronts and a toy pistol in the belt. Marching in *en bloc* you'd be surprised how effective this can be.[47]

As ever, the details are important to success: *fluffy* slip mats, not smooth ones, for example. And she is certainly right about the baby. This miniature *pièce de résistance* converts an otherwise trite fancy-dress idea into something noticeable.

She gives the same treatment to other timeworn characters, always adding a personal reminiscence or aside to convince the reader of their efficacy. 'They were hallmarked prize-winners from the very first,' she remarks at rigging out two little girls as the 'Princes in the Tower' by threading elastic through the hem of their black velvet party frocks to loop up as doublet and trunk hose. For Red Riding Hood, 'the great trick is to borrow an Alsatian dog.' For a gypsy family she recommends introducing a horse. Two people beneath an army blanket with battery light bulbs in the eyes and a soda siphon in the nose give 'the most terrific effect'.[48] A few of the Butlin book's ideas do seem novel and Essex is effusive about camouflaging a red-haired man as a gingernut biscuit. Huntley & Palmer's biscuit labels are pinned to brown dungarees along with a sign reading, 'Doesn't this take the biscuit?'[49]

124 'I am matchless so is Butlins', an ingenious costume at a Butlin's holiday camp, 1950s.

The ultimate aim was always to catch the eyes of the judges and win a prize (illus. 124). This is in perfect accord with the ethos of holiday camps, as was the emphasis on family fancy dress. Though siblings and couples often dressed as a thematic pair, the family aspect is not given much prominence elsewhere: Essex's writing reinforces the concept of the multi-generational togetherness that holiday camps typified in the immediate post-war world. She understood this and also made a point of acknowledging the difficulty of getting some men, especially married men with children, to dress up. Despite, or maybe as an act of resistance against, involvement in clumsy concert parties and revues in the armed forces, and in stark contrast to the exclusive masculine participation in traditionally inspired festivals, it seems that some men were more reluctant than women to take part in holiday-camp parades. For Butlin's campers, the family ensemble was thus an ingenious solution to inclusion. Conversely, Essex is totally unabashed by dressing a man as a 'fair'wy' in a bunched-up nightdress, tinsel and a wig of dusting brushes.[50] Male to female cross-dressing, another throwback to army and navy days, could be a part of holiday-camp high jinks as well.

Warming to her theme, Essex insists: 'It is not sufficient to dress up; people who are going to get prizes are the ones who go into it prepared to *live* the part for the evening, and that is one of the essentials.'[51] The 'Indian' family make a striking entrance with 'tom-toms', the little 'Princes in the Tower' stand huddled together timidly, and a couple of spivs in raked trilbies and loud ties, a topical costume in the war years and just after, bark out their black-market wares. Since the assimilation of moving pictures into ordinary lives, bodily repose was not now the only option where fancy dress was concerned. Increasingly, costumed characters affected exaggerated poses and launched themselves into activity. Billy Butlin, with his sponsorship of carnival, his enthusiastic embrace of moving pictures and his sharp-witted thinking about all-inclusive breaks at holiday camps persuaded tens of thousands of holidaymakers into fancy dress and helped to keep the practice alive.

Eight

THE CHARACTERS OF FANCY DRESS: THREE CASE STUDIES

At the Blackpool Carnival in 1923, the theatrical costumier S. B. Watts had reason to feel thoroughly gratified because several of the floats the firm had dressed were highly commended and their 'Cowboy and Indian' cavalcade won first prize.[1] 'Cowboys and Indians' came to occupy a central place in the fancy-dress pantheon and, by the time of the Blackpool carnival, they were well established. One of the most striking things about fancy-dress outfits is not their ever-changing novelty but the oft-repeated appearances of the same characters in different permutations. Originality and innovation, for sure, played a part but central to our story are a stockpile of dependable outfits that endured for many years, and a few reached right across our period and beyond. Out of the many long-established costumes that became the backbone of the fancy-dress repository in Britain, the following instructive examples – 'Cowboys and Indians', Pierrot and animal disguise – give us clues as to why and how they were co-opted as costume and the reasons for their endurance. Their narratives show similarities with one another as well as with the barrage of characters not included in this scrutiny but each takes several twists and turns that makes it unique and sets it against a specific backdrop of time and place.

'Cowboys and Indians' are widely perceived to be yoked together. This recognition of their pairing came about only around 1900, and both characters continued to operate separately on occasion. Whereas Jack and Jill, for example, are always seen in fancy dress as a pair – a lone Jack is unlikely to attend a party without his water-fetching partner – Native Americans and cowboys did not invariably appear as a twosome for the obvious reason that the latter term was coined only in the late nineteenth century to denote a new kind of worker, a cattle handler in the American West. So 'Indian' dress-up pre-dates that of their rancher adversaries. Prior to our period, the Native American had an early commanding presence in the costume roster, with the allegorical figure of 'America' depicted as a Native American, though the medium was not usually fancy dress but fine art or statuary. Grand portraiture rendered British sitters as proponents of empire and, in the eighteenth century, many decked themselves out in Native American dress, or at least a parody of it, fabricating an ensemble from artefacts culled from different tribes, as demonstrated by William Bowles, pictured in the Introduction.[2] These early sitters would not have sanctioned the term 'fancy dress' for their awesome ensembles and neither would John Buchan, author of the popular derring-do novel *The Thirty-Nine Steps* and Governor-General of Canada (1935–40), who was photographed by Yousuf Karsh in 1937 wearing resplendent First Nation plumes.[3] The rationale behind such self-fashioning is complex and inconsistent but, where fancy dress is concerned, the idea of feathers became forever inextricably linked to the depiction of Native Americans and dressing in their likeness came later to be known as 'feathering up'. Increasingly from the nineteenth century onwards, costumed merrymakers depicting the land of 'America' did not dress in feathers but in stars and stripes (illus. 125). They did not renounce the Native American, however, and their allegiance to the character, together with misreadings and crass simplifications of the clothing, remained strong.

125 A young woman dressed in the stars and stripes of America, photographed by R. O. Wilson, Consett, County Durham, 1920s. The banner is embroidered with the title of a popular American song, 'The Ragtime Goblin Man', first recorded in 1912.

As with other fancy-dress personae, the staying power of the 'Indian' had a lot to do with the costume's very individual qualities that immediately marked it out, though its many distinctions across divergent First Nation peoples went unheeded. When George Catlin brought his Indian Gallery to the Egyptian Hall in London in the 1840s, the British public had already been exposed to all manner of

126 Ernest Nelson Perrett won first prize dressed as an 'Indian' at an unnamed carnival, *c.* 1916.

Americana, and 'the Indian' in both real and delusional presentations was a remarkably attractive subject for fancy dress. Sensing that static exhibitions of pictures and artefacts could not compete with the sensational live shows that vied for the public's attention at the time, Catlin first employed two Englishmen to appear in tribal trappings and then added groups of Native Americans wearing authentic garments and accessories. Native American land-rights activists and Christian converts also visited Britain, unintentionally inviting copycat dressers.[4] These and several other Native Americans were in Britain well before the publication of Ardern Holt's books. In Holt's 1887 volume of women's fancy dress, 'American Indian Queen' is astonishingly decked out in a fringed leather dress and diadem of eagle and vulture feathers while, in the same edition, 'Pocahontas' is given leggings of porcupine quills. The 'Indian Chief' and 'Sioux Chief' in Holt's 1882 *Gentlemen's Fancy Dress* each have a tomahawk, the distinctive single-handed axe that, along with the bow and arrow, flagged up 'Indian' in all subsequent versions of male fancy dress.[5]

These costume descriptions follow, at least in part, some of the representations that the public might have seen but, more sensationally, a hundred Native Americans crossed the Atlantic in 1887 and toured with William Frederick Cody (1846–1917) in his show *Buffalo Bill's Wild West*, an extravaganza that also brought the 'cowboy' to prominence. At the show grounds, the public wandered freely into the Native American troupe's encampments and, conversely, off-duty entertainers became tourists mingling in the streets with ordinary citizens.[6] The sensory excitement generated by these Native Americans is well captured by an image from Ormskirk in Lancashire.[7] Buffalo Bill's show passed through this typical market town on a later visit to Britain in 1904 and gawpers stopped to witness the Native Americans in their crested finery, sitting atop a 'Wild West' stagecoach. Why wouldn't you want to 'feather up' too? (illus. 126).

Certain features of 'Indian' clothing became enshrined and perpetuated in fancy dress. Beading, fringing and feathers were the key to character recognition, with face-painting becoming inescapable by the 1900s. The Butterick manual *Masquerade and Carnival* of 1892, itself emanating from America, includes wolf teeth as part of the habiliment of the costume for a 'North American Indian' and adds: 'the eyebrows may be blackened to meet at the center, and the face may be painted beneath the lower eyelids to produce a properly savage expression.'[8] This 'savage' mien was retained in 'Indian' fancy dress and Native American performers in the *Wild West* phenomenon were mostly depicted as the aggressors. But, alongside this more belligerent aspect, Native Americans were also perceived as upstanding and uncorrupted. Dressing in their likeness was seen as an act of commemoration in the face of their presumed near-extinction. Grey Owl, mentioned in the Introduction, was just such an example. Whether sympathetically portrayed or otherwise, the costume had a particular magnetism, with grease paint and powder defining the outfit as much as beads and feathers.

The Native American character enfolded the famous and mellifluously named Hiawatha in its embrace. Henry Wadsworth Longfellow's 1855 poem, its familiar verse rhythms based on those of the Finnish epic *Kalevala*, concerned the life of an Ojibwe Indian, his mother, Ncomis, and his wife, Minnehaha. The specific subject of Longfellow's *The Song of Hiawatha* had inspired almost instant artistic interpretations in America, though an illustrated edition of the book was not available to a British public until 1891 when Frederic Remington's rather free pictures of Native Americans were included with the text. The Remington edition is to the point where fancy dress is concerned because, as well as rendering episodes from the poem's narrative, one illustration per canto, the right margin of each page contains detailed drawings of artefacts connected with the indigenous way of life: tools, weapons, pictograms, garments and headdresses of all kinds. These details are always important for fantasy dressers. As well as book illustrations, Native Americans were favourite subjects for picture postcards and the power of such cards as a factor in sustaining interest in certain recurring fancy-dress themes was paramount. Characters from *The Song of Hiawatha* were featured in at least two series produced by the firm of Raphael Tuck alone. The images from 1904 and 1911–12, some of them painted by a prolific illustrator called Joseph Finnemore (1860–1939), show bold portrayals in bright colours, each with a relevant stanza from the poem printed across the card's surface (illus. 127). These imposing renderings in the form of inexpensive postcards were a blueprint for Native American dressing up.

127 Hiawatha depicted on a postcard published by Raphael Tuck, 1904.

By the time the Tuck postcards were produced, the book-length narrative poem was already immensely celebrated and the character of Hiawatha was made even more popular when Longfellow's words were set to music by Samuel Coleridge-Taylor (1875–1912).[9] Even after 'cowboy' became a viable fancy-dress possibility, the tenacity of Coleridge-Taylor's trilogy of cantatas, also called *The Song of Hiawatha* and composed between 1898 and 1900, ensured there were costumed 'Indians' that paid little or no attention to the gun-slinging cowboy partner we know from late 1920s and '30s cinema. Such was the case in London from 1924 to the outbreak of the Second World War.

During those years, the Royal Albert Hall witnessed a truly extraordinary example of fancy-dress junketing not only on the concert platform itself but throughout the hall's vast auditorium. From the

London boroughs and from the suburbs and beyond, enthusiasts of the phenomenon that was Coleridge-Taylor's *Hiawatha* cantata pursued a romanticized embodiment of the Native American. Unrecorded photographically, they descended on South Kensington dressed as Native Americans, or rather, their version of what they thought these peoples looked like.[10] By the 1920s, if not before, the authenticity of the stories and Longfellow's reshaping of Indian ethnography were being brought into question, but none of this deterred the aficionados at the Royal Albert Hall. Richard Gordon-Smith records his father, David's, reminiscences of the *Hiawatha* extravagant presentations:

> Attendance at the Royal Albert Hall during the 1924–1939 period was probably not frequent, but *Hiawatha* was something that everyone went to, so they [his father and grandparents] duly 'feathered up' with thousands of others to take the train from Brixton to Kensington . . . Cheap, affordable entertainment on the spectacular scale of the annual *Hiawatha* fortnights were therefore greatly valued. My father told of one such expedition and said that the performance reminded him more of a circus than a concert, with conductor (Sir) Malcolm Sargent as the ring master. The audience, most of them in versions of Native American fancy dress – axes, bows and papooses included – joined in with some of the better-known numbers, which participation Sargent partially encouraged.[11]

The Hiawatha spectacles were performed in other cities too. The Brighton and Hove Harmonic Society, for one, regularly staged Thomas Fairbairn's original Albert Hall production in the 1930s.[12] The sentimental combination of Longfellow's words and Coleridge-Taylor's melodies fed into the affection and nostalgia for 'Indian' customs and made manifest the public's fascination with these North American peoples. Just at the time their habitual manner of living was threatened, they were represented by Europeans in costume. This is a recurring pattern: a way of life on the edge of extinction reinvented by foreigners in fancy dress.

Even while adults were singing along to Coleridge-Taylor's score in the aisles of the Royal Albert Hall, *The Song of Hiawatha* was becoming both a story told to children and a children's fancy-dress choice. At around this time, the upstanding 'Sioux Chief' is often being replaced by an expendable 'Indian': a white-created 'Indian', now often called a 'Red Indian', who gets killed by the cavalry. So 'Indian', as an imaginative persona realized in costume, had an atypical trajectory in that its pairing with 'cowboy', a new character for fancy dress from the time of Cody's *Buffalo Bill*, lent it a prolonged lease of life that was later dependent to a very large extent on the moving-image genre of the Western. This is to oversimplify but in general Holt's chieftains and queens, costumed in materials that were far too expensive for most party-goers, became the cunning Native American whose trademark bow and arrow or tomahawk balanced the cowboy's fast-shooting gun. The character shifted generations, becoming – if not exclusively, then in large part – a children's costume, with paper patterns for 'Red Indian' readily available. From the 1920s, abundant requisite accessories could be had from fancy-dress suppliers with, for instance, Theatricals, the felicitous name of a novelty firm in Birmingham, offering brown, black, red and speckled feathers, tomahawks and pipes of peace. Gamba, the theatrical and ballet shoe manufacturer, sold moccasins in various colours.[13] By the time of the Second World War, children could be rigged out in off-the-peg 'Indian' outfits and these, along with cowboy suits, were readily available in toyshops and department stores.

Turning now to look at the history of cowboy costume, the character's initiation into the fancy-dress muster was, at first, in large part due to *Buffalo Bill's Wild West*. This daredevil equestrian and sharpshooter show was seen by as many as 40,000 people a day on its lengthy European tours from the late 1880s until the early 1900s. It was not universally praised by Europe's press, though it thrilled British audiences, among them Victoria, the queen who loved to dress up. *Buffalo Bill* was the beginning of a partnership of 'cowboy' and 'Indian' that was to come into full flowering as fancy dress towards the latter end of our period and beyond. An early instance of a lone cowboy, though, is a Mr Bevan at the Artists' Fancy Ball, the precursor to the Chelsea Arts Club Ball, in 1889. Bevan's cowboy is not singled out for particular comment in the newspaper report, suggesting that his character was recognizable if not commonplace at this time.[14] Initially, the main promoter of the cowboy myth sometimes lent his name to the costume: 'Buffalo Bill' appeared as a male character costume in Butterick's 1892 book: 'Large, loose-fitting coat, buckskin trousers, top boots, large soft felt hat, fur girdle, hunting bag and rifle.'[15]

A year prior to the Butterick iteration, G. A. Henty (1832–1902), a widely read author of adventure stories, had paid tribute to the cowboy in his book *Redskin and Cowboy: A Tale of the Western Plains*. Owen Wister's best-selling novel published in 1902 was a more serious narrative about the 'West', and Wister's eponymous hero, the Virginian, heralded the cowboy as a legendary American man of courage. Even before he wrote the novel, Wister's cowboy and his mode of living on the open plains was all but over, a familiar sign that his attire could be pressed into service as fancy dress. Here is Wister's evocative description of the novel's central character: 'Lounging against the wall was a slim young giant, more beautiful than pictures. His broad, soft hat was pushed back; a loose-knotted, dull-scarlet handkerchief sagged from his throat, and one casual thumb was hooked in the cartridge-belt that slanted across his hips.'[16] These clothes and this kind of posturing would be endlessly reinterpreted in fancy dress (illus. 128).

128 Three men in fancy dress, c. 1900. The cowboy wears fleecy chaps, while his cross-dressed companion may be a cancan dancer, and the third seems to be a mix of Indian potentate and Gordon Highlander.

Wister's novel itself might not have been read by everyone who dressed as cowboys but many other fictional cowboy heroes followed in the Virginian's wake and became compellingly popular when they were transferred to comics, the big screen and then television either side of the Second World War. Hopalong Cassidy, a fictional character who featured in 66 Hollywood films from the mid-1930s and then on television, was originally a cowboy protagonist from a 1904 short story

129 A trio of young women dressed for the 'Wild West'. The costumes and stuffed horse were provided by The Fancy Dress Studio in London, 1910–25.

and it was around that time that *Weldon's Fancy Dress for Children* first illustrated a costume called 'cow boy'. He looks more like a rancher than the later stereotype, wears a 'Buffalo Bill hat' and carries a length of rope but no gun.[17] The cowboy was rife for endless replication in fancy dress.

Though children shared the cowboy genre with adults, some of the earliest visual references to cowboy impersonators are grown-ups posing for the camera in what appear at first to be highly plausible garments. While William 'Bill' Cody himself was togged out in a fringed leather suit and showy over-the-knee boots, other performing frontiersmen in his and other travelling shows wore the now-obligatory soft shirt and neckerchief along with chaps, a quite marvellous item of clothing new to many in Britain and seemingly irresistible to masqueraders. Chaps, designed to protect the legs from low, tangled thorn bushes (*chaparro*), are leggings worn on top of trousers, and the particular style seen in these early twentieth-century dress-up photographs are fashioned from fleece, giving the legs a bulky appearance. These chaps' inherent bizarreness attracted attention. Taking advantage of the mood surrounding the dazzling pageantry of professional cowboy performances, photography studios equipped themselves with this novelty outfit. One such was the Erdington Studio at 22 Dundee Street in Carnoustie, a Scottish seaside resort near Dundee where Buffalo Bill presented his bravura displays in 1904. The Carnoustie studio sent their photographer and, we presume, all the props and costumes to the nearby Ministry of Defence Barry Buddon Training Area to snap off-duty soldiers accoutred as cowboys.[18] Several photographic postcards survive of these posing squaddies, and cowboy get-ups were a standard in studios across the country.

It is unsurprising that the look extended to women. At the turn of the nineteenth century, Annie Oakley (1860–1926), she of the whizzing bullets, had worn a skirt for her audacious gun-toting performances, and some faux cowgirls chose to wear skirts as well. However, swinging skirts, plaid shirts and boots, the sartorial attributes of a cowgirl, only really became a definite British fancy-dress fixture with the London premiere in 1947 of *Annie Get Your Gun*, the musical of Annie's life. Prior to that, women fancy dressers mostly posed in trousers to impersonate cowboys. Again, this was prompted by the easy availability of the costume at photographers' studios. One in Marine Parade, Southend-on-Sea, even billed itself as 'Whitaker's "Cowboy" Fancy Dress Studios',

130 A group of young women dressed in a variety of fancy dress costumes, several in men's guise, posing against a studio backcloth depicting a seaside resort, 1920s.

and The Fancy Dress Studio in London's Oxford Street, its name a testimony to the faddish infatuation with dressing up for the camera, has bequeathed several images to us showing young women tricked out in much the same cowboy style as the men. One of these shows three women wedged together in front of the camera lens along with a stuffed horse (illus. 129). The offbeat nature of the disguise and its drift towards gender crossing must have been part of its seductiveness. Who were these women? Did they work as shop assistants in the big Oxford Street stores? Were they dressing up in their lunch hour, carefully removing their smart work clothes and donning chaps? Had they come up from the suburbs on a Saturday for a shopping spree and a lark? Likely they had seen photographic postcards of American women performance riders in chaps and maybe even witnessed the sensational trick rider Tad Lucas (Barbara Inez Barnes, 1902–1990) at London's Wembley Stadium in 1924. They left us a souvenir of their fleeting time as cowboys and that is all we know.

A telling photograph of another group of young women demonstrates the magnetism of the cowboy genre and it also encapsulates the interwar feeling for dressing up as a diversion from the mundane routine of everyday life (illus. 130). From this image, we get a clue as to the stock of fancy dress held by studios in the 1920s. Five of the group are cowboys dressed in togs similar to those from The Fancy Dress Studio, and there are two Scots in tartan kilts, a Welsh girl, an Irish girl, a sailor and assorted Pierrots. Most appear to be women in men's guise or at least sexually equivocal. The photographer was able to accommodate male and female customers by utilizing the same costumes for both, though we cannot assume that all women wanted to cross-dress: the studio determined the gender. We can say, however, that this image marks a critical, if gentle, moment of change for fancy dress, echoing altered sartorial mores that began to be felt in the opening years of the twentieth century and were given momentum by the upheaval of the First World War.

Pierrot, a character duplicated several times over in the cowboy line-up and as indestructible as the legendary rider, had an enormously long life in fancy dress, with the high point of infatuation being compressed into the decades between the two World Wars (illus. 131). From the First World War on, Pierrot imitators in ruffs and pompoms often outnumbered other characters at fancy-dress get-togethers. As early as 1891, at Covent Garden's opening carnival ball of the season, often a predictor of future trends, there was 'every variety of the clown family, the ubiquitous Pierrot predominating'.[19] In 1904, one newspaper entry commented on half a dozen Pierrots at the more modest Shipley Sociable Ball in Leeds.[20] By the 1920s, Pierrot variants were

131 Two young women dressed as classic Pierrots, 1910–20.

well established everywhere, the name itself almost synonymous with fancy dress. In 1928, the *Aberdeen Press and Journal* captured the ongoing craze well with a report headed 'Jazz Pierrots Predominated at the Students' Carnival':

> A casual glance round the Mitchell Hall on Saturday night showed dozens and dozens of pierrots far removed

> in semblance from the original pierrot as to be almost unrecognisable. The conventional pierrot has been sacrificed to a jazz age. No longer does he appear in simple white suit, with its black pom-poms in sets of three on conical hat, straight coat and trousers, and with his white ruff. Gone was the white suit, and in its place suits of satin, silk, and even woven tissue of every possible colour – vivid hues for preference. Brilliant greens jostled with glaring scarlet, dazzling yellow against vivid blue, and the gigantic ruffle standing out in all its stiff bravado no way resembled the pathetically dropping ruffle of the pierrot of bygone days. There were pierrots and pierrettes in cherry and black, emerald and black, yellow and blue, yellow and green.[21]

At the mania's high point there were social functions solely dedicated to Pierrot. The Esplanade Assembly Rooms in Portsmouth advertised a Pierrot night in December 1920, and a Pierrot dance revel was held at the Metropole in Hastings in February 1922.[22]

This inescapable character, originating in the Italian *commedia dell'arte* and appearing in English proto-pantomime by the eighteenth century, accrued multifarious associations across the years and was relentlessly reiterated in the interwar period. Like many character costumes, the transfigured Pierrot suit paid tribute to numerous influences from both high and low culture, and the fancy-dress character is an amalgam of everything Pierrot-esque that had gone before. He pays homage to Watteau's paintings, Nadar's photographs, Schoenberg's *Pierrot lunaire* and all the Pierrots of Romantic, Decadent, Symbolist and Modernist art and theatre. A foundational moment, though not the first one, for the reception of Pierrot into the realm of fancy dress occurred in London in 1891 when the French actress Jane May impersonated the character in a mime production, *L'Enfant prodigue.*

Widely circulated photographs show her with white face make-up, ruff and skullcap.[23] May's interpretation was in a line of descent from the innovatory mime artist Jean-Gaspard Deburau (1796–1846), who devised a different, more emotionally intense, persona for Pierrot as later immortalized in the film *Les Enfants du paradis* (1945).

The success of *L'Enfant prodigue* at the Prince of Wales Theatre in London led to a second cast touring several big provincial cities, giving the be-ruffed and distinctive-looking penitent wide appeal. Fashion, a sister to fancy dress, quickly appropriated all things Pierrot and the frilled collar, instantly recognizable as belonging to his world, was taken up by the fashion columns from the 1890s. Its regular appearance as a fashion item over many years reinforced its appeal as fancy dress.[24]

If Jane May's blanched figure in *L'Enfant prodigue* provided one of the catalysts for Pierrot's rebirth and his embrace by party-goers in Britain, another stimulant to the fad for Pierrot fancy dress was provided by a contemporary seaside spectacle that was exclusively British but was in part the antithesis of the silent Pierrot. Clifford Essex (1869–*c.* 1946), a banjo-playing performer, is credited with the invention of the Pierrot Troupe in 1891, a significant year for the character. *L'Enfant prodigue* plainly motivated him. His band of musical entertainers seem to be the first group to have dressed identically in ruffled collars, conical hats and loose-fitting garments decorated with pompoms but many more were to follow. Working around Britain's coastal resorts during the summer season, their noisy variety sets worked against the spirit of mute loneliness so associated with the French mime heritage. These troubadours' costumes, however, adhered to a classic image of Pierrot.

All this fed into the fantasies of fancy dressers who took Pierrot to their hearts and, increasingly from the beginning of the twentieth century, fashioned him into multiple permutations, blending him with other characters from the *commedia dell'arte* as well as giving him a modern twist. Many of these Pierrot emulators bore little resemblance to any of the ancestral models but, as we have seen time and again, one of the qualities of fancy dress is its ability to improvise, adapt and make over. This is precisely what had happened to the original Pierrot himself as he moved from one country to another over three or more centuries. By comparison, the height of the Pierrot fixation in Britain was short-lived.

Throughout the late 1910s and the 1920s, Pierrot was represented in some form at every Chelsea Arts Club Ball, an annual event that very much defined the flavour of the era.[25] Their victory ball in 1919 encapsulates the confused profusion of ideas behind the Pierrot figure as a fancy-dress choice. Pierrot, with his outsize ruff, is quickly discernible in all the press photographs.[26] His costume is no longer plain white and his sadness has become elation. It was the traditional chequers of Harlequin that seems to have provided the theme for the entire 1919 Chelsea ball (illus. 132). The geometric coloured shapes and stripes were, in fact, a deliberate tribute to Norman Wilkinson (1878–1971) rather than Harlequin. Wilkinson was the marine artist who devised the wartime dazzle camouflage for First World War navy ships and the Chelsea gathering was consequently given the radiant designation 'Dazzle Ball'. *The Graphic*, in high-flown language, described the occasion as 'a token, unmistakable, if bizarre, of some of the things which the dark years have achieved, of the setting free of the spirits which dwell within the form of things'.[27] These clear-cut motifs would soon appear everywhere. In Ramsgate, on the Kent coast, the *Thanet Advertiser* newspaper asked:

132 Pierrot and Harlequin at the Dazzle Ball, Chelsea Arts Club's victory celebration, Royal Albert Hall, London, *The Sphere*, Saturday, 22 March 1919.

133 Pierrot costumes from *Leach's Fancy Dress* (1922).

> What is a Dazzle Ball? . . . The garb of both ladies and gentlemen will be fashioned by means of stripes and spots, squares and other cubist effects that are calculated to form a brilliant and dazzling scene. All the colours of the rainbow in slabs and slashes. That's a Dazzle Ball.[28]

These markings were transferred to Pierrot himself (illus. 133).

As part of the free-spiritedness of the post-First World War years, when the roles of men and women, in some instances, became blurred, the sexually ambivalent Pierrot, whether pale or patterned, offered up a legitimate model for gender ambiguity. Fancy dress, often conservative, seized on Pierrot's malleable anima. *Leach's Fancy Dress* magazines of the 1920s and '30s provide a charmed encounter with the character and, while the love-entangled trio of Harlequin, Columbine and Pierrot had certainly appeared in pre-twentieth century costume books, Pierrot, of all the three, is given particular prominence during the twentieth century. His insistent presence in the later magazines such as *Leach's* signalled a changed direction for fancy dress in the 1900s, a major shift in the perception and execution of dressing up. In 1922, *Leach's* roundly dismisses historical characters and peasant costume as passé but this does not wholly prepare us for the many diverting images of prettified Pierrots that appear in the pages of the magazine, their youth and liveliness a long way from Ardern Holt's models. Now Pierrot's costume and persona are presented as more in line with what *Leach's* termed 'the unconquerable spirit of youth and gaiety'.[29] The white clown's idealism and poetic sensibility became submerged beneath his new external appearance, which was recast as altogether more cheerful and optimistic, decked out in patterned and vivid-coloured garments. Pierrot as the high avatar of the pale and listless was frequently lost during the interwar period, and many party-goers perhaps knew nothing of his origins. The deluge of different Pierrots is witness to the public's restlessness for constant change as well as their attentiveness to the details and nuances of dress.

In what forms was Pierrot reincarnated and how, in practical terms, were these new costumes configured? The feminine 'Pierrette' (sometimes spelled with two 'r's, sometimes with one) appears very frequently in the 1920s. She had featured in Thomas Hailes Lacy's *Female Costumes Historical, National and Dramatic*, published in London in 1865 and taken from an earlier French source. Lacy shows 'Pierrette' in a white skirt, a garment common to most characters so

134 'Bubbles' as Pierrot wearing exaggerated 'Jazz Trousers' stiffened at the sides, 1920s.

designated in the nineteenth century. By the second decade of the twentieth century, on the cusp of the disputes surrounding women wearing trousers, there is a mix of confident female Pierrots and Pierrettes sweeping through the pages of the pattern books, sometimes in skirts but often in trousers, far outnumbering their male counterparts. Pierrette's trousers could be highly idiosyncratic: broad at the hip, narrowing at the ankle or at the knee, sometimes tied in with pompoms, an almost jodhpur-like cut (illus. 134). *Leach's Fancy Dress* of 1920 has 'Jazz Pierrette', 'Carnival Pierrette' and 'Black Pierrette' all wearing versions of the fanciful trousers, identified by *Leach's* as being comfortable for dancing.[30] Trousers as everyday wear for women were a novelty and still unacceptable in many circles so this particular loose cut may have been tolerated as a kind of intermediate stage between skirts and the real thing.

Whatever mixed messages there were with respect to gender, one thing is clear: legs were certainly on show as they had never been before. *Leach's* pictured a 'Liberty Pierrette' and a 'Harlequinette' in extremely short skirts in 1920 and they were to become even shorter in the next decade.[31] Only circus and music-hall performers had previously revealed so much, though swimwear was starting to shrink in dimensions in the 1920s followed by other sportswear. Opportunities for bodily exposure, coupled with unconventional costume shapes, were presented in these catalogues as part of the 'anything goes' attitude of the Roaring

Twenties. Modish-sounding names added to the quirkiness: *The Lady* featured 'Pierrette of the Present' and 'Modern Pierrot', for example, and *Leach's*, among many other names, presented 'Madcap Pierrette', 'Glad Eye Pierrot', with an eye design all across the costume, 'Razzle Dazzle Pierrette' and 'Futuristic Pierrot'. These fantastical Pierrots, all from the mid-1920s, were of their time and did not last. Individual party-goers, like the Countess of Monte Cristo, devised equally preposterous outfits not found in the pattern books. The thrice-married, self-styled countess (Mrs Smith-Wilkinson from Nottingham) showed her 'futurist pierrot fancy dress' to an unnamed wonderstruck *Sunday Post* correspondent. The countess's then husband embroidered it himself, taking three months to stitch roses on the front, and pink carnations and forget-me-nots on the back and round the neck. 'One side [of the costume] forms a skirt in black satin and the other side a black silk georgette trouser with little frills all the way up,' reported the paper in 1921.[32]

For a while, up to the Great Depression, consumer demand acknowledged no bounds and the dynamism of 1920s urban culture sparked novelty and a break with the past. That fancy dress should light upon Pierrot as its agent of modernity is significant because, although he could fit right in with the credo of the age as regards sentiment and gender, he was also a figure of tradition. Indeed, Pierrot and Pierrette were both subject to historicizing so *Leach's*, for example, proposed 'Victorian Pierrette' in 1922 and 1934, and 'Pompadour Pierrette', 'Hooped Pierrette', 'Vandyke Pierrette' and 'Crinoline Pierrette' in 1924. Understanding that the general style of the Pierrot costume was in demand, these interwar fancy-dress magazines creatively incorporated the character's favourite features into many of their other suggested designs. Even though they are not named as Pierrot, *Leach's* 'Saturnine', 'Stars and Stripes' and 'Jockey' are all depicted in ruffs.[33] The characteristic trousers we noted earlier and which came to be termed 'Jazz

Trousers' were used in an array of outfits that were, both in name and in appearance, far from those of the traditional Pierrot character. He goes on evolving through the late 1920s and '30s, when we get, for example, the absurdly named Pertinette, a fancy-dress character which promiscuously combines traditional Pierrot attributes with overt femininity and sauciness. Appearing in *Leach's* several times, and perhaps even invented by them, Pertinette is shown with fashionably bobbed hair, wearing multi-coloured checked trousers, a low-cut black satin bodice and strappy, high heels.[34]

Pierrot, Pierrette and a medley of Pierrot progeny feature time and again in descriptions of fancy-dress gatherings up and down the country, his suit and accessories providing flexible boundaries for a variety of outfits that acknowledged the chalk-white archetype, if only in some small way. Pierrot pompoms, ruffs, skullcaps and conical hats were the recognizable elements extracted from the original and combined with other costume components. The trick was to appear new and innovatory while retaining something of the prototype. 'Not seen in Bexhill' was perhaps the most important piece of information regarding two Pierrot costumes in the 'For Sale' columns of a local paper.[35]

By the time these Pierrot suits were up for sale in 1931, it was well acknowledged that the character could provide a gradation of fancy-dress opportunities. A column devoted to dressing up in the *Fife Free Press* from that same year had this to say: 'The old joke about everyone going as a pierrot now loses its point, for pierrots are just as varied as any other dress, and there are a hundred and one different ways in which you may array yourself and still earn the title as going as a pierrot or a pierrette.' Encouraging the trend, the Fife newspaper offered its readers a Pierrot paper pattern for a shilling, together with directions for cutting out and making up.[36] Newspapers, magazines and pattern books fuelled the Pierrot fever in this and other ways. Suppliers and costumiers were also quick to capitalize on the compulsive trend, ever attentive to their customers' quest for the new. Providers and consumers alike became attuned to the fine gradations of Pierrot accoutrements. Stockists sold a benumbing array of pompoms, ruffs, folly bells, sateen skullcaps and conical hats. As advertised in *The Lady* in the mid-1920s, Burkinshaw of Liverpool, as a typical example, offered a pack of six 2-inch wool pompoms in every colour, and silk ones for twice the price. They also stocked a variety of ruffs, their most luxurious being triple-frilled. For those home dressmakers using paper patterns supplied by *Leach's*, *Weldon's* and *The Lady*, Burkinshaw stocked fabric in nineteen different Harlequin and Jazz designs. Many other firms offered similar though minutely different merchandise.

It is easy to see why the costume became so popular so quickly. The eccentric outfit with all its whimsical trappings was just the thing to bring a new urgency to fancy-dress parties after the First World War. It was different from other forms of dress, even other fancy dress. More than any other costume style, this is the one that gets mentioned most in the press, and visual evidence for its wide currency is overwhelming, with still and moving pictures confirming that Pierrot had become omnipresent.[37]

Another fancy-dress choice that came to full fruition a little later than Pierrot and outpaced him into modern times was the animal disguise, conspicuous in a crowd and, in its twentieth-century incarnation, hugely amusing. From way back, people have simulated the attributes and features of animals, and we humans have long cherished the notion of communicating with them and being understood by them.[38] Folklore is crowded with examples of humans in animal guise, from the Padstow Hobby Horse in the southwest of the British Isles to the Festival of the Horse far to the north in Orkney.[39]

The idea of pretending to be something other than fully human was certainly being introduced into the British dressing-up repertoire by the time of Ardern Holt's influential manuals of the 1880s. All the way

135 A float with young women dressed as bees and butterflies, Ilford Hospital Carnival, July 1908. Another 'insect' and a 'Pearly King' walk beside the wagon with collecting boxes.

through our period, insects and birds were acceptable guises, though the way they were portrayed changed over time and, increasingly through the course of the twentieth century, larger animals came to be a recognized subdivision of the fancy-dress anthology. The story of fancy-dress creatures is one of progression: at first costumes only alluded to them but, later, garments were fashioned to imitate animal characteristics more closely.

The long lists of winged things in the early manuals (there are around forty insects and birds described in Holt's 1896 book) do not match up with the surviving visual evidence: butterflies and dragonflies are the most conspicuous in the pictorial record along with wasps, bees and hornets, their stripiness a gift for distinct outfits (illus. 135). Holt even included a fancy costume called 'Insectifuga': 'This can be represented by every variety of insect, dotted over a black or white tulle evening dress intersected with gold; fireflies imprisoned in the veil.'[40] Costume choices were becoming more playful by Holt's final edition but even so there is little that is unbecoming about even this insect-repelling character. It is still predicated on the notion of a formal ball-dress and it copies Parisian fancy-dress fashion plates ornamented with birds and flying insects. These seductive images were widely disseminated in English-language publications and I suggest that their allure as fancy costumes was due to that most covetable of appendages, a pair of wings.

Humans might have bodies with flexible limbs but an exoskeleton eludes them, and the many thrilling connotations of wings – soaring, flying, lighter-than-air – stirs the imagination of the earth-bound. Angels and fairies have a similar aura of possible elevation about them. In the fancy-dress sphere, these winged beings are sometimes indistinguishable from one another. They represent a delusion, of course, but the feel of wings on your back fosters a sense of limitless possibilities.

Another facet contributing to the popularity of insects with costume masqueraders must lie with the artfulness of the microscope. Like the camera, the microscope – a much older contrivance – changed people's ways of looking at the world and, from the second half of the nineteenth century, these optical instruments were available to middle-class families to use at home along with commercially mounted specimens of Lepidoptera and other orders of insects. A tiny butterfly with shimmering wings could be enlarged in all its fragile detail by means of a microscopic lens.[41] Fancy-dress costume monumentalized it.

Miss Tootsie Sloper paid tribute to the butterfly in a less serious manner. The frock-conscious daughter of the fictional comic character Ally Sloper designed a wondrous butterfly costume in 1887 as part of her 'Fashion Fancies' series reproduced in *Ally Sloper's Half-Holiday*.[42] It had exaggerated sleeves for wings and was worn with striped stockings.

136 Woman dressed as a butterfly, photographed by the firm of Carbonara, Liverpool, February 1924.

Tootsie frequently incorporated animal shapes as well as insects into her fantasy garments and all of these 'Fancies' were shot through with humour and reflected the contemporary vestiary tempo. Her 'Polar Regions' costume is pictured in the Introduction.

It would be another decade or more before butterfly fancy dress came close to resembling the nectar-feeding creature. Even after that time, it was portrayed as more human than insect, an unavoidable aspect of most animal fancy dress however well it was designed. Whichever way it was realized, the butterfly was always associated with young women and girls – boys, who are not recorded as butterflies, dressed up as stingers and buzzers along with girls – and designated 'pretty', 'attractive' or 'artistic'. Deemed 'most artistic' at a juvenile ball in 1903, the butterfly costume of Miss Irene Port had glittering antennae.[43] We might think this defining appendage essential to a butterfly portrayal but, like the fairy wings discussed in Chapter One, they were not always in evidence. Fancy-dress guides make little mention of them at first but sometimes give the butterfly a wand, an accessory of the fairy realm.[44] There is much fancy-dress miscegenation between fairies, insects and flowers, and flower fairies were legion. Many different butterfly incarnations appeared at fancy-dress balls of all kinds and, as the idea of dressing as a butterfly began to lose its novelty value, other attributes to do with attractive patterning and wing ornamentation came into play to ensure its survival as a prize-winning costume choice.

As the butterfly fancy dress developed, small wings were replaced by something much more dramatic. A page of designs from *Leach's* children's catalogue of 1922 shows a bevy of small girls, all of them with fanciful and differently shaped wings. *Leach's* helpfully gives a back view illustration of each costume.[45] Fancy dressers began to pose with outstretched butterfly wings, facilitating fake fluttering and flying as well as showing off the decoration to best advantage (illus. 136). Satin cross-gartering or silk harem trousers were often brought into service for the lower part of the insect. The butterfly was to hold its own as a popular outfit through to the Second World War, though more newsworthy costume types sometimes edged it to the sidelines. Mary Cave's butterfly at the Devizes Carnival in 1934 was a lucky winner, even though she was up against several entrants whose outfits were much more topical: 'Mickey and Minnie Mouse', 'Will's Cigarettes' and 'Nippy', the Lyons Tea Shop waitress in her distinguishing uniform.[46]

The bat, embedded in British fancy dress by the 1890s, was one of the outfits that heralded a turn away from gender-specific characters: both male and female adults and children wore it. It represents a kind of halfway house between insects and animals.[47] Other creatures from the animal kingdom were late entrants into the costume pantheon despite animals and animal images of all sorts permeating society during our period. Productive farm animals and transport horses were an integral part of the countryside and city streets, and more exotic animals from the far reaches of the British empire were familiar to most Victorians and Edwardians. Menageries and circuses widened the circle of types of animals they could see, as did the opening of London Zoo to the general public in 1847.[48] Keepers dressed up as colonial tiger-shooters and foreign custodians in their traditional dress attended to the animals under their charge. Sophisticated taxidermy gave deceased animals a kind of immortality, and Walter Potter (1835–1918) opened up this grimly weird world with his *tableaux* of dressed dead kittens.[49]

In 1874, one of Queen Victoria's sons, the Duke of Connaught, sported the pelt of a large cat over his head and the creature's long tail swept the ground. He looked as if he might be mimicking a leopard when he attended the Marlborough House Ball.[50] In fact, he was taking part in the Fairy Tale Quadrille and was playing the Beast, a pseudo-animal-cum-prince, opposite Miss Graham's Beauty. Nearly a decade later, Holt's *Gentlemen's Fancy Dress* would be quoting the duke's outfit as exemplary for the Beast prince.[51] While writers on dress often take Holt's volumes to be foundational, it is good to be reminded that they popularized but did not invent dressing up.

The first mention of a true animal outfit in Ardern Holt's women's costume book is also a character from a fairy story: 'White Cat'.[52] Known in many different versions, *The White Cat* shows up in Britain throughout the nineteenth and early twentieth centuries both as a story and as a pantomime. James Robinson Planché, whose multi-faceted career as a dramatist, costume designer, *tableaux vivants* creator and advisor to Queen Victoria touches everywhere on our own story of fancy dress, translated *The White Cat* into English in 1855, giving a boost to the princess/cat persona's popularity. Holt's cat, with her delightful fur-trimmed attire, follows the fashion norms of the day rather than the outlines of a cat, but the costume does conjure up at least some semblance of non-humanness with pointed ears and a velvet collar hung with bells. There is no obvious tail; neither are there paws. A greater emulative closeness to an animal could have been troublesome. There is a sense that fancy dress might wish to distance itself from pagan animal rituals, for example, or the unsophisticated culture surrounding rural animal husbandry in a now rapidly industrializing and urbanized Britain. Despite all this, 'White Cat' in Marie Schild's 1881 costume book seems nearer to a mouser than a princess. This costume for a six-year-old girl includes a small bird worn on the head and a caged mouse.[53] There does not seem to be anything quite like an all-in-one animal suit for amateur fancy dress much prior to 1891. In that year, Master Pincus attended the Leeds Children's Fancy Dress Ball dressed as a cat and, in 1892, Butterick's *Masquerade and Carnival: Their Customs and Costumes* featured a 'white cat' alongside an illustration of a girl unmistakably dressed in a bifurcated suit with eared hood and tail.[54]

Like traditional tales, children's books were full of clothed, talking and emotion-driven animals whose stories often instilled morals and correct behaviour in their young readers. The animal characters in Lewis Carroll's *Alice* books are wonderfully chaotic and some children must have been drawn to these figures in preference to Alice herself, whose clothes and appearance were rather everyday until the passage of time historicized her attire.[55] We first meet some of the *Alice* characters in Holt's 1887 edition, where the descriptions, vague as to how they might be contrived, presume an acquaintance with some of the famous book's illustrations.[56]

Whatever the strictures on dressing up as something non-human, there is no doubt that the late Victorian and Edwardian periods were years of unabated interest in animals. While some party-goers might have been reluctant to dress up *as* animals, they were not averse to dressing up their pets. Pet-keeping and breeding were endlessly absorbing preoccupations and, at the turn of the twentieth century, one dog fancier had no qualms about disguising himself as an animal. A breeder and exhibitor of Dalmatians and, beyond question, a star of this book, Dr Wheeler-O'Bryen took the prize for the best character costume at a ball, dressed as one of his delightfully spotted canines (illus. 137). The tail-coated evening suit is surmounted with a moulded head that completely covers the dog-lover's features.

137 Dr Wheeler-O'Bryen, a breeder of Dalmatians, dressed as one of his dogs for a costume ball, *c.* 1900, from Charles Lane, *Dog Shows and Doggy People* (1902).

Wheeler-O'Bryen aside, it was perhaps pantomime, transformed from the harlequinade in the 1840s, that proved to be a fruitful inspiration for the more disruptive genre of animal costume. Some pantomime animals, originally characters from fairy tales and traditional stories, shared certain attributes with humans and joined the ranks of fancy dress. Puss in Boots, the celebrity cat in a plumed hat, stole the limelight in pantomime, and his swagger and bravado appealed to costumed revellers. His musketeer-like garments defined the character perhaps more than any cat features and, although pantomime posters show him with a tail, this appendage is not invariably mentioned in the costume books. A young guest at the children's annual Lord Mayor's Ball at the Mansion House in 1892 *does* sport a tail, and in place of the swashbuckling hat, he wears a hood sewn with ears, eyes and whiskers. The characteristic high boots are retained to distinguish him as Puss.[57]

Animal roles in pantomime are known as 'skin parts' and their enveloping costumes were skilfully made by professionals to allow movement and vision. Two-person cows and horses cavorted in tandem on pantomime stages along with Mother Goose, cats and dogs. Performers specialized in these taxing roles, and the comic quirkiness of a man in an animal suit undoubtedly encouraged amateurs to emulate the style. One of the first proper animal costumes was the poodle, a favourite breed of pet dog. In truth, it is questionable how much this costume ever materialized as fancy dress in the nineteenth century; it certainly appeared in the listings but was complicated to make, involving frizzed hair and many tiny ruches for the coat.[58] Its inclusion must have been due to the widespread adulation of the breed with its highly distinctive haircut as well as to Charles Lauri's anthropomorphic pantomime act. Lauri (1860–1903) was a renowned animal impersonator and left an account of just how difficult his suits were to make and wear.[59] This might, in part, account for the party-goer's initial disinclination to don complete animal cover-ups.

The first years of the twentieth century do seem to herald the beginnings of the all-enveloping animal suit as fancy dress. The 'Dancing Bear' at the Chard carnival in 1891 may have worn an all-in-one suit though there is no picture. Likewise, there is no illustration of Master Keene, who attended the Mansion House Juvenile Ball in 1903 'in the skin of an electric monkey, with an electric light at the tip of the tail', a wonderfully zany costume for such a traditional gathering.[60] In 1909, a participant in the Tottenham Prince of Wales Hospital Carnival was photographed dressed up in a bear suit (illus. 138). In that same year, an Up Helly Aa squad rigged themselves out in monkey suits and from then on Shetland would see an array of animal disguises through the years, as pictured in Chapter Three. At the 1913 Chelsea Arts Club Ball,

138 Two people dressed as a bear and its keeper, participants in Tottenham Prince of Wales Hospital Carnival, posing for a studio photograph by William Atkinson Jr, London, 1909.

139 Gerald and Donald Johns in cat suits, Dairen (modern-day Dalian), China, 1928–9. They are holding a Felix the Cat toy and the brothers may have been impersonating this favourite cartoon character.

Mrs Cole was completely disguised as a polar bear while her husband enacted the part of 'zoo keeper'.[61]

Such total concealment was not comprehensively reflected at all fancy-dress get-togethers. Heads and masks were cumbersome and hot, and sometimes the point of dressing up was to be recognized rather than totally disguised. However, there was no stopping the trend for animal characters, and caps and hoods that left the face uncovered were

26

Weldon's Fancy Dress for Children

D81622
Witch
8 to 14 yrs.

66359
Frog
4 to 12 yrs.

78455
Red Riding Hood
4 to 10 yrs.

39235
Rabbit
6 to 16 yrs.

63892
Wolf
4 to 16 yrs.

Weldon's fancy dress patterns are 1/- each post free, and include directions for making, suggested colour schemes and quantities of materials required. Orders accompanied by remittance to cover cost, should be sent to Weldons, Ltd., 30-32 Southampton Street, Strand, London, W.C.2

72793
"Alice"
9 to 14 yrs.

72803
"The Mad Hatter"
9 to 14 yrs.

75719
The White Rabbit
(Alice in Wonderland)
4 to 10 yrs.

41564
Tabby Cat
4 to 16 yrs.

75732
Mouse
4 to 10 yrs.

140 Page from *Weldon's Fancy Dress for Children* showing several different animal suits, characters from *Alice's Adventures in Wonderland* and other outfits, 1940s.

HERE you see two variations of the Clown's costume beloved of men since time began, and certainly beloved by the women often entrusted with the making. Use printed cotton fabric in the traditional red and white. The Pantomime Clown has many frills edged with red ribbon or braid. Unless nature has been very unkind in the matter of hair he had better wear a wig. His compatriot from the Circus rejoices in a one-piece costume of white blobbed with red. His felt hat is unadorned, but his make-up is a thing of beauty, attained after much labour with rouge and flour.

All these costumes are cut to fit small and medium men.

No. 18,697
Pantomime Clown.

No. 8,131
Lobster

No. 18,057
Harlequin.

No. 18,696
Circus Clown.

A MOST realistic lobste clad in a shell of pin sateen of the approve shade. The body marking are painted in, and the trouse legs tied in place and slightl pouched to continue the effec which is completed by realisti whiskers sewn in with the le seam and made of dyed hors hair or raffia. A formidabl pair of pincers provide head-dress worthy of th occasion.

HARLEQUIN, No. 18,057, mashed in the approved fashion, wearing a little black "waistcoat" and diamond-patterned trousers and sleeves. When bought the material boasted only black, red, orange and blue, but the use of two bottles of gold paint has made it glitter in approved Drury Lane fashion. Collar and cuffs of white.

Masks, wigs, and carnival novelties from W. Clarkson, Wardour Street, London, W.

Page 10—Fancy Dress Book.

141 A lobster outfit for a man from *Leach's Fancy Dress* (1922).

common. These were much more suitable and safer for children (illus. 139). As the years went by, children noticeably laid claim to animal fancy dress. Changing attitudes to animals coupled with a loosening of what was sartorially acceptable and possible fanned the desire for new characters. Weldons produced children's patterns for a raft of animals, including a frog, goldfish, monkey, moth, mouse, penguin, puppy, owl, spring chicken, tabby cat, tiger and wolf (illus. 140). Children had a greater opportunity to show off their creature camouflage when drama, dancing and singing became worthwhile educational pursuits in schools and clubs.

Adults were not excluded from animal fun, however, and their greater size lent their zoic costumes an air of surreal comedy. Recommended as suitable for hotel dances at Swiss winter resorts, a marvellous lobster outfit for a woman was featured in *The Tatler* in 1911.[62] Despite its ludicrous appearance, it did resemble the modish hobble skirts fashionable at the time, another example of the meeting of fashion and fancy dress. Lobster fancy dress seems to have been a particular favourite for both men and women and continued to appear in the catalogues. From 1922, *Leach's Fancy Dress*, for example, featured the fetching crustacean for a male party-goer clad in pink sateen with the body markings painted in and the trouser legs tied up at intervals, giving a pouchy effect (illus. 141). A hood surmounted with what *Leach's* termed a 'formidable pair of pincers' completed the outfit.[63]

EPILOGUE

Fancy dress certainly did not slip away from the sartorial stage in the decades after Queen Elizabeth II's coronation in 1953. In the course of writing this book, many people who were children at that time have been eager to tell me how they remember dressing up for birthday parties, or of their other experiences of fancy dress. One colleague, the daughter of a vicar, recalls a dressing-up box containing a gypsy outfit, a fabulous Spanish flamenco dress, several 'Red Indian' outfits and a little Miss Muffet complete with stuffed spider, proving that old favourites continued to hold sway. Another friend produced a photograph of her family trip to Volendam in the Netherlands around 1960 when she, her sister and a friend posed as Dutch girls in a studio setting. They purchased the costumes and brought them back to England as souvenirs. A less than happy experience of dressing up is recounted by a family member who to this day shudders with humiliation at the memory of the costume hurriedly improvised from tea-towels by a determined mother for a children's fancy-dress competition during a transatlantic crossing on the *Queen Elizabeth* in 1964.

But there is still a real sense that, from the mid-1950s onwards, new media and new influences were brought to bear in ways that altered the terrain described in this book. Quite clearly, one of the most important of these was the widespread adoption of television as the main form of home entertainment. The 'Davy Crockett' hat, with its pendant tail at the back, was such a craze among young boys in Britain that 5,000 a day were being sold when the television series about this American woodsman aired in Britain. 'Dr Kildare', 'Dr Who', 'Dalek' and many more television characters besides would join the 'king of the wild frontier' in the repertoire of fancy dress over the subsequent decades. These were above all *children's* characters since, although adults clearly did continue to dress up in the 1950s, '60s and '70s, particularly in the context of student rags, which conspicuously flourished at this time, it was as a childish form of fun that fancy dress survived most prominently in the immediate post-war decades. Although the evidence is anecdotal, in contrast to fancy dress of earlier periods, it seems that a distinct feature of some children's costumes right the way through the second half of the twentieth century is that they were occasionally, even often, worn in everyday situations. The Marvel hero or Disney princess in the supermarket aisle is an unremarkable sight.

Apart from television and cinema, another factor that has fostered a dynamic fancy-dress revival of a distinct kind is the changing demographic of Britain. Racially motivated attacks on people arriving to work in British cities from the West Indies spurred on these new immigrants to organize events that took pride in their Caribbean heritage. The Notting Hill Carnival grew out of this desire for community cohesion, and the truly fabulous costumes, different in many obvious ways from the fancy dress described in this book, mark another direction for dressing up. Similarly, the Chinese diaspora and people from the Indian sub-continent, to name just two influential groups, have enriched the fancy-dress repertoire in thoughtful and inspiring ways.

From the 1980s and through to the present, a huge resurgence in the practices of dressing up by adults has assumed proportions that neither Ardern Holt nor the 'feathered-up' audiences for *Hiawatha* could ever have imagined. Some of this is clearly related to the commercialization of Halloween as an occasion for bacchanalian and costumed jollification. The rise and rise of the ritualized 'Stag Night' and, perhaps even more, 'Hen Night' has given a huge boost to the number of occasions on which fancy dress signals the abandonment of everyday restraints. The proliferation of fancy-dress shops and now fancy-dress websites, frequently offering a particular form of sexualised costume – endless variations on 'Sexy Nurse/Secretary/Policewoman/Librarian' are prominent – takes fancy dress into realms of imagined and actual transgression that are very much part of the contemporary world.

It is nowadays quite common for forms of fancy dress to be worn at demonstrations (think of the dystopian 'Handmaidens' of Margaret Atwood novels) and protests (Extinction Rebellion has its own repertoire of costumed figures, even living statues), as well as at music festivals and gigs (illus. 142). Phenomena like the steampunk movement have their own very distinctive dress codes, mixing Victorian and dystopian styles

142 Women dressed as Handmaidens protesting the U.S. president Donald Trump's UK state visit, London, June 2019.

143 Whitby Steampunk Weekend, North Yorkshire, July 2018.

(illus. 143). And the prevalence of numerous forms of cosplay ('costume play'), where participants wear specific character costumes from popular literature or performances, has its roots in the vibrant media landscape of contemporary Japan. This speaks to a globalization of fancy dress, where the same costumes, drawn from anime as well as from the Marvel Universe, are worn in Shanghai and Seattle and Sunderland.[1] At the same time, globalization has been accompanied by an awareness of the perils of cultural appropriation, where 'dressing up as X' no longer seems quite like the innocent pleasure it once did, and the kinds of cheerfully blatant racism which marked the popular culture of Britain in the past will not now go unchallenged, even as they stubbornly refuse to disappear.

Other anxieties and disquietudes now attend on fancy dress too. The overtly gendered nature of the marketing of costumes has been the subject of new challenges while simultaneously confirming the divisions of the past.[2] And the cult of the Disney princess, with hundreds of little girls in identical costumes attending singalong screenings of *Frozen*, or phalanxes of Harry Potters turning up at primary schools across the land for World Book Day, often cost hard-pressed parents significant sums of money. This is all part of the process whereby fancy dress has become an arm of the global entertainment industry, as much as it is an opportunity for individual creativity or the display of craft skills.

But continuities with the past also remain. Many events not recorded in this book – the Jewish holiday of Purim and the Preston Guild celebrations being just two examples – survive and flourish with fancy dress a significant constituent (illus. 144). Perhaps World Book Day is just the current incarnation of Empire Day, both equally approved of by teachers and official guardians of national culture like the BBC. The dressing up of fans of the various incarnations of *The Rocky Horror Show*, in imitation of the characters on stage or screen, is perhaps a modern equivalent of the audiences of 'Red Indians' who attended those performances of Samuel Coleridge-Taylor's cantata at the Royal Albert Hall between the wars. Events like the Lewes and Bridgwater carnivals, and Up Helly Aa in Shetland, continue to flourish and indeed attract large crowds of spectators; some of these events now receive funding from such gatekeepers of approved culture as the Arts Council and the National Lottery, even if others, by their refusal

144 Celebrating the Jewish festival of Purim in Stamford Hill, London, March 2017. The man's *shtreimel* hat gets a global makeover, while his son as an airline pilot and his daughter in a Japanese kimono develop the international theme.

to admit women as participants to what are still all-male events, fall outside the norms of contemporary society, remain purely self-funded. And Britain's city centres are fuller than they ever were in the past of 'living sculptures', their gold-painted Yodas and Darth Vaders a perhaps remote descendant, but still arguably a descendant, of the *poses plastiques* and *tableaux vivants* of the Victorian and Edwardian drawing room. Above all, getting dressed up remains an opportunity to be photographed, as even the most cursory search online will immediately show you. The approval, and sometimes disapproval, which it evokes is beyond doubt precisely the point of fancy dress, and that remains too. It seems unlikely to go away any time soon.

REFERENCES

Introduction **FANCY DRESS DEFINED**

1 Hilaire and Meyer Hiler, *Bibliography of Costume* (New York, 1939), pp. xii–xiii.

2 For many perceptive examples of what fancy dress is and is not, together with etymological derivations, see Benjamin Wild, *Carnival to Catwalk: Global Reflections on Fancy Dress Costume* (London, 2020), unpaginated electronic copy, Introduction. Wild's insightful volume appeared after this present work was essentially finished but it repays close study, especially as regards its global and theoretical orientation.

3 Judith R. Walkowitz, *Nights Out: Life in Cosmopolitan London* (New Haven, CT, 2012); Matt Houlbrook, *Queer London: Perils and Pleasures in the Sexual Metropolis, 1918–1957* (Chicago, IL, 2006).

4 For pageants: Angela Bartie, Linda Fleming, Mark Freeman and Alexander Hutton, eds, *Restaging the Past: Historical Pageants, Culture and Society in Modern Britain* (London, 2020); for re-enactments: Pat Poppy, 'Fancy Dress? Costume for Re-Enactment', *Costume*, XXXI (1997), pp. 100–104.

5 Angus McLaren, 'Smoke and Mirrors: Willy Clarkson and the Role of Disguises in Inter-War England', *Journal of Social History*, XL/3 (2007), pp. 597–618; John Gudenian, 'Bermans & Nathans: Costume and the Entertainment World', *Costume*, XV (1981), pp. 60–66.

6 Michael Silvestri, 'The Thrill of "Simply Dressing Up": The Indian Police, Disguise and Intelligence Work in Colonial India', *Journal of Colonialism and Colonial History*, II/2 (2001), e-journal at http://muse.jhu.edu/journals.

7 Verity Wilson, 'Western Modes and Asian Clothes: Reflections on Borrowing Other People's Dress', *Costume*, XXXVI (2002), pp. 139–57.

8 For many other examples: Alison Smith, ed., *Artists and Empire: Facing Britain's Imperial Past*, exh. cat., Tate Britain (London, 2015).

9 Linda Colley, *Captives: Britain, Empire and the World, 1600–1850* (London, 2002), pp. 9–10.

10 Judith Walkowitz, 'The Indian Woman, the Flower Girl, and the Jew: Photojournalism in Edwardian London', *Victorian Studies*, XLII (1998/9), pp. 3–46.

11 Marjorie Garber, *Vested Interests: Cross-Dressing and Cultural Anxiety* (London, 1992).

12 Michael Warboys, Julie-Marie Strange and Neil Pemberton, *The Invention of the Modern Dog: Breed and Blood in Victorian Britain* (Baltimore, MD, 2018), pp. 45–8.

13 P.A.W. Collins, 'Queen Mab's Chariot Among the Steam Engines: Dickens and "Fancy"', *English Studies*, XLII/1–6 (1961), pp. 78–90.

14 Newark House Museum, Leicester, #C533–1969.

15 Sara Stevenson and Helen Bennett, *Van Dyck in Check Trousers: Fancy Dress in Art and Life*, exh. cat., Scottish National Portrait Gallery, Edinburgh (1978), p. 87.

16 Anthea Jarvis and Patricia Raine, *Fancy Dress* (Aylesbury, 1984); Bethan Bide, 'Signs of Wear: Encountering Memory in the Worn Materiality of a Museum Fashion Collection', *Fashion Theory*, XXI/4 (2017), pp. 449–76.

17 *Ipswich Journal*, Saturday 9 December 1893, p. 2.

18 Catherine Hindson, *London's West End Actresses and the Origins of Celebrity Charity, 1880–1920* (Iowa City, IA, 2016), pp. 101–24.

19 Richard W. Schoch, *Queen Victoria and the Theatre of Her Age* (Basingstoke, 2004), p. 17.

20 Cynthia Cooper, *Magnificent Entertainments: Fancy Dress Balls of Canada's Governors General, 1876–1898* (Fredericton, New Brunswick, 1997), pp. 28–9.

21 Nancy Martha West, *Kodak and the Lens of Nostalgia* (Charlottesville, VA, 2000), chap. 4.

22 For a scholarly view on photographic perception see the several works of Jonathan Crary.

23 Barak Y. Orbach, 'The Johnson–Jeffries Fight and Censorship of Black Supremacy', *NYU Journal of Law and Liberty* (2010), pp. 270–346, at https://ssrn.com/abstract.

24 *London Daily News*, Saturday 14 September 1907, p. 7; for Indians in Edwardian Britain see Walkowitz, 'The Indian Woman', p. 8.

25 Barbara Adam, 'Time', *Theory, Culture and Society*, XXIII/2–3 (2006), pp. 111–26.

26 *Western Times*, Friday 13 November 1925, p. 3.

27 For Covent Garden prizes: *Morning Post*, Monday 21 January 1901, p. 4; for Cinema Fancy Dress Ball: *Sunderland Daily Echo and Shipping Gazette*, Wednesday 4 March 1936, p. 5; for Burnley Harvest Dance: *Burnley Express*, Saturday 15 September 1945, p. 6; 'Marie Lloyd Presenting Prizes for the Best Fancy Dresses at Mr E. Slights Fancy Dress Ball, Kings Hall, Hackney, Mar. 18th 1908', *History in Pictures*, postcard #E-113 at www.history-in-pictures.co.uk, accessed 5 March 2020.

28 Carly Eck, 'Headlines Make Fashion: The Use of Newsprint Fabric and Newspaper Clippings in Fashion and Fancy Dress', *Costume*, XLIII (2009), pp. 138–49.

29 Sara Stevenson, *Hill and Adamson's The Fishermen and Women of the Firth of Forth* (Edinburgh, 1991); Rachel Worth, 'Some Issues in the Representation of Rural Working-Class Dress in British Nineteenth-Century Photography', *Revue belge de philologie et d'histoire*, LXXXVII/3–4 (2009), pp. 775–91 (pp. 780–81).

30 Stephen Knott, 'Fancy Dress as an Amateur Craft', *Performance Research*, XXV/1 (2020), pp. 10–17.

31 Robert Bud, Paul Greenhalgh, Frank James and Morag Shiach, eds, *Being Modern: The Cultural Impact of Science in the Early Twentieth Century* (London, 2018), pp. 1–19.

32 Charles Dickens, 'Managers and Music-Halls', *All the Year Round*, IV/23 (March 1861), pp. 558–61 (p. 559) at Dickens Journals Online, www.djo.org.uk.

33 London Transport Museum #1983/4/331; Victoria and Albert Museum, London #T.263–1987.

34 For further examples of dress in fiction: Celia Marshik, *At the Mercy of Their Clothes: Modernism, the Middlebrow, and British Garment Culture* (New York, 2017), pp. 114–44.

One **BALLS AND PARTIES**

1 Metropolitan Museum of Art, New York #2007.284.

2 For examples: *Hampshire Advertiser*, Saturday 17 January 1857, p. 5; *Banffshire Journal and General Advertiser*, Tuesday 14 October 1879, p. 6.

3 Photostream of 'ronramstew', p. 37, at www.flickr.com/explore, accessed 28 January 2021.

4 Marina Warner, *Stranger Magic: Charmed States and the 'Arabian Nights'* (London, 2012), especially the Glossary, pp. 437–8.

5 Anthea Jarvis and Patricia Raine, *Fancy Dress* (Aylesbury, 1984), pp. 26–9.

6 C. Willett Cunnington, *English Women's Clothing in the Nineteenth Century* [London, 1937] (Mineola, NY, 1990), pp. 261–3, 302; both London and provincial newspapers reported the sale of Dickens's Dolly Varden portrait, for example: *London Evening Standard*, Monday 11 July 1870, p. 6, and *Falkirk Herald*, Thursday 14 July 1870, p. 7.

7 Thomas Cardoza, *Intrepid Women: Cantinières and Vivandières of the French Army* (Bloomington, IN, 2010).

8 For the link between fancy dress, folk tales and pantomime: Jennifer Schacker, *Staging Fairyland: Folklore, Children's Entertainment, and Nineteenth-Century Pantomime* (Detroit, MI, 2018), pp. 45–56.

9 Audrey Linkman, *The Victorians: Photographic Portraits* (London, 1993), pp. 37–46.

10 'Fancy Dress Photographs by Sussex Photographers', www.photohistory-sussex.co.uk, accessed 10 June 2015.

11 The Exeter ball appears in the following accounts: *Exeter and Plymouth Gazette*, Friday 17 January 1873, p. 5; *Exeter Flying Post*, Wednesday 15 January 1873, p. 5; *Exeter and Plymouth Gazette*, Friday 31 January 1873, p. 5; *Exeter and Plymouth Gazette*, Friday 18 April 1873, p. 6; *Exeter Flying Post*, Wednesday 16 April 1873, p. 5; Owen Angel's name appears many times in the Exeter newspapers through the 1850s, '60s and '70s.

12 Royal Collections Trust #RCIN 2914285, #RCIN 2914286.

13 *Liverpool Daily Post*, Friday 12 January 1877, pp. 5–6; *Liverpool Mercury*, Friday 12 January 1877, p. 6.

14 *Liverpool Mercury*, Wednesday 3 January 1877, p. 3.

15 *Liverpool Mercury*, Thursday 8 November 1877, p. 6; *Liverpool Daily Post*, Thursday 4 January 1877, p. 1.

16 *Liverpool Daily Post*, Thursday 4 January 1877, p. 1.

17 State Library of South Australia #B 7723/388–398.

18 For balls in Leicester and at Hatfield House: Jarvis and Raine, *Fancy Dress*, pp. 26–7; for a ball in Leeds: Leeds Museums and Galleries, blog: Kitty Ross, 'The Children's Fancy Dress Ball', 19 December 2016.

19 Sara Stevenson and Helen Bennett, *Van Dyck in Check Trousers: Fancy Dress in Art and Life*, exh. cat., Scottish National Portrait Gallery, Edinburgh (1978), pp. 19–30.

20 Ann Mozley Moyal, *Clear Across Australia: A History of Telecommunications* (Melbourne, 1984).

21 *The Sphere*, Saturday 17 January 1925, p. 5.

22 British Pathé historical collection #851.26 (13 January 1936); The Lord Mayor's Children's Ball album, 1936: Victoria and Albert Museum, Bethnal Green Museum of Childhood, London #B.222:1–1996.

23 Royal Collection Trust #RCIN 913335.

24 London Metropolitan Archives #CLA/057/03/028–029.

25 *Cheshire Observer*, Saturday 1 January 1927, p. 4.

26 Royal Collection Trust #RCIN 74860.

27 *The Times*, Saturday 3 July 1897, p. 12; a comprehensive list of sitters, their backgrounds and costumes, together with images from the Victoria and Albert Museum, London: Russell Harris, 'A Great Ball in 1897', www.rvondeh.dircon.co.uk/incalmprose/ball, accessed 5 February 2020; Sophia Murphy, *The Duchess of Devonshire's Ball* (London, 1984).

28 Nancy J. Troy, *Couture Culture: A Study in Modern Art and Fashion* (Cambridge, MA, 2003), pp. 80–191.

29 Martin Spies, 'Late Victorian Aristocrats and the Racial Other: The Devonshire House Ball of 1897', *Race and Class*, LVII/4 (2016), pp. 95–103.

30 Fancy dress balls for royal servants were regularly organized at Sandringham, the country retreat of British monarchs, for example: *Evening Star*, Friday 31 December 1909, p. 3.

31 Anthea Jarvis, '"There was a Young Man of Bengal . . .": The Vogue for Fancy Dress, 1830–1950', *Costume*, XVI (1982), pp. 33–46 (pp. 34–40); Cynthia Cooper, *Magnificent Entertainments: Fancy Dress Balls of Canada's Governors General, 1876–1898* (Fredericton, New Brunswick, 1997); Bridget Brereton, 'The Trinidad Carnival in the Late Nineteenth Century', in *Carnival: Culture in Action. The Trinidad Experience*, ed. Milla Cozart Riggio (New York and Abingdon, 2004), pp. 53–63 (p. 61); Bradley Shope, 'Masquerading Sophistication: Fancy Dress Balls of Britain's Raj', *Journal of Imperial and Commonwealth History*, XXXIX/3 (2011), pp. 375–92.

32 Bridget J. Elliott, 'Covent Garden Follies: Beardsley's Masquerade Images of Posers and Voyeurs', *Oxford Art Journal*, IX/1 (1986), pp. 38–48 (pp. 41–4).

33 *The Bystander*, Wednesday 12 November 1913, p. 32.
34 The classic account is Terry Castle, *Masquerade and Civilization: The Carnivalesque in Eighteenth-Century English Culture and Fiction* (Stanford, CA, 1986).
35 *Taunton Courier and Western Advertiser*, Wednesday 4 February 1903, p. 2.
36 For prices, prizes and constructed costumes: Framley Steelcroft, 'Some Curious Fancy Dresses', *Strand Magazine* (January–June 1895), pp. 694–702; for butterfly costume and runners-up: *The Referee*, Sunday 5 December 1897, p. 3.
37 Catherine Hindson, *London's West End Actresses and the Origins of Celebrity Charity, 1880–1920* (Iowa City, IA, 2016), pp. 101–24.
38 *Yorkshire Post and Leeds Intelligencer*, Wednesday 6 February 1929, p. 12; *Coventry Evening Telegraph*, Wednesday 12 October 1932, p. 6.
39 *The Tatler*, Wednesday 4 December 1918, p. 7.
40 *Pall Mall Gazette*, Friday 22 November 1918, p. 7; *The Globe*, Monday 25 November 1918, p. 2.
41 For nurses' protest: *Daily Record*, Tuesday 26 November 1918, p. 3; for Sheppard's letter: *The Times*, 20 October 1925, p. 15.
42 *Daily Mirror*, Friday 28 November 1930, p. 1.
43 Matt Houlbrook, *Queer London: Perils and Pleasures in the Sexual Metropolis, 1918–1957* (Chicago, IL, 2006), pp. 266–9; Lady Malcolm's Servants' Ball Archive Display at Bishopsgate Institute, London, June–December 2016, www.duckie.co.uk/vintage.
44 *Illustrated Police News*, Saturday 9 October 1880, pp. 1–2.
45 British Pathé historical collection #269.24 (8 February 1923); #456.15 (4 March 1926); #826.24 (19 December 1929).
46 *Western Morning News*, Thursday 8 February 1923, p. 5; *The Sketch*, Wednesday 14 February 1923, p. 36.
47 *Isle of Wight Observer*, Saturday 16 February 1895, p. 8.
48 *Nottingham Journal*, Thursday 19 February 1920, p. 5; *Motherwell Times*, Friday 4 April 1924, p. 5; *Milngavie and Bearsden Herald*, Friday 15 November 1929, p. 8; *Leeds Mercury*, Monday 3 March 1930, p. 3; *Lincolnshire Echo*, Friday 1 March 1935, p. 3; *Morpeth Herald*, Friday 29 January 1937, p. 5.
49 Nicole Baur and Joseph Melling, 'Dressing and Addressing the Mental Patient: The Uses of Clothing in the Admission, Care and Employment of Residents in English Provincial Mental Hospitals, *c.* 1860–1960', *Textile History*, XLV/2 (2014), pp. 145–70 (p. 164).
50 *Chelmsford Chronicle*, Friday 21 January 1910, p. 2.

Two POSES AND TABLEAUX

1 The Brothers Mayhew, *Acting Charades or Deeds Not Words: A Christmas Game to Make a Long Evening Short* (London, 1850), pp. 2–3, 145.
2 Henry Dalton, *The Book of Drawing-Room Plays and Evening Amusements: A Comprehensive Manual of In-Door Recreation, with Scenic Illustrations by E. H. Corbould and G. du Maurier* (London, 1868), pp. 12, 14, 35, 44.
3 For Palace Theatre: *Morning Post*, Wednesday 9 May 1894, p. 3; for Royal Academy: *Yorkshire Post and Leeds Intelligencer*, Tuesday 24 June 1930, p. 10; *A Musical Clown:* Harris Museum and Art Gallery, Preston #PRSMG:P357; *Silver and Gold*: Birmingham Museums Trust #1930P333.
4 *Yorkshire Post and Leeds Intelligencer*, Saturday 4 June 1870, p. 5.
5 Kate Flint, *The Victorians and the Visual Imagination* (Cambridge, 2000), pp. 227, 234.
6 *Strand Magazine* (July 1891), pp. 3–8.
7 *Evening Star*, Wednesday 9 January 1907, p. 3.
8 *Pall Mall Gazette*, Saturday 12 May 1894, p. 3, and Friday 1 March 1889, p. 6.
9 For the relationship between art, photography and *tableaux*: Carol Jacobi, *Painting With Light: Art*

and Photography from the Pre-Raphaelites to the Modern Age (London, 2016); for the stereograph: Denis Pellerin and Brian May, *The Poor Man's Picture Gallery: Stereoscopy Versus Painting in the Nineteenth Century* (London, 2014), pp. 149–51; for the popular ballad: Roud Folk Song Index 2336; for one example as a *tableau*: *Derbyshire Times and Chesterfield Herald*, Saturday 8 May 1897, p. 6.

10 *Strand Magazine* (July 1891), pp. 3–8 (pp. 4–5).

11 Dalton, *The Book of Drawing-Room Plays*, pp. 139–41.

12 Richard W. Schoch, *Queen Victoria and the Theatre of Her Age* (Basingstoke, 2004).

13 Margaret Homans, *Royal Representations: Queen Victoria and British Culture, 1837–1876* (Chicago, IL, 1998).

14 Charles Harrison, *Theatricals and Tableaux Vivants for Amateurs* (London, 1882), pp. 114–18.

15 *Dorking and Leatherhead Advertiser*, Saturday 28 November 1891, p. 5.

16 *Ally Sloper's Half-Holiday*, Saturday 24 November 1888, p. 4.

17 G. J. Goodrick, *Tableaux Vivants and Living Waxworks with Directions for Stage Management* (London, *c.* 1895), pp. 22, 27, 29.

18 George Bradford Bartlett, *Mrs Jarley's Far-Famed Collection of Waxworks* (London, 1873–89), p. 4.

19 *Bexhill-on-Sea Observer*, Saturday 3 September 1910, p. 9.

20 *Essex Standard*, Saturday 31 December 1892, p. 7; *Leominster News and North West Herefordshire and Radnorshire Advertiser*, Friday 23 December 1892, p. 3.

21 Naomi Paxton, *The Methuen Drama Book of Suffrage Plays: Taking the Stage* (London, 2018), pp. xvi–xvii.

22 Josephine Kane, *The Architecture of Pleasure: British Amusement Parks, 1900–1939* (Farnham, 2013), pp. 17–79.

23 For the implications surrounding the female body: Lynda Nead, *The Haunted Gallery: Painting, Photography, Film, c. 1900* (New Haven, CT, and London, 2007), pp. 69–81.

24 The standard scholarly account remains Marina Warner, *Monuments and Maidens: The Allegory of the Female Form* (London, 1996).

25 Kate Nichols, *Greece and Rome at the Crystal Palace: Classical Sculpture in Modern Britain, 1854–1936* (Oxford, 2015).

26 David Huxley, 'Music Hall Art: "La Milo", Nudity and the *pose plastique*, 1905–1915', *Early Popular Visual Culture*, XI (2013), pp. 218–36.

27 O. J. Wendlandt, *Living Statuary; How It May Be Successfully Produced by Amateurs* (Manchester, 1896), pp. 4, 16.

28 Anne Hollander, *Seeing Through Clothes* (Berkeley, CA, and London, 1993), pp. 1–13.

29 Wendlandt, *Living Statuary*, p. 26.

30 Ibid., p. 21.

31 Robyne Calvert, '"The Artistic Aspect of Dress": The Story of the Healthy and Artistic Dress Union', *Costume*, LIV/2 (2020), pp. 175–201.

32 Wendlandt, *Living Statuary*, pp. 1–17.

33 'Living Statuary', *Every Woman's Encyclopaedia* (London, 1910–12), vol. VI, pp. 4145–8 (p. 4148).

34 Wendlandt, *Living Statuary*, pp. 11–13.

35 'Living Statuary', pp. 4146–7.

36 Butterick, *Masquerade and Carnival: Their Customs and Costumes* (London and New York, 1892), p. 21.

37 Audrey Linkman, *Photography and Death* (London, 2011).

38 *Dundee Evening Telegraph*, Friday 17 February 1893, p. 2.

39 *Strand Magazine* (July 1891), pp. 3–8 (p. 8).

40 Charles Harrison, *Theatricals and Tableaux Vivants*, p. 113 and back matter.

41 *The Graphic*, Saturday 25 February 1882, p. 12.

42 For the wide influence of the *Arabian Nights*: Philip F. Kennedy and Marina Warner, eds, *Scheherazade's*

Children: Global Encounters with the Arabian Nights (New York, 2013).

43 Cynthia Rowena Starey, *Bethlehem Tableaux as Played in a Somersetshire Village* (London, 1920), pp. 8–18.

44 For a stimulating example of what can be gained from addressing the question of lighting technology: Kate Flint, *Flash! Photography, Writing, and Surprising Illumination* (Oxford, 2017).

45 Sara Stevenson, *The Personal Art of David Octavius Hill* (New Haven, CT, and London, 2002).

46 University of Texas, The Harry Ransom Center for the Humanities, Photography Collections #964:0641:0001.

47 Ellen Handy, *Pictorial Effect, Naturalistic Vision: The Photographs and Theories of Henry Peach Robinson and Peter Henry Emerson*, exh. cat., Chrysler Museum of Art, Norfolk, VA (1994).

48 Marta Weiss, 'The Diversity of Expression and the Wondrous Power of the Art of Photography in the Albums of Richard Cockle Lucas', *History of Photography*, XXXVII/4 (2013), pp. 431–44.

49 Juliet Hacking, *Princes of Victorian Bohemia: Photographs by David Wilkie Wynfield* (London, 2000).

50 Diane Waggoner, *Lewis Carroll's Photography and Modern Childhood* (Princeton, NJ, 2020); Carol Mavor, *Becoming: The Photographs of Clementina, Viscountess Hawarden* (Durham, NC, and London, 1999); Jeffrey Rosen, *Julia Margaret Cameron's 'Fancy Subjects': Photographic Allegories of Victorian Identity and Empire* (Manchester, 2016).

51 Jeremy Coote and Christopher Morton, '"Dressed as a New Zealander", or an Ethnographic Mischmasch? Notes and Reflections on Two Photographs by Charles Dodgson (Lewis Carroll)', *Journal of Museum Ethnography*, XXVIII (2015), pp. 150–72.

52 Waggoner, *Lewis Carroll's Photography*, pp. 32, 162–4.

53 Adrian Woodhouse, *Angus McBean: Face-Maker* (Richmond, Surrey, 2006), pp. 44–5, 54–5.

54 Annebella Pollen, *The Kindred of the Kibbo Kift: Intellectual Barbarians* (London, 2006).

55 Woodhouse, *Angus McBean*, pp. 43, 121.

Three GUY FAWKES AND UP HELLY AA

1 For the history and myth of the Guy Fawkes celebration: James Sharpe, *Remember, Remember: A Cultural History of Guy Fawkes Day* (Cambridge, MA, 2005).

2 *The Procession of the Lewes Bonfire Boys*, lithograph by Thomas Henwood (1797–1861), 1853: Yale Center for British Art #B1978.43.246.

3 Steve Roud, *The English Year: A Month-By-Month Guide to the Nation's Customs and Festivals, from May Day to Mischief Night* (London, 2008), p. 452.

4 *Western Daily Press*, Monday 8 November 1880, p. 3.

5 For the effect of flares at Bridgwater: British Pathé historical collection, Reuters-Gaumont British Newsreel #VLVA5LI6HTFNPGBCE9OVHSZO8R4RE (7 November 1938).

6 *Taunton Courier and Western Advertiser*, Wednesday 13 November 1935, p. 3.

7 The standard scholarly text is Callum G. Brown, *Up-Helly-Aa: Custom, Culture and Community in Shetland* (Manchester, 1998).

8 For a comprehensive view of the construction of the Viking Age in Victorian Britain: Andrew Wahn, *The Vikings and the Victorians: Inventing the Old North in Nineteenth-Century Britain* (Rochester, NY, 2000).

9 *Greenock Telegraph and Clyde Shipping Gazette*, Tuesday 19 October 1897, p. 3.

10 Brian Smith, 'Shetland in Saga-Time: Rereading the *Orkneyinga Saga*', *Northern Studies*, XXV (1988), pp. 21–41, http://ssns.org.uk.

11 *Shetland Times*, Saturday 11 March 1905, p. 5.

12 *Shetland Times*, Saturday 13 January 1906, p. 4.

13 *The Sphere*, Saturday 10 February 1906, p. 4.
14 Carl Emil Doepler, Richard Wagner and Clara Steinitz, *Der Ring des Nibelungen von Richard Wagner: Figurinen Erfunden und Gezeichnet* (Berlin, 1889); Peter Cook, ed. and trans., *A Memoir of Bayreuth, 1876: related by Carl Emil Doepler including illustrations of his costume designs for the first production of the 'Ring'* (London, 1979).
15 *Shetland Times*, Saturday 10 October 1896, p. 2.
16 Venetia Newell, 'Up Helly Aa: A Shetland Winter Festival', *Arv*, XXXIV (1978), pp. 37–97 (pp. 63–5).
17 Roberta Frank, 'The Invention of the Viking Horned Helmet', in *International Scandinavian and Medieval Studies in Memory of Gerd Wolfgang Weber*, ed. Michael Dallapiazza, Olaf Hansen, Preben Meulengracht-Sørensen and Yvonne S. Bonnetain (Trieste, 2000), pp. 199–208.
18 For the first Jarl's outfit and subsequent information about its refashioning: www.uphellyaa.org; for the visual record of successive Jarls and all the squads: Shetland Museum and Archives, www.shetlandmuseumandarchives.org.uk, both accessed 16 March 2020.
19 For H. J. Anderson: Shetland Museum and Archives #UH00333; for Laurence Sandison: #ST00200; for A. P. Hawick: #00009MJ.
20 For several images of Peter Moar and A.R.M. Mathewson: Shetland Museum and Archives Photo Library.
21 Olwyn Owen and Christopher Lowe, *Kebister: The Four-Thousand-Year-Old Story of One Shetland Township*, Society of Antiquaries of Scotland (Edinburgh, 1999), p. 8.
22 Shetland Museum and Archives #PO5888, #PO5894.
23 *Shetland Times*, Monday 5 May 1873, p. 4.
24 *Shetland Times*, Saturday 16 January 1897, p. 2.
25 For elaborate costuming: *Shetland Times*, Monday 12 January 1874, p. 2, and Saturday 8 January 1876, p. 2; for early matching outfits: *Shetland Times*, Saturday 11 January 1879, p. 2; for lancers: Shetland Museum and Archives #A00107.
26 Aileen Ribeiro, *Dress in Eighteenth-Century Europe, 1715–1789* (London, 1984), pp. 165, 174.
27 Shetland Museum and Archives #UH00062.
28 For suffragette squads: *Shetland Times*, Saturday 30 January 1909, p. 5, and Saturday 6 February 1909, p. 5; for *jūjitsu* on Shetland: *Shetland Times*, Saturday 23 January 1909, p. 7, and Saturday 2 January 1909, p. 4; *Every Woman's Encyclopaedia* (London, 1910–12), vol. 1, pp. 446, 687.
29 Lynn Abrams, *Myth and Materiality in a Woman's World: Shetland, 1800–2000* (Manchester, 2005).
30 *Shetland Times*, Saturday 4 April 1908, p. 1.
31 *Shetland Times*, Saturday 4 February 1911, p. 5.
32 Shetland Museum and Archives #UH00170.
33 For diabolo: Shetland Museum and Archives #UH00036; for pogo: #UH00208.
34 For cookery classes: Shetland Museum and Archives #UH00130; for water supply: #UH00302; for council housing: #SM00318.
35 For 'Sole Savers': Shetland Museum and Archives #00047UP.
36 For monkeys: Shetland Museum and Archives #UH00075; for March Hares: #UH00239 and #00012UP; for chanticleers: #UH00231; for penguins: #UH00283.
37 'Old Norse Vikings Festival', Gaumont Graphic #1656 (1927), https://player.bfi.org.uk.
38 *The Scotsman*, Thursday 27 January 1938, p. 12.

Four CARNIVALS AND RAGS

1 For one example: 'Southend Carnival Procession', August 1929, https://player.bfi.org.uk.
2 *Bridlington Free Press*, Saturday 22 April 1876, p. 2.
3 *Sunderland Daily Echo and Shipping Gazette*, Saturday 20 October 1877, p. 1.
4 *Bristol Mercury*, Monday 20 August 1888, p. 3.

5 *Hunts Post*, Saturday 17 July 1897, p. 4; *Bedfordshire Times and Independent*, Saturday 19 June 1897, p. 10.
6 Trick riding, some in fancy dress, was popular with amateurs: Isabel Marks, *Fancy Cycling: Trick Riding for Amateurs* (London, 1901).
7 *Evening Star*, Thursday 15 September 1898, p. 3.
8 *Banbury Guardian*, Thursday 8 August 1907, p. 6.
9 Ibid.
10 *Derbyshire Times and Chesterfield Herald*, Saturday 16 September 1899, p. 8.
11 *Penny Illustrated Paper*, Saturday 10 February 1883, p. 13.
12 *Lake's Falmouth Packet and Cornwall Advertiser*, Saturday 29 August 1885, p. 9.
13 *Isle of Wight County Press and South of England Reporter*, Saturday 18 August 1888, p. 8.
14 *Isle of Wight County Press and South of England Reporter*, Saturday 10 August 1889, p. 7.
15 *Chard and Ilminster News*, Saturday 7 November 1891, p.5.
16 Dion Georgiou, 'Only A Local Affair: Imagining and Enacting Locality Through London's Boer War Carnivals', *Urban History*, XLV/2 (2018), pp. 100–127.
17 *Portsmouth Evening News*, Friday 24 August 1900, p. 4.
18 *Cricket and Football Field*, Saturday 1 August 1908, p. 8.
19 Peter Bailey, '*Ally Sloper's Half-Holiday*: Comic Art in the 1880s', *History Workshop*, XVI/1 (1983), pp. 4–32.
20 *Isle of Wight County Press and South of England Reporter*, Saturday 15 September 1906, p. 8.
21 *Chelmsford Chronicle*, Friday 18 August 1911, p. 5.
22 *Southend Calling*, a film history of Southend Carnival at www.carnivalarchive.org.uk, accessed 20 November 2019, no longer accessible.
23 *Illustrated Sporting and Dramatic News*, Saturday 6 September 1930, p. 3.
24 British Pathé historical collection #865.09 (31 August 1931).
25 For Hebden Bridge: *Todmorden and District News*, Friday 17 August 1934, p. 6; for Williton: *West Somerset Free Press*, Saturday 14 November 1908, p. 6; for Wells swans: photograph by Bert Philips in Wells and Mendip Museum, www.somersetlive.co.uk, accessed 14 February 2021.
26 *Western Times*, Friday 10 November 1922, p. 3.
27 *Daily Herald*, Thursday 29 August 1929, p. 2.
28 *Chelmsford Chronicle*, Friday 29 August 1930, p. 9.
29 *Daily Herald*, Thursday 28 August 1930, p. 2.
30 County Borough of Southend-on-Sea, *Hospitals Carnival: Official Handbook* (Southend, 1930), pp. 17, 19, at www.carnivalarchive.org.uk, accessed 9 December 2019.
31 *Chelmsford Chronicle*, Friday 25 August 1939, p. 8; *Birmingham Daily Gazette*, Tuesday 22 August 1939, p. 7.
32 Julie V. Gottlieb, 'Neville Chamberlain's Umbrella: "Object" Lessons in the History of Appeasement', *Twentieth Century British History*, XXVII/3 (2016), pp. 357–88.
33 *Ballymena Observer*, Friday 9 July 1948, p. 7.
34 *Essex Newsman*, Tuesday 9 September 1947, p. 3.
35 *London Daily News*, Friday 8 March 1912, p. 7.
36 *Liverpool Echo*, Tuesday 23 June 1914, p. 6.
37 British Pathé historical collection #272.14 (29 June 1922).
38 For Bradford queen: *Yorkshire Post and Leeds Intelligencer*, Monday 23 May 1927, p. 11; for fairy: *Sheffield Independent*, Monday 8 November 1937, p. 3; for Mae West: British Pathé historical collection #1424.05 (8 March 1948).
39 *Sheffield Independent*, Wednesday 4 November 1936, p. 1.
40 British Pathé historical collection #1269.11 (26 September 1949) and #1377.13 (28 August 1950).
41 *Hull Daily Mail*, Thursday 4 May 1950, p. 6.

Five **CORONATIONS AND CELEBRATIONS**

1 *Hampshire Advertiser*, Saturday 2 July 1887, p. 6.
2 *Dundee Courier*, Wednesday 18 June 1902, p. 7.
3 *Fraserburgh Herald and Northern Counties' Advertiser*, Tuesday 17 June 1902, p. 4.
4 *Herts and Cambs Reporter and Royston Crow*, Friday 15 August 1902, p. 8.
5 Nicola J. Thomas, 'Embodying Imperial Spectacle: Dressing Lady Curzon, Vicereine of India 1899–1905', *Cultural Geographies*, XIV/3 (2007), pp. 369–400.
6 *Daily Telegraph and Courier*, Tuesday 13 June 1911, p. 8.
7 The standard work remains Lisa Tickner, *The Spectacle of Women: Imagery of the Suffrage Campaign, 1907–14* (London, 1987).
8 *Longford Journal*, Saturday 1 July 1911, p. 6.
9 *Edinburgh Evening News*, Tuesday 27 June 1911, p. 1.
10 *Liverpool Evening Express*, Saturday 24 June 1911, p. 2.
11 *Ealing Gazette and West Middlesex Observer*, Saturday 29 July 1916, p. 8; for a postcard from The Fancy Dress Studio: Victoria and Albert Museum, London #B.289–2013.
12 Croxley Green History Project, www.croxleygreenhistory.co.uk, accessed 15 December 2019.
13 British Pathé historical collection, Reuters-Gaumont Graphic Newsreel #VLVACF3GCDXN5DR3KD3AQIHO7B4ZJ (1 January 1927).
14 Jim English, 'Empire Day in Britain, 1904–1958', *Historical Journal*, XLIX/1 (2006), pp. 247–76.
15 For charity matinees and balls: M. Macdonagh, *London During the Great War: The Diary of a Journalist* (London, 1935), pp. 71–2; Luci Gosling, 'Motley and Morale: The Role of Fancy Dress in the First World War', https://blog.maryevans.com, 10 December 2015.
16 *Middlesex Chronicle*, Saturday 17 February 1917, p. 2.
17 *Ripley and Heanor News and Ilkeston Division Free Press*, Friday 14 August 1942, p. 4.
18 *Lancashire Evening Post*, Tuesday 30 May 1944, p. 1.
19 Deborah Sugg Ryan 'Spectacle, the Public and the Crowd: Pageants and Exhibitions in 1908', in *The Edwardian Sense: Art, Design and Spectacle in Britain, 1901–1910*, ed. M. Hatt and M. O'Neill (New Haven, CT, 2010), pp. 43–71.
20 Angela Bartie, Linda Fleming, Mark Freeman, Tom Hulme, Paul Readman and Charlotte Tupman, '"And Those Who Live, How Shall I Tell Their Fame?" Historical Pageants, Collective Remembrance and the First World War, 1919–39', *Historical Research*, XC (2017), pp. 636–61.
21 *Nottingham Evening Post*, Tuesday 24 June 1919, p. 5.
22 Deborah Hedgecock and Robert Waite, *Haringey at War: Images of London* (Stroud, 2004), p. 60.
23 The gypsy dress was donated to Haringey Archives/ Bruce Castle Museum by Grace Boyce's daughter, Elizabeth Sells.
24 *Coventry Evening Telegraph*, Monday 21 July 1919, p. 2.
25 For Gamages and Jeannie Jackson: Luci Gosling, 'Motley & Morale' blog.
26 Peace Celebration Float, Masterton, https://nzhistory.govt.nz, accessed 21 March 2020.
27 National Library of Scotland, Moving Image Archive, Fyfe and Fyfe, *Galashiels Historical Peace Pageant*, #0760 (2 August 1919).
28 For mock funeral: Museums Victoria #7177; for an example of a Kaiser effigy: *Cambridge Daily News*, Tuesday 12 November 1918, p. 4; for an example of a soldier with a *Pickelhaube*: *Oxford Journal Illustrated*, 9407 (20 January 1915), p. 6.
29 Sara Stevenson and Helen Bennett, *Van Dyck in Check Trousers: Fancy Dress in Art and Life*, exh. cat., Scottish National Portrait Gallery, Edinburgh (1978), pp. 4–8.
30 'ScotsSue', 'Earlston Clown Band On Parade Across the Borders', https://auldearlston.blogspot.com, 6 July 2018.

31 Patricia Campbell Warner, *When the Girls Came Out to Play: The Birth of American Sportswear* (Amherst, MA, 2006), pp. 149–57; Katrina Jungnickel, *Bikes and Bloomers: Victorian Women Inventors and Their Extraordinary Cycle Wear* (London, 2018).

32 Beck Hemsley, '"Out Guising": Gender Transgression in Warwickshire Postcards', www.ourwarwickshire.org.uk, accessed 9 May 2020.

33 For sailor suit: National Portrait Gallery, London #AX160071.

34 Elaine Aston, 'Male Impersonation in the Music Hall: The Case of Vesta Tilley', *New Theatre Quarterly*, IV/15 (1988), pp. 247–57.

35 Christopher Breward, *The Hidden Consumer: Masculinities, Fashion and City Life* (Manchester, 1999), pp. 241–2.

36 For Elizabeth Ann Robertson: Marion Wright's ('lincslady22') maternal grandparents' album, www.flickr.com/explore, accessed 12 December 2020; for Margaret Mitchell in her husband's uniform: Hedgecock and Waite, *Haringey at War: Images of London*, p. 29.

37 Imperial War Museum amateur film footage: the Warwickshire Yeomanry in Palestine #ID MGH 2622 (1939) and HMS *Kent* visiting Ceylon #ID MGH 4571 (1940).

38 For Henlow 'Hitler': Henlow and RAF Henlow, Bedfordshire/1945 VJ Day #10 www.ampthillimages.com; for two Führers: Yorkshire Film Archive, Debenham & Co., 'Hull Victory Celebrations, 1945' (May 1945); for Churchill lookalike: Sutton History Celebrations, Heritage #2, Celebrations, www.suttonbeauty.org.uk , accessed 22 March 2020; for Churchill, Montgomery and Truman: National Library of Scotland, Moving Image Archive, attributed to Ben H. Humble, *Dumbarton, 1944–1946*, #1871.

39 For an example of amateur colour film shot by RAF Leading Aircraftsman R. W. Johnson and his father, William Johnson, during VE Day in London: Imperial War Museum #MGH 5125 (8 May 1945/6–16 June 1946).

40 For Worthing Victory Tea: *Worthing Herald*, Friday 31 August 1945, p. 4; for Edmonton celebrations: 'Street Peace Parties Following Victory in WW2', www.1900s.org.uk, accessed 22 March 2020.

41 For this and other examples: Victoria Haddock, 'VE Day Fashions', *Costume Society Newsletter* (Autumn, 2020), pp. 16–17.

42 See Yorkshire Film Archive, Debenham & Co., 'Hull Victory Celebrations, 1945' (May 1945).

43 Imperial War Museum, #Art. IWM ART LD 2850.

44 Shari Roberts, '"The Lady in the Tutti-Frutti Hat": Carmen Miranda, a Spectacle of Ethnicity', *Cinema Journal*, XXXII/3 (1993), pp. 3–23.

45 Christopher B. Balme, 'Dressing the Hula: Iconography, Performance and Cultural Identity Formation in Late Nineteenth Century Hawaii', *Paideuma: Mitteilungen zur Kulturkunde*, XLV (1999), pp. 233–55, especially p. 247.

46 S. Brawley and C. Dixon, *Hollywood's South Seas and the Pacific War: Searching for Dorothy Lamour* (New York, 2012), especially chap. 4.

Six THE BUSINESS OF FANCY DRESS: THE NINETEENTH CENTURY

1 *Manchester Courier and Lancashire General Advertiser*, Saturday 12 April 1845, p. 1.

2 *The Stage*, Thursday 11 January 1894, p. 24.

3 *Western Times*, Saturday 12 October 1878, p. 1; *Hampshire Chronicle*, Saturday 7 June 1884, p. 4; *Dundee Evening Telegraph*, Saturday 16 September 1893, p. 4.

4 *Worthing Gazette*, Wednesday 29 March 1899, p. 4.

5 *Liverpool Mercury*, Saturday 6 January 1883, p. 1.

6 *Bath Chronicle and Weekly Gazette*, Thursday 16 October 1856, p. 8.

7 Notice of North Woolwich Gardens Grand Masquerade Garden Party, 1887, British Library, Evanion Collection #Evan. 1365; Francis Patrick Martin, *The Revellers' Return, Charities Day*, *c.* 1934, McLean Museum and Art Gallery, Greenock #1977.995 depicts people in fancy dress in a Glasgow underground railway carriage.
8 *London Evening Standard*, Thursday 27 January 1898, p. 6.
9 John Gudenian, 'Bermans & Nathans: Costume and the Entertainment World', *Costume*, XV (1981), pp. 60–66 (p. 61).
10 All the information about suppliers and their stock is derived from advertisements in the front and back matter of the fancy-dress guides by Harrison, Holt, Schild and Aria cited in the text.
11 Marianne Van Remoortel, 'Who Do You Think They Were? What Genealogy Databases Can Do for Victorian Periodical Studies', in *Researching the Nineteenth-Century Periodical Press: Case Studies*, ed. Alexis Easley, Andrew King and John Morton (London and New York, 2018), pp. 131–44 (p. 135).
12 *Walsall Advertiser*, Saturday 24 December 1887, p. 2.
13 *The Spectator*, 7 January 1888, p. 39.
14 Ardern Holt, *Fancy Dresses Described or What to Wear at Fancy Balls* (London, 1882), p. 1.
15 Ibid., p. 9.
16 Holt, *Fancy Dresses Described* (1896), pp. 190, 196, 279.
17 Holt, *Fancy Dresses Described* (1882), Introduction, pp. 1–9; Ardern Holt, *Gentlemen's Fancy Dress: How to Choose It* (London, 1882), Introduction, pp. 1–4.
18 Holt, *Fancy Dresses Described* (1882), pp. 14, 19–21.
19 For 'New Woman' and Victorian fancy dress revelation generally: Rebecca N. Mitchell, 'The Victorian Fancy Dress Ball, 1870–1900', *Fashion Theory*, XXI/3 (2016), pp. 291–315.
20 Holt, *Fancy Dresses Described* (1882), pp. 31, 78.
21 Holt, *Fancy Dresses Described* (1882), Normandy peasant, p. 100; Ellen Terry, pp. 112–13; Donna Vittoria Colonna, p. 146.
22 Holt, *Fancy Dresses Described* (1882), p. 51.
23 *The Argus* (Melbourne, Australia), Friday 5 October 1866, p. 5.
24 Aileen Ribeiro, *Dress in Eighteenth-Century Europe, 1715–1789* (London, 1984), p. 182.
25 For example: *The World of Fashion*, colour and black-and-white plates in the February and March issues (1845).
26 Léon Sault designs for the House of Worth: Victoria and Albert Museum, London, https://collections.vam.ac.uk, accessed 29 April 2020.
27 Anthea Jarvis, '"There was a Young Man of Bengal . . .": The Vogue for Fancy Dress, 1830–1950', *Costume*, XVI (1982), pp. 33–46 (pp. 35–6).
28 *The Argus* (Melbourne, Australia), Friday 5 October 1866, p. 6.
29 *Blackburn Standard*, Saturday 14 January 1888, p. 6.
30 Holt, *Fancy Dresses Described* (1882), p. 169; Holt (1896), pp. 307–12.
31 Kevin L. Seligman, 'Dressmakers' Patterns: The English Commercial Paper Pattern Industry, 1878–1950', *Costume*, XXXVII/1 (2003), pp. 95–113 (p. 97).
32 [Marie Schild], *Male Character Costumes for Fancy Dress Balls and Private Theatricals* (London, 1884), p. 9.
33 Marie Schild, *Album of Fancy Costumes* (London, 1881): paper models, pp. vii, 109; costume prints, pp. 109–10; Australian agent, p. vii.
34 Holt, *Fancy Dresses Described* (1896), p. 23.
35 For American paper pattern pioneers and some discussion of English firms: Joy Spanabel Emery, *A History of the Paper Pattern Industry: The Home Dressmaking Fashion Revolution* (London, 2017), pp. 29–43, 49, 60, 85.
36 For an American view: Beverly Gordon, *The Saturated World: Aesthetic Meaning, Intimate*

Objects, Women's Lives, 1890–1940 (Knoxville, TN, 2006), pp. 107–38.

37 Todd M. Endelman, 'The Frankaus of London: A Study in Radical Assimilation, 1837–1967', *Jewish History*, VIII/1–2, The Robert Cohen Memorial Volume (1994), pp. 117–54.

38 Mrs Aria, *Costume: Fanciful, Historical, Theatrical* (London, 1906), p. 183.

39 Ibid., pp. 180, 183–5.

40 Ibid., p. 188.

41 Ibid., p. 180.

42 Ibid., p. vii.

43 Ibid., pp. 182–3.

44 Margaret Maynard, '"A Dream of Fair Women": Revival Dress and the Formation of Late Victorian Images of Femininity', *Art History*, XII/3 (1989), pp. 322–41; Rebecca N. Mitchell, 'The Victorian Fancy Dress Ball', p. 298.

45 'Magazines and Catalogues', at www.thejohnbrightcollection.co.uk, accessed 20 January 2021.

46 Barbara Burman, 'Home Sewing and *Fashions for All*, 1908–1937', *Costume*, XXVIII/1 (1994), pp. 71–80.

47 *Pick-Me-Up*, Saturday 27 January 1894, p. 286.

Seven THE BUSINESS OF FANCY DRESS: THE TWENTIETH CENTURY

1 Mary E. Davis, *Classic Chic: Music, Fashion, and Modernism* (Berkeley, CA, 2006), p. 163.

2 Virginia Nicholson, *Among the Bohemians: Experiments in Living, 1900–1939* (London, 2003), pp. 128–9, illus. p. 269.

3 Maurice Mouvet, *Maurice's Art of Dancing: An Autobiographical Sketch with Complete Descriptions of Modern Dances and Full Illustrations Showing the Various Steps and Positions* (New York, 1915), pp. 26–33; *London Daily News*, Monday 30 November 1908, p. 1.

4 *Leach's Fancy Dress* (1934), p. 9.

5 *Leach's Fancy Dress*, Special Supplement (December 1922), p. 1.

6 *Leach's Fancy Dress* (1924–5), pp. 11, 34.

7 *The Lady Book of Fancy Dresses* (*c.* 1924), p. 2.

8 *The Lady Book of Fancy Dresses* (*c.* 1925), p. 26.

9 *Skegness Standard*, Wednesday 15 September 1948, p. 3.

10 *Yorkshire Post and Leeds Intelligencer*, Monday 22 December 1930, p. 6.

11 *Leach's Fancy Dress* (1933), p. 7.

12 *Weldon's Fancy Dress for Ladies and Gentlemen* (*c.* 1930), p. 21.

13 Katrina Honeyman, 'Suits for the Boys: The Leeds Multiple Tailors and the Making of Boys' Wear, 1890–1940', *Textile History*, XLII/1 (2011), pp. 50–68 (pp. 58–9).

14 *Leach's Fancy Dress* (1923), p. 20.

15 Barbara Burman, 'Introduction' to *The Culture of Sewing: Gender, Consumption and Home Dressmaking*, ed. Barbara Burman (Oxford, 1999), pp. 6–12.

16 *Worthing Herald*, Saturday 20 August 1932, p. 3.

17 For cut-outs and impromptu costumes: *Leach's Fancy Dress* (1933), pp. 14–15, 20, 22; for improvisation: *Leach's Fancy Dress* (1922), p. 30.

18 *The Lady Book of Fancy Dresses* (*c.* 1925), p. 16.

19 *Leach's Fancy Dress* (1933), p. 7.

20 *Bournemouth and Southampton Graphic*, Friday 5 February 1932, p. 11.

21 *Birmingham Daily Gazette*, Wednesday 29 January 1930, p. 8; Charles Graves, '"Motley's the Only Wear": The Boom in the Fancy Dress Industry: An Old-Established Costumier's with a Hundred Thousand Dresses Always Ready to be Donned', *The Sphere*, Saturday 30 September 1933, p. 16.

22 Agnes M. Miall, *Making Clothes for Children: Every Mother's Practical Guide to the Art of Making and Mending for the Children from Babyhood to*

Adolescence, with Chapters on Nursery Equipment and Furnishings and Fancy Dress (London, 1934), pp. 150–51.

23 'Let the Kiddies Dress Up', *Wife and Home* (1933), in *Some Things for the Children*, ed. Jane Waller (London, 1974), pp. 111–12.

24 *Western Morning News*, Monday 25 November 1929, p. 6.

25 Sotheby's Cecil Beaton Studio Archive.

26 Cecil Beaton, 'Suggestions for Fancy Dress', *Vogue*, 'Younger Generation Number', 22 December 1937.

27 James R. Crompton & Brothers, Elton Mills, Bury, Lancashire: *Grace's Guide to British Industrial History*, www.gracesguide.co.uk, accessed 26 November 2019.

28 Beverly Gordon, *The Saturated World: Aesthetic Meaning, Intimate Objects, Women's Lives, 1890–1940* (Knoxville, TN, 2006), pp. 107–8.

29 The archives of Dennison Manufacturing Company are held at the Framingham History Center, Framingham, Massachusetts, and at the Baker Library, Harvard Business School, Boston, Massachusetts. My thanks to Nancy Prince and Patricia Levin at Framingham for alerting me to the Selfridges connection and supplying a copy of Miss Bissell's letter.

30 Dennison Manufacturing, *How to Make Crepe Paper Costumes* (Framingham, MA, 1925), p. 20.

31 *Leach's Fancy Dress* (1922), p. 25, and (1925), p. 39.

32 *How to Make Crepe Paper Costumes* (1925), p. 1.

33 *Northampton Chronicle and Echo*, Friday 19 June 1925, p. 2.

34 *Belfast News-Letter*, Tuesday 24 January 1922, p. 7; *Belfast News-Letter*, Thursday 2 February 1922, p. 1.

35 *Northampton Chronicle and Echo*, Wednesday 24 June 1931, p. 3.

36 Laura Stagliola, Framingham History Center blog, 9 August, 2013, https://framinghamhistory.org.

37 *Chelmsford Chronicle*, Friday 24 June 1938, p. 3.

38 British Pathé historical collection #974.17 (23 March 1933).

39 Hazel Hurst, *Crepe-Craft in the Home: A Hint Book for Modern Women* (London, 1935).

40 Sarah Cheang, '"Our Missionary Wembley": China, Local Community and the British Missionary Empire, 1901–1924', *East Asian History*, XXXII–XXXIII (2006/7), pp. 177–98.

41 'London Missionary Society, *Missionary Scenes* (London, 1927), pp. 4, 6, in Cheang, '"Our Missionary Wembley"', p. 192.

42 United Council for Missionary Education, *Let's Dress Up! Dressing Up with Costumes of Many Countries* (London, 1949), pp. 1–38.

43 Ibid., p. 39.

44 Ibid., pp. 40–46.

45 *Skegness Standard*, Wednesday 23 September 1931, p. 3; *Skegness Standard*, Wednesday 22 June 1932, p. 2; *Skegness Standard*, Wednesday 29 June 1932, p. 5.

46 Sandra Trudgen Dawson, *Holiday Camps in Twentieth-Century Britain: Packaging Pleasure* (Manchester, 2011).

47 Mary Essex, 'Fancy Dress for Nothing', in *The Butlin Holiday Book, 1949–50*, ed. Lyle Blair (London, 1950), pp. 154–71 (p. 160).

48 Ibid., pp. 162–3.

49 Ibid., p. 156.

50 Ibid., p. 158.

51 Ibid., p. 162.

Eight THE CHARACTERS OF FANCY DRESS: THREE CASE STUDIES

1 *Leach's Fancy Dress* (1923), p. 31.

2 Beth Fowkes Tobin, *Picturing Imperial Power: Colonial Subjects in Eighteenth-Century British Painting* (Durham, NC, and London, 1999), pp. 81–109.

3 National Portrait Gallery, London #P490 (79).

4 Kate Flint, *The Transatlantic Indian, 1776–1930* (Princeton, NJ, 2009), pp. 53–85 for portraits, p. 4 for land rights activists, pp. 198, 220 for missionary visitors; for a portrait of the Revd Peter Jones, a Christian convert, in Ojibwe dress, 1845: Scottish National Portrait Gallery #PGP HA 420.
5 Ardern Holt, *Fancy Dresses Described or What to Wear at Fancy Balls* (London, 1882), p. 72; Holt, *Fancy Dresses Described* (1887), p. 180; Ardern Holt, *Gentlemen's Fancy Dress: How to Choose It* (London, 1882), pp. 32, 60.
6 L. G. Moses, *Wild West Shows and the Image of American Indians* (Albuquerque, NM, 1996), pp. 43–8.
7 Dot Broady-Hawkes, '"Buffalo Bill's Wild West and Congress of Rough Riders of the World" Travelling Show, September 1904', http://ormskirkbygonetimes.co.uk, 25 November 2015.
8 Butterick, *Masquerade and Carnival: Their Customs and Costumes* (London and New York, 1892), p. 39.
9 Jeffrey Green, *Samuel Coleridge-Taylor: A Musical Life* (London, 2011).
10 For photographs of performers: London Metropolitan Archive #301826–29, #301838–9, #301840, 42, 49, 50.
11 Richard Gordon-Smith, 'Recalling My Father's Reminiscences on Hiawatha', Samuel Coleridge-Taylor Foundation, https://sctf.org.uk, 27 June 2011. Malcolm Sargent conducted the Last Night of the Proms at the Royal Albert Hall in a similar vein from 1947 and continued to champion Coleridge-Taylor.
12 Claire Wintle, 'Visiting the Empire at the Provincial Museum, 1900–1950', in *Curating Empire: Museums and the British Imperial Experience*, ed. Sarah Longair and John McAleer (Manchester, 2012), pp. 37–55 (pp. 46–7).
13 For Theatricals: *The Lady Book of Fancy Dresses* (1923–4), p. 38; for Gamba: *The Lady Book of Fancy Dresses* (1923–4), p. 30.
14 *The Star*, Saturday 16 February 1889, p. 4.
15 Butterick, *Masquerade and Carnival*, p. 172.
16 Owen Wister, *The Virginian* (Oxford, 2009), pp. 12–13.
17 *Weldon's Fancy Dress for Children* (London, second series, *c.* 1900), pp. 83–4.
18 Buffalo Bill's Wild West in Scotland Newsflash, www.snbba.co.uk/bb.html, accessed 26 February 2021.
19 *London Daily News*, Thursday 31 December 1891, p. 6.
20 *Shipley Times and Express*, Friday 29 January 1904, p. 4.
21 *Aberdeen Press and Journal*, Monday 23 April 1928, p. 2.
22 *Portsmouth Evening News*, Wednesday 1 December 1920, p. 6; *Hastings and St Leonards Observer*, Saturday 25 February 1922, p. 10.
23 *Illustrated London News*, 2 May 1891, p. 12; Victoria and Albert Museum, London #S.137:632–2007.
24 For one example: *Pontefract Advertiser*, Saturday 18 April 1891, p. 3 syndicated from the *Daily News*.
25 The Chelsea Arts Balls, https://chelseaartsclub.com, accessed 29 March 2020.
26 *The Tatler*, Wednesday 19 March 1919, p. 7; *The Sphere*, Saturday 22 March 1919, p. 6.
27 *The Graphic*, 22 March 1919, p. 18.
28 *Thanet Advertiser*, Saturday 26 April 1919, p. 6.
29 *Leach's Fancy Dress* (1922), colour supplement, p. 1.
30 *Leach's Fancy Dress* (1920), p. 9; *Leach's* (1922), Frontispiece.
31 *Leach's Fancy Dress* (1920), p. 9.
32 'The Countess of Monte Cristo: Mrs Smith Wilkinson Talks About Her Romantic Career and Wonderful Wardrobe' *Sunday Post*, Sunday 17 July 1921, p. 16.
33 *Leach's Fancy Dress* (1927–8), pp. 7, 9.
34 Ibid., p. 17.
35 *Hastings and St Leonards Observer*, Saturday 17 January 1931, p. 13.
36 *Fife Free Press*, Saturday 3 January 1931, p. 2.

37 For one example: 'Light-Hearted Students from the University College Parade [around] Town at their Annual Rag', British Pathé historical collection #206.25 (1 March 1920).
38 Ulrich Raulff, trans. Ruth Ahmedzai Kemp, *Farewell to the Horse: The Final Century of Our Relationship* (London, 2017), p. 214.
39 Steve Roud, *The English Year: A Month-by-Month Guide to the Nation's Customs and Festivals, from May Day to Mischief Night* (London, 2008).
40 Holt, *Fancy Dresses Described* (1896), p. 134.
41 Laura Forsberg, 'Nature's Invisibilia: The Victorian Microscope and the Miniature Fairy', *Victorian Studies*, LVII/4 (2015), pp. 638–66.
42 *Ally Sloper's Half-Holiday*, Saturday 23 April 1887, p. 2.
43 *Kirkintilloch Herald*, Wednesday 2 December 1903, p. 6.
44 Holt, *Fancy Dresses Described* (1882), p. 29.
45 *Leach's Fancy Dress* (1922), p. 14.
46 *Wiltshire Times and Trowbridge Advertiser*, Saturday 1 September 1934, p. 9.
47 For bat pictures: Anthea Jarvis and Patricia Raine, *Fancy Dress* (Aylesbury, 1984), p. 28; The Lord Mayor's Children's Ball album, 1936, Victoria and Albert Museum, Bethnal Green Museum of Childhood #B.222:1–1996, no. 47.
48 For a full account: Caroline Grigson, *Menagerie: The History of Exotic Animals in England* (Oxford, 2016).
49 Pat Morris, *Walter Potter's Curious World of Taxidermy*, ed. Joanna Ebenstein (London, 2013).
50 National Portrait Gallery, London #x26135.
51 Holt, *Gentlemen's Fancy Dress* (London, 1882), p. 10.
52 Holt, *Fancy Dresses Described* (1882), p. 151.
53 Marie Schild, *Album of Fancy Costumes* (London, 1881), p. 106.
54 Leeds Museums and Galleries, blog: Kitty Ross, 'The Children's Fancy Dress Ball', 19 December 2016; Butterick, *Masquerade and Carnival*, p. 142.
55 Kiera Vaclavik, 'The Dress of the Book: Children's Literature, Fashion and Fancy Dress', in *Beyond the Book: Transforming Children's Literature*, ed. Bridget Carrington and Jennifer Harding (Cambridge, 2014), pp. 62–76.
56 Holt, *Fancy Dresses Described* (1887), p. 238.
57 *Illustrated London News*, 18 January 1892, p. 12.
58 Butterick, *Masquerade and Carnival*, p. 167; Holt, *Fancy Dresses Described* (1896), p. 204.
59 *Strand Magazine* (December 1894), pp. 671–2.
60 *The Queen*, Saturday 17 January 1903, p. 24.
61 *The Sketch*, Wednesday 5 March 1913, pp. 4–5.
62 *The Tatler*, Wednesday 29 November 1911, p. 60.
63 *Leach's Fancy Dress* (1922), p. 10.

EPILOGUE

1 Benjamin Wild, *Carnival to Catwalk: Global Reflections on Fancy Dress Costume* (London, 2020).
2 Annebella Pollen, 'Performing Spectacular Girlhood: Mass-Produced Dressing-Up Costumes and the Commodification of Imagination', *Textile History*, XLII/2 (2011), pp. 162–80.

BIBLIOGRAPHY

Abrams, Lynn, *Myth and Materiality in a Woman's World: Shetland, 1800–2000* (Manchester, 2005)

Adam, Barbara, 'Time', *Theory, Culture and Society*, XXIII/2–3 (2006), pp. 111–26

Aria, Mrs E., *Costume: Fanciful, Historical, Theatrical* (London, 1906)

Aston, Elaine, 'Male Impersonation in the Music Hall: The Case of Vesta Tilley', *New Theatre Quarterly*, IV/15 (1988), pp. 247–57

Bailey, Peter, '*Ally Sloper's Half-Holiday*: Comic Art in the 1880s', *History Workshop*, XVI/1 (1983), pp. 4–32

Balme, Christopher B., 'Dressing the Hula: Iconography, Performance and Cultural Identity Formation in Late Nineteenth Century Hawaii', *Paideuma: Mitteilungen zur Kulturkunde*, XLV (1999), pp. 233–55

Bartie, Angela, Linda Fleming, Mark Freeman, Tom Hulme, Paul Readman and Charlotte Tupman, '"And Those Who Live, How Shall I Tell Their Fame?" Historical Pageants, Collective Remembrance and the First World War, 1919–39', *Historical Research*, XC (2017), pp. 636–61

—, Linda Fleming, Mark Freeman and Alexander Hutton, eds, *Restaging the Past: Historical Pageants, Culture and Society in Modern Britain* (London, 2020)

Bartlett, George Bradford, *Mrs Jarley's Far-Famed Collection of Waxworks* (London, 1873–89)

Baur, Nicole, and Joseph Melling, 'Dressing and Addressing the Mental Patient: The Uses of Clothing in the Admission, Care and Employment of Residents in English Provincial Mental Hospitals, *c.* 1860–1960', *Textile History*, XLV/2 (2014), pp. 145–70

Bide, Bethan, 'Signs of Wear: Encountering Memory in the Worn Materiality of a Museum Fashion Collection', *Fashion Theory*, XXI/4 (2017), pp. 449–76

Brawley, S., and C. Dixon, *Hollywood's South Seas and the Pacific War: Searching for Dorothy Lamour* (New York, 2012)

Brereton, Bridget, 'The Trinidad Carnival in the Late Nineteenth Century', in *Carnival: Culture in Action: The Trinidad Experience*, ed. Milla Cozart Riggio (New York and Abingdon, 2004), pp. 53–63

Breward, Christopher, *The Hidden Consumer: Masculinities, Fashion and City Life* (Manchester, 1999)

Brown, Callum G., *Up-Helly-Aa: Custom, Culture and Community in Shetland* (Manchester, 1998)

Bud, Robert, Paul Greenhalgh, Frank James and Morag Shiach, eds, *Being Modern: The Cultural Impact of Science in the Early Twentieth Century* (London, 2018)

Burman, Barbara, 'Home Sewing and *Fashions for All*, 1908–1937', *Costume*, XXVIII/1 (1994), pp. 71–80

—, ed., *The Culture of Sewing: Gender, Consumption and Home Dressmaking* (Oxford, 1999)

Butterick, *Masquerade and Carnival: Their Customs and Costumes* (London and New York, 1892)

Calvert, Robyne, '"The Artistic Aspect of Dress": The Story of the Healthy and Artistic Dress Union', *Costume*, LIV/2 (2020), pp. 175–201

Cardoza, Thomas, *Intrepid Women: Cantinières and Vivandières of the French Army* (Bloomington, IN, 2010)

Castle, Terry, *Masquerade and Civilization: The Carnivalesque in Eighteenth-Century English Culture and Fiction* (Stanford, CA, 1986)

Cheang, Sarah, '"Our Missionary Wembley": China, Local Community and the British Missionary Empire, 1901–1924', *East Asian History*, XXXII–XXXIII (2006/7), pp. 177–98

Colley, Linda, *Captives: Britain, Empire and the World, 1600–1850* (London, 2002)

Collins, P.A.W., 'Queen Mab's Chariot Among the Steam Engines: Dickens and "Fancy"', *English Studies*, XLII/1–6 (1961), pp. 78–90

Cook, Peter, ed. and trans., *A Memoir of Bayreuth, 1876: related by Carl Emil Doepler including illustrations of his costume designs for the first production of the 'Ring'* (London, 1979)

Cooper, Cynthia, *Magnificent Entertainments: Fancy Dress Balls of Canada's Governors General, 1876–1898* (Fredericton, New Brunswick, 1997)

Coote, Jeremy, and Christopher Morton, '"Dressed as a New Zealander", or an Ethnographic Mischmasch? Notes and Reflections on Two Photographs by Charles Dodgson (Lewis Carroll)', *Journal of Museum Ethnography*, XXVIII (2015), pp. 150–72

Crary, Jonathan, *Techniques of the Observer: On Vision and Modernity in the Nineteenth Century* (Cambridge, MA, and London, 1990)

Cunnington, C. Willett, *English Women's Clothing in the Nineteenth Century* [London, 1937] (Mineola, NY, 1990)

Dalton, Henry, *The Book of Drawing-Room Plays and Evening Amusements: A Comprehensive Manual of In-Door Recreation, with Scenic Illustrations by E. H. Corbould and G. du Maurier* (London, 1868)

Davis, Mary E., *Classic Chic: Music, Fashion, and Modernism* (Berkeley, CA, 2006)

Dennison Manufacturing, *How to Make Crepe Paper Costumes* (Framingham, MA, 1925)

Doepler, Carl Emil, Richard Wagner and Clara Steinitz, *Der Ring des Nibelungen von Richard Wagner: Figurinen Erfunden und Gezeichnet* (Berlin, 1889)

Eck, Carly, 'Headlines Make Fashion: The Use of Newsprint Fabric and Newspaper Clippings in Fashion and Fancy Dress', *Costume*, XLIII (2009), pp. 138–49

Elliott, Bridget J., 'Covent Garden Follies: Beardsley's Masquerade Images of Posers and Voyeurs', *Oxford Art Journal*, IX/9/1 (1986), pp. 38–48

Endelman, Todd M., 'The Frankaus of London: A Study in Radical Assimilation, 1837–1967', *Jewish History*, VIII/1–2, The Robert Cohen Memorial Volume (1994), pp. 117–54

English, Jim, 'Empire Day in Britain, 1904–1958', *Historical Journal*, XLIX/1 (2006), pp. 247–76

Essex, Mary, 'Fancy Dress for Nothing', in *The Butlin Holiday Book 1949–50*, ed. Lyle Blair (London, 1950), pp. 154–71

Flint, Kate, *The Victorians and the Visual Imagination* (Cambridge, 2000)

—, *The Transatlantic Indian, 1776–1930* (Princeton, NJ, 2009)

—, *Flash! Photography, Writing, and Surprising Illumination* (Oxford, 2017)

Forsberg, Laura, 'Nature's Invisibilia: The Victorian Microscope and the Miniature Fairy', *Victorian Studies*, LVII/4 (2015), pp. 638–66

Fowkes Tobin, Beth, *Picturing Imperial Power: Colonial Subjects in Eighteenth-Century British Painting* (Durham, NC, and London, 1999)

Frank, Roberta, 'The Invention of the Viking Horned Helmet', in *International Scandinavian and Medieval Studies in Memory of Gerd Wolfgang Weber*, ed. Michael Dallapiazza, Olaf Hansen, Preben Meulengracht-Sørensen and Yvonne S. Bonnetain (Trieste, 2000), pp. 199–208

Garber, Marjorie, *Vested Interests: Cross-Dressing and Cultural Anxiety* (London, 1992)

Georgiou, Dion, 'Only a Local Affair: Imagining and Enacting Locality through London's Boer War Carnivals', *Urban History*, XLV/2 (2018), pp. 100–127

Goodrick, G. J., *Tableaux Vivants and Living Waxworks with Directions for Stage Management* (London, *c.* 1895)

Gordon, Beverly, *The Saturated World: Aesthetic Meaning, Intimate Objects, Women's Lives, 1890–1940* (Knoxville, TN, 2006)

Gottlieb, Julie V., 'Neville Chamberlain's Umbrella: "Object" Lessons in the History of Appeasement', *Twentieth Century British History*, XXVII/3 (2016), pp. 357–88

Green, Jeffrey, *Samuel Coleridge-Taylor: A Musical Life* (London, 2011)

Grigson, Caroline, *Menagerie: The History of Exotic Animals in England* (Oxford, 2016)

Gudenian, John, 'Bermans & Nathans: Costume and the Entertainment World', *Costume*, XV (1981), pp. 60–66

Hacking, Juliet, *Princes of Victorian Bohemia: Photographs by David Wilkie Wynfield* (London, 2000)

Haddock, Victoria, 'VE Day Fashions', *Costume Society Newsletter* (Autumn 2020), pp. 16–17

Handy, Ellen, *Pictorial Effect, Naturalistic Vision: The Photographs and Theories of Henry Peach Robinson and Peter Henry Emerson*, exh. cat., Chrysler Museum of Art, Norfolk, VA (1994)

Harrison, Charles, *Theatricals and Tableaux Vivants for Amateurs* (London, 1882)

Hedgecock, Deborah, and Robert Waite, *Haringey at War: Images of London* (Stroud, 2004)

Hiler, Hilaire and Meyer, *Bibliography of Costume* (New York, 1939)

Hindson, Catherine, *London's West End Actresses and the Origins of Celebrity Charity, 1880–1920* (Iowa City, IA, 2016)

Hollander, Anne, *Seeing Through Clothes* [New York, 1978] (Berkeley, CA, and London, 1993)

Holt, Ardern, *Fancy Dresses Described or What to Wear at Fancy Balls* (London, 6 edns: 1879, 1880, 1882, 1884, 1887, 1896)

—, *Gentlemen's Fancy Dress: How to Choose It* (London, 1882)

Homans, Margaret, *Royal Representations: Queen Victoria and British Culture, 1837–1876* (Chicago, IL, 1998)

Honeyman, Katrina, 'Suits for the Boys: The Leeds Multiple Tailors and the Making of Boys' Wear 1890–1940', *Textile History*, XLII/1 (2011), pp. 50–68

Houlbrook, Matt, *Queer London: Perils and Pleasures in the Sexual Metropolis, 1918–1957* (Chicago, IL, 2006)

Hurst, Hazel, *Crepe-Craft in the Home: A Hint Book for Modern Women* (London, 1935)

Huxley, David, 'Music Hall Art: "La Milo", Nudity and the *pose plastique* 1905–1915', *Early Popular Visual Culture*, XI (2013), pp. 218–36

Jacobi, Carol, *Painting With Light: Art and Photography from the Pre-Raphaelites to the Modern Age* (London, 2016)

Jarvis, Anthea, '"There was a Young Man of Bengal . . .": The Vogue for Fancy Dress, 1830–1950', *Costume*, XVI (1982), pp. 33–46

—, and Patricia Raine, *Fancy Dress* (Aylesbury, 1984)

Jungnickel, Katrina, *Bikes and Bloomers: Victorian Women Inventors and Their Extraordinary Cycle Wear* (London, 2018)

Kane, Josephine, *The Architecture of Pleasure: British Amusement Parks, 1900–1939* (Farnham, 2013)

Kennedy, Philip F., and Marina Warner, eds, *Scheherazade's Children: Global Encounters with the Arabian Nights* (New York, 2013)

Knott, Stephen, 'Fancy Dress as an Amateur Craft', *Performance Research*, XXV/1 (2020), pp. 10–17

The Lady Book of Fancy Dresses (1924–30)

Leach's Fancy Dress and *Leach's Fancy Dress for Children* (1920–36)

Linkman, Audrey, *The Victorians: Photographic Portraits* (London, 1993)

—, *Photography and Death* (London, 2011)

Macdonagh, M., *London During the Great War: The Diary of a Journalist* (London, 1935)

McLaren, Angus, 'Smoke and Mirrors: Willy Clarkson and the Role of Disguises in Inter-War England', *Journal of Social History*, XL/3 (2007), pp. 597–618

Marks, Isabel, *Fancy Cycling: Trick Riding for Amateurs* (London, 1901)

Marshik, Celia, *At the Mercy of Their Clothes: Modernism, the Middlebrow, and British Garment Culture* (New York, 2017)

Mavor, Carol, *Becoming: The Photographs of Clementina, Viscountess Hawarden* (Durham, NC, and London, 1999)

The Mayhew Brothers, *Acting Charades or Deeds Not Words: A Christmas Game to Make a Long Evening Short* (London, 1850)

Maynard, Margaret, '"A Dream of Fair Women": Revival Dress and the Formation of Late Victorian Images of Femininity', *Art History*, XII/3 (1989), pp. 322–41

Miall, Agnes M., *Making Clothes for Children: Every Mother's Practical Guide to the Art of Making and Mending for the Children from Babyhood to Adolescence, with Chapters on Nursery Equipment and Furnishings and Fancy Dress* (London, 1934)

Mitchell, Rebecca N., 'The Victorian Fancy Dress Ball, 1870–1900', *Fashion Theory*, XXI/3 (2016), pp. 291–315

Morris, Pat, *Walter Potter's Curious World of Taxidermy*, ed. Joanna Ebenstein (London, 2013)

Moses, L. G., *Wild West Shows and the Image of American Indians* (Albuquerque, NM, 1996)

Mouvet, Maurice, *Maurice's Art of Dancing: An Autobiographical Sketch with Complete Descriptions of Modern Dances and Full Illustrations Showing the Various Steps and Positions* (New York, 1915)

Mozley Moyal, Ann, *Clear Across Australia: A History of Telecommunications* (Melbourne, 1984)

Murphy, Sophia, *The Duchess of Devonshire's Ball* (London, 1984)

Nead, Lynda, *The Haunted Gallery: Painting, Photography, Film, c. 1900* (New Haven, CT, and London, 2007)

Newell, Venetia, 'Up Helly Aa: A Shetland Winter Festival', *Arv*, XXXIV (1978), pp. 37–97

Nichols, Kate, *Greece and Rome at the Crystal Palace: Classical Sculpture in Modern Britain, 1854–1936* (Oxford, 2015)

Nicholson, Virginia, *Among the Bohemians: Experiments in Living, 1900–1939* (London, 2003)

Orbach, Barak Y., 'The Johnson–Jeffries Fight and Censorship of Black Supremacy', *NYU Journal of Law and Liberty* (2010), pp. 270–346, at https://ssrn.com/abstract

Owen, Olwyn, and Christopher Lowe, *Kebister: The Four-Thousand-Year-Old Story of One Shetland Township*, Society of Antiquaries of Scotland (Edinburgh, 1999)

Paxton, Naomi, *The Methuen Drama Book of Suffrage Plays: Taking the Stage* (London, 2018)

Pellerin, Denis, and Brian May, *The Poor Man's Picture Gallery: Stereoscopy Versus Painting in the Nineteenth Century* (London, 2014)

Pollen, Annebella, *The Kindred of the Kibbo Kift: Intellectual Barbarians* (London, 2006)

—, 'Performing Spectacular Girlhood: Mass-Produced Dressing-Up Costumes and the Commodification of Imagination', *Textile History*, XLII/2 (2011), pp. 162–80

Poppy, Pat, 'Fancy Dress? Costume for Re-Enactment', *Costume*, XXXI (1997), pp. 100–104

Raulff, Ulrich, *Farewell to the Horse: The Final Century of Our Relationship* , trans. Ruth Ahmedzai Kemp (London, 2017)

Ribeiro, Aileen, *Dress in Eighteenth-Century Europe, 1715–1789* (London, 1984)

Roberts, Shari, '"The Lady in the Tutti-Frutti Hat": Carmen Miranda, a Spectacle of Ethnicity', *Cinema Journal*, XXXII/3 (1993), pp. 3–23

Rosen, Jeffrey, *Julia Margaret Cameron's 'Fancy Subjects': Photographic Allegories of Victorian Identity and Empire* (Manchester, 2016)

Roud, Steve, *The English Year: A Month-by-Month Guide to the Nation's Customs and Festivals, from May Day to Mischief Night* (London, 2008)

Schacker, Jennifer, *Staging Fairyland: Folklore, Children's Entertainment, and Nineteenth-Century Pantomime* (Detroit, MI, 2018)

Schild, Marie, *Album of Fancy Costumes* (London, 1881)

—, *Male Character Costumes for Fancy Dress Balls and Private Theatricals* (London, 1884)

Schoch, Richard W., *Queen Victoria and the Theatre of Her Age* (Basingstoke, 2004)

Seligman, Kevin L., 'Dressmakers' Patterns: The English Commercial Paper Pattern Industry, 1878–1950', *Costume*, XXXVII/1 (2003), pp. 95–113

Sharpe, James, *Remember, Remember: A Cultural History of Guy Fawkes Day* (Cambridge, MA, 2005)

Shope, Bradley, 'Masquerading Sophistication: Fancy Dress Balls of Britain's Raj', *Journal of Imperial and Commonwealth History*, XXXIX/3 (2011), pp. 375–92

Silvestri, Michael, 'The Thrill of "Simply Dressing Up": The Indian Police, Disguise and Intelligence Work in Colonial India', *Journal of Colonialism and Colonial History*, II/2 (2001), e-journal at http://muse.jhu.edu/journals

Smith, Alison, ed., *Artists and Empire: Facing Britain's Imperial Past*, exh. cat., Tate Britain (London, 2015)

Smith, Brian, 'Shetland in Saga-Time: Rereading the *Orkneyinga Saga*', *Northern Studies*, XXV (1988), pp. 21–41, at http://ssns.org.uk

Spanabel Emery, Joy, *A History of the Paper Pattern Industry: The Home Dressmaking Fashion Revolution* (London, 2017)

Spies, Martin, 'Late Victorian Aristocrats and the Racial Other: The Devonshire House Ball of 1897', *Race and Class*, LVII/4 (2016), pp. 95–103

Starey, Cynthia Rowena, *Bethlehem Tableaux as Played in a Somersetshire Village* (London, 1920)

Stevenson, Sara, *Hill and Adamson's The Fishermen and Women of the Firth of Forth* (Edinburgh, 1991)

—, *The Personal Art of David Octavius Hill* (New Haven, CT, and London, 2002)

—, and Helen Bennett, *Van Dyck in Check Trousers: Fancy Dress in Art and Life*, exh. cat., Scottish National Portrait Gallery, Edinburgh (1978)

Sugg Ryan, Deborah, 'Spectacle, the Public and the Crowd: Pageants and Exhibitions in 1908', in *The Edwardian Sense: Art, Design and Spectacle in Britain, 1901–1910,* ed. M. Hatt and M. O'Neill (New Haven, CT, 2010), pp. 43–71

Thomas, Nicola J., 'Embodying Imperial Spectacle: Dressing Lady Curzon, Vicereine of India, 1899–1905', *Cultural Geographies*, XIV/3 (2007), pp. 369–400

Tickner, Lisa, *The Spectacle of Women: Imagery of the Suffrage Campaign, 1907–14* (London, 1987)

Troy, Nancy J., *Couture Culture: A Study in Modern Art and Fashion* (Cambridge, MA, 2003)

Trudgen Dawson, Sandra, *Holiday Camps in Twentieth-Century Britain: Packaging Pleasure* (Manchester, 2011)

United Council for Missionary Education, *Let's Dress Up! Dressing Up with Costumes of Many Countries* (London, 1949)

Vaclavik, Kiera, 'The Dress of the Book: Children's Literature, Fashion and Fancy Dress', in *Beyond the Book: Transforming Children's Literature*, ed. Bridget Carrington and Jennifer Harding (Cambridge, 2014), pp. 62–76

Van Remoortel, Marianne, 'Who Do You Think They Were?: What Genealogy Databases Can Do for Victorian Periodical Studies', in *Researching the Nineteenth-Century Periodical Press: Case Studies*, ed. Alexis Easley, Andrew King and John Morton (London and New York, 2018), pp. 131–44

Waggoner, Diane, *Lewis Carroll's Photography and Modern Childhood* (Princeton, NJ, 2020)

Wahn, Andrew, *The Vikings and the Victorians: Inventing the Old North in Nineteenth-Century Britain* (Rochester, NY, 2000)

Walkowitz, Judith R., 'The Indian Woman, the Flower Girl, and the Jew: Photojournalism in Edwardian London', *Victorian Studies*, XLII (1998/9), pp. 3–46

—, *Nights Out: Life in Cosmopolitan London* (New Haven, CT, 2012)

Waller, Jane ed., *Some Things for the Children* (London, 1974)

Warboys, Michael, Julie-Marie Strange and Neil Pemberton, *The Invention of the Modern Dog: Breed and Blood in Victorian Britain* (Baltimore, MD, 2018)

Warner, Marina, *Monuments and Maidens: The Allegory of the Female Form* (London, 1996)

—, *Stranger Magic: Charmed States and the 'Arabian Nights'* (London, 2012)

Warner, Patricia Campbell, *When the Girls Came Out to Play: The Birth of American Sportswear* (Amherst, MA, 2006)

Weiss, Marta, '"The Diversity of Expression and the Wondrous Power of the Art of Photography" in the Albums of Richard Cockle Lucas', *History of Photography*, XXXVII/4 (2013), pp. 431–44

Weldon's 350 Ideas for Fancy Dresses (n.d., 1917–20s)

Weldon's Children's Fancy Dress (n.d., *c.* 1924–37)

Weldon's Fancy Dress for Children and *Weldon's Practical Fancy Dress for Children*, 1st and 2nd series (n.d., *c.* 1880–1900)

Weldon's Fancy Dress for Ladies and Gentlemen (n.d., *c.* 1925–40)

Weldon's Fancy Dress for Ladies and *Weldon's Practical Fancy Dress for Ladies*, 1st and 2nd series (n.d., *c.* 1880–1900)

Wendlandt, O. J., *Living Statuary; How It May Be Successfully Produced by Amateurs* (Manchester, 1896)

West, Nancy Martha, *Kodak and the Lens of Nostalgia* (Charlottesville, VA, 2000)

Wild, Benjamin, *Carnival to Catwalk: Global Reflections on Fancy Dress Costume* (London, 2020)

Wilson, Verity, 'Western Modes and Asian Clothes: Reflections on Borrowing Other People's Dress', *Costume*, XXXVI (2002), pp. 139–57

Wintle, Claire, 'Visiting the Empire at the Provincial Museum, 1900–1950', in *Curating Empire: Museums and the British Imperial Experience*, ed. Sarah Longair and John McAleer (Manchester, 2012), pp. 37–55

Woodhouse, Adrian, *Angus McBean: Face-Maker* (Richmond, Surrey, 2006)

Worth, Rachel, 'Some Issues in the Representation of Rural Working-Class Dress in British Nineteenth-Century Photography', *Revue belge de philologie et d'histoire*, LXXXVII/3–4 (2009), pp. 775–91

ACKNOWLEDGEMENTS

For inspiration and help in writing this book, I have many people to thank.

Reminiscences, suggestions and information came from Stephen Bartley at the Chelsea Arts Club Archive; Mary Brooks at Durham University; William Clunas; Elizabeth Edwards; Fiona Graham at Newarke House Museum, Leicester; Deborah Hedgecock at Bruce Castle Museum, Haringey; Josie Kane; Julie Anne Lambert at the Bodleian Library's John Johnson Collection; Paula Martin at Arlington Court; Elizabeth Miller; Lisa Monnas; Laura Peers; Nancy Prince and Patricia Levin at Framingham History Center, Massachusetts; Jennifer Schacker; Julie-Marie Strange.

Assistance with images came from many sources: I am particularly grateful to Gail Durbin for the care that went into the formation of her photographic collection, which played a valuable role in the research of this book. My gratitude also goes to Jamie Carstairs, who generously shared his own collection of images with me, as well as making the material in Bristol University's Special Collections available. Jean Pile and Penelope Byrde went to enormous trouble to capture a digital image of a photograph stuck in an album. I also offer my thanks to the following for help with images: Antoinette Ashworth of the Gosport Society; Phil Beard; Robert Bickers, whose Historical Photographs of China project at Bristol University is a model of Internet archiving; John Bright, Barbara Kloos and Elizabeth Owen of the John Bright Collection; Tim Crook at Goldsmiths' College; Tom Cunningham; Steve Delves; Rita Jones of the Bridgwater Guy Fawkes Carnival Committee; Chris Nicoletti at Cranhill Arts, Glasgow; Annebella Pollen; David Simkin; Mustafa Suleman; Ian Tait at Shetland Museum and Archives; Philip Warren and Sarah Nicol at Leicester Museums.

While work was in progress Barbara Burman, Claire O'Mahony and Elizabeth Miller read draft chapters, and Craig Clunas and Penelope Byrde, my co-editor at *Costume* from 2009 to 2014, read the entire manuscript when it was nearing completion. I appreciate their constructive and critical engagement.

Staff of the Bodleian Library, University of Oxford and the London Metropolitan Archives were always patient and helpful.

I am grateful to the British Academy, the Paul Mellon Centre for Studies in British Art and the Pasold Research Fund for awarding me publication grants, and to Vivian Constantinopoulos at Reaktion Books for seeing the potential in the project.

PHOTO ACKNOWLEDGEMENTS

The author and publishers wish to express their thanks to the below sources of illustrative material and/or permission to reproduce it:

Alamy: 1 (Chronicle), 25 (Artokorolo), 34 (Chronicle), 104 (Heritage Image Partnership Ltd), 107 (Neil Setchfield – Vintage), 124 (Thislife Pictures), 126 (Will Perrett), 142 (Guy Corbishley), 143 (Bailey Cooper Photography), 144 (photo Amer Ghazzai); author's collection: 24, 37, 39, 40, 42, 43, 62, 69, 70, 75, 82, 89, 93, 94, 100, 101, 102, 103, 105, 106, 116, 120, 121, 122, 123, 127, 128; Biggleswade History Society, Bedfordshire and Luton Archive Service Collection: 63, 64; Blake Museum, Bridgwater: 50; The Bodleian Library, University of Oxford: 7, 26, 41, 81 (John Johnson Collection), 98, 109, 110, 133, 137, 141; Bridgeman Images: 11 (Chatsworth Settlement Trustees), 36 (© Look and Learn); Bridgwater Guy Fawkes Carnival Committee: 49, 51; The British Library Board, The British Newspaper Archive: 10; Bruce Castle Museum, Haringey Archive and Museum Service: 76, 138; Bukit Panjang Government School Collection/ National Archives of Singapore: 2; Jamie Carstairs: 67; The Cecil Beaton Studio Archive at Sotheby's: 117; Cheshire Archives and Local Studies: 73; Tim Crook: 33; Gail Durbin: 15, 65, 66, 72, 83, 84, 99, 111, 118, 119, 125, 129, 130, 131, 134, 136; Getty Images: 3 (Popperfoto), 13 (Warner/Mirrorpix), 31 (Topical Press Agency/Hulton Archive), 32 (Fox Photos/ Hulton Archive), 53 (Imagno/Hulton Archive), 88 (Topical Press Agency), 135 (photo Bob Thomas/Popperfoto); Harry Ransom Center, The University of Texas at Austin: 44; History in Pictures: 78; Irish Sheet Music Archives: 16; The John Bright Collection: 12, 95; Look and Learn: 22, 27 (MegaMaxArt); Mary Evans Picture Library: 9 (Peter Higginbotham Collection), 28 (© Illustrated London News Ltd), 35 (© Illustrated London News Ltd), 74 (Grenville Collins Postcard Collection), 79 (© Illustrated London News Ltd), 108 (Peter and Dawn Cope Collection), 113 (The Land of Lost Content Collection), 114, 115 (Peter and Dawn Cope Collection), 132 (© Illustrated London News Ltd), 140 (The Land of Lost Content Collection); The Metropolitan Museum of Art, New York: 17, 18, 19; Mirrorpix/*Daily Mirror*, 28 November 1930: 29, 30; National Gallery of Art, Washington: 45; National Portrait Gallery, London: 23, 46, 47, 48; The National Trust for Scotland: 4; National Trust Images: 8; Northampton Museums and Art Gallery: 68; Oxfordshire History Centre: 90; Jean Pile (née Alder): 92; Annebella Pollen: 5; Royal Botanic Garden Edinburgh Archives: 6 (The Farrer Family Collection); Royal Collection

Trust: 38 (Her Majesty Queen Elizabeth II); Shetland Museum and Archives: 52, 54, 55, 56, 57, 58, 59, 60, 61; State Library of Queensland: 87; State Library of South Australia: 14, 20, 21, 89, 96; University of Bristol Library: 112 (Historical Photographs of China/ Special Collections), 139 (Historical Photographs of China/ Special Collections); Valence House Museum, Barking and Dagenham Archives: 86; Victoria and Albert Museum, London: 97; Warwickshire County Record Office: 71, 77, 85; West Sussex Record Office: 91.

INDEX

Illustration numbers are indicated by *italics*